D0847553

structures of syntax, character, scene, and plot by means of sound and images, is explored in detail as it occurred in the novels. The ways in which Woolf's esthetics, ethics, and metaphysics evolved in unison during a lifetime of craft and thought are traced.

The sources of evolution, in terms of experiment and response to the seminal ideas of contemporary poets, artists, scientists, and mystics, are brought out. Perhaps most importantly, the hitherto neglected evolution of Woolf's thought, which was in fact, as Dr. Alexander shows, a genuine philosophical progress, is clearly traced.

* * *

Jean Alexander is Associate Professor of English at the University of Calgary.

THE VENTURE OF FORM IN THE NOVELS
OF VIRGINIA WOOLF

Kennikat Press
National University Publications
Series in Literary Criticism

General Editor
Eugene Goodheart
Professor of Literature, Massachusetts Institute of Technology

by Jean Alexander

AFFIDAVITS OF GENIUS
Edgar Allan Poe and the French Critics
(1971)

JEAN ALEXANDER

The Venture of Form
In the Novels of
VIRGINIA WOOLF

WITHDRAWN

National University Publications
KENNIKAT PRESS • 1974
Port Washington, N.Y. • London

DELTA COLLEGE
LEARNING RESOURCES CENTER

MAR - 1975

PR 6045 .O72 Z536 1974

Alexander, Jean, 1926-

The venture of form in the
novels of Virginia Woolf

Copyright © 1974 by Jean Alexander. All Rights Reserved. No Part of this
publication may be reproduced, stored in a retrieval system, or transmitted,
in any form or by any means, electronic, mechanical, photocopying, record-
ing, or otherwise, without the prior written permission of the publisher.

Library of Congress Catalog Card No. 73-83260
ISBN: 0-8046-9052-9

Manufactured in the United States of America

Published by
Kennikat Press Corp.
Port Washington, N.Y./London

Contents

Illustrations

These illustrations are to be found in *A Christian Rosenkreutz Anthology*, ed. Paul M. Allen (Blauvelt, N.Y., 1968).

*THE VENTURE OF FORM IN THE NOVELS
OF VIRGINIA WOOLF*

Acknowledgment

For research grants enabling me to examine the unpublished diaries of Virginia Woolf in the Berg Collection of the New York Public Library, I am grateful to the University of Calgary; and for courtesy in allowing me to examine the diaries I thank Dr. Lola Szladits, Curator of the Berg Collection.

Introduction

Since the chapters of this book are close studies of individual novels and pairs of novels, it is well to warn the reader in advance that the studies are not disjunct, and to indicate the nature of the approach I have taken and the continuity found in the work of Virginia Woolf. I have not recapitulated the substantial critical work already done by others, nor made a stylistic examination; style and sensibility in the work of Woolf have until now received most of the critical attention. Biography, personality, and milieu have been studiously avoided in the following chapters because I believe these factors have proved misleading as a guide to Virginia Woolf's fiction.

The biographical approach to the work of any author is of uncertain value, and requires the restraint of other approaches, but the biographical approach to the work of a woman poses additional problems of such seriousness that biography can be a hindrance rather than a help. I refer to the basic fact that a woman's active life, especially if the woman lived before the First World War, did not reflect her mind, her choice in the way that a man's life tended to reflect his choice. For example, Thoby Stephen chose the intellectual influence of G. E. Moore, and chose the Cambridge companions who would subsequently see Virginia [Stephen] Woolf in London. Virginia Stephen welcomed G. E. Moore, J. M. Keynes, E. M. Forster as people brought

1

to her home. Although her association with these men became one of affection or respect, her feeling did not necessarily imply intellectual or artistic agreement or influence. Like Lily Briscoe in *To the Lighthouse,* she could admire their beautiful boots without buying the kitchen table of their reality. Accounts of the rather fierce young woman who silently attended to the long nights of conversation in Gordon Square or Fitzroy Square (as well as the record of her own fiction and criticism) should warn us that much of the influence of the young thinkers to whom she listened was a negative influence; that is, she was stimulated but aroused to opposition. More complex, but related, is the powerful influence of Leslie Stephen, her father—with whom she had an ambiguous relationship, even in childhood—which resulted in his daughter's having an intense double battle, struggling against the domestic tyrant but also against the entire weight of the nineteenth century embodied in him. This was the primary negative influence which had to be transcended. Writing on her father's birthday in 1928, Virginia Woolf was to say: "He would have been 96, 96, yes, today . . . but mercifully was not. His life would have entirely ended mine. What would have happened? No writing, no books. . . ."[1]

In general, the young Virginia Stephen was sustained in her creative life by forces beyond the rather narrow scope of her active life, but within the range of active possibilities open to her she took the most decisive step of departure: she married Leonard Woolf, the man most alien to the old order of her early environment. For more reasons than one, she was bent on losing her maiden name. However, even Leonard Woolf was hostile to some of the forms of her thought; in certain areas Woolf's diaries are reticent; the visionary could find expression only in fiction.[2]

The same kind of problem arises with the question of literary influences. Even after Virginia Woolf ceased to earn a living as a reviewer, she read widely and eagerly; but her reading of Hardy, Freud, Proust, and Joyce did not mean that she was learning from these writers. For example, it seems clear that Jung rather than Freud was the psycho-analytic mind with whom Virginia Woolf could feel harmony; and the idiot child in *Between the Acts,* defined by a sophisticated member of the audience as "the unconscious," is a gently satiric thrust at Freudian concepts. Similarly, the efforts that have been made to see Woolf writing within the theoretical structure of Proust's *A la recherche du temps perdue* ignore the fact, recounted in *A Writer's Diary,* that Woolf read Proust as escape literature, in the sense that he took her far from her own work. The connections made between Joyce and Woolf are even more problematical; possibly Woolf learned something about technique from Joyce, but the configurations of the two minds were so radically different that even a direct technical influence was not possible. Of her contemporaries, Virginia Woolf felt herself most akin to D. H. Lawrence; the pursuit of this hint might take us farther than any of the more obvious technical and philosophic approaches linking Joyce and Woolf. The most fertile influences upon Virginia Woolf as she passed beyond the stage of tutelage came from outside the confines of the Bloomsbury group, and the writers who most excited her were men with a strong contemplative and visionary inclination, Chekhov and Yeats. Moreover, the ambivalence of Virginia Woolf's attitude to Katherine Mansfield partially masks an influence which is also spiritual, but less visionary than psychological in its effect. These influences deserve further exploration, but are outside the range of the present study.

From the beginning of her work, the radical if unobtrusive state of rebellion of the young woman is evident as a philosophic problem rather than as an incentive to social action, and it takes a direction familiar to us now, after several decades of existentialist literature.[3] The refusal of the inherited system is shown by rejection of the forms of its thought. Distrust of the rational mind, its systems, and the

institutions it gives rise to is perhaps the most all-pervasive
existentialist attitude; in Woolf's fiction it is to be found in
style, structure, and characters, as well as in explicit statement. The entire range of dead ideas and habits is suggested in "The Mark on the Wall," as well as a profound
epistemological skepticism.

> . . . But these generalizations are very worthless. The military
> sound of the word is enough. It recalls leading articles, cabinet
> ministers—a whole class of things indeed which, as a child, one
> thought the thing itself, the standard thing, the real thing, from
> which one could not depart save at the risk of nameless damnation.
> . . . There was a rule for everything. . . .
> . . . .
> And what is knowledge? What are our learned men save the
> descendants of witches and hermits who crouched in caves and in
> woods brewing herbs, interrogating shrew-mice and writing down
> the language of the stars? And the less we honour them as our
> superstitions dwindle and our respect for beauty and health of
> mind increases . . . Yes, one could imagine a very pleasant world
> . . . A world without professors or specialists or house-keepers
> with the profiles of policemen, a world which one could slice with
> one's thought as a fish slices the water with his fin, . . .[4]

All intellectuals in Virginia Woolf's novels have arid hearts
and pseudo-relationships, from St. John Hirst in *The Voyage
Out* to Edward in *The Years*. Scholars are the most hope-
lessly inhuman, and the limitations of abstract man are
nowhere so relentlessly clear as in Mr. Ramsay in *To the
Lighthouse*.

But Woolf's attack on generalization encompasses more.
It includes the most rudimentary actions of the mind making
practical categories with which to cope with experience:
birds, fruit, time, and love. All these substitute a concept
for an experience. When Rachel asks in *The Voyage Out,*
"What is it to be in love?" Woolf proceeds to test the abstraction. The refusal of society's generalizations—habits, duties,
roles, and institutions—is implicit in her treatment of major
characters and in her refusal after *Night and Day* to deal in
fiction with the falsities of social action. This aspect of her
rebellion against rational systems is very simple and clear,

often taking the form of a satiric aside, like this one from
Jacob's Room:

> Anyhow . . . it must come as a shock about the age of twenty—
> the world of the elderly—thrown up in such black outline upon
> what we are; upon the reality; . . . upon the obstinate irrepressible
> conviction which makes youth so intolerably disagreeable—"I am
> what I am, and intend to be it," for which there will be no form
> in the world unless Jacob makes one for himself. The Plumers will
> try to prevent him from making it. Wells and Shaw and the serious
> sixpenny weeklies will sit on its head.[5]

This is a key passage, not only for its rebellion against the
life-denying ideas and institutions but also for its statement
about form, to which we will return in chapter 2. Woolf's
insistent fidelity to experience, beginning with physical, perceptual experience, is an implicit questioning of reality as
traditionally taught.

The dangers of a plunge into unclassified experience are
not immediately apparent, but the doubting of knowledge
is obviously a perilous enterprise, since it threatens even the
reality of experience. Here we return to "The Mark on the
Wall" because it is an early experiment, and self-consciously
so, with knowledge, fancy, and experience.

> But for that mark, I'm not sure about it; I don't believe it was
> made by a nail after all; it's too big, too round, for that. I might
> get up, but if I got up and looked at it, ten to one I shouldn't be
> able to say for certain; because once a thing's done, no one ever
> knows how it happened. Oh! dear me, the mystery of life; the
> inaccuracy of thought![6]

Because this is very playful, we are not shattered by the
anxiety or terror of the instability of our world. Yet these
few lines reveal succinctly the slipperiness of experience.
What is experienced by the dreamer beside the fire? The
perception itself is uncertain. The cause is unknown. The
response of the dreamer is an associational stream of fancies.
The experience, then, is as factitious as a generalization, and
far more unstable. If ideas and rules are safe and fixed but
unreal, and experience is unfixed but partly imaginary, where
is one to look for truth? Virginia Woolf is perhaps more in

sympathy with the visionary scientist than with the philosopher. It is certain that Sir James Jeans expresses some of the
terrors of the exploring mind, and enumerates problems with
which Woolf's fiction grapples:

> Standing on our microscopic fragment of a grain of sand, we
> attempt to discover the nature and purpose of the universe which
> surrounds our home in space and time. Our first impression is
> something akin to terror. We find the universe terrifying because
> of its vast meaningless distances, terrifying because of its incon-
> ceivably long vistas of time which dwarf human history to the
> twinkling of an eye, terrifying because of our extreme loneliness,
> and because of the material insignificance of our home in space—
> a millionth part of a grain of sand out of all the sea-sand in the
> world. But above all else, we find the universe terrifying because
> it appears to be indifferent to life like our own; emotion, ambition
> and achievement, art and religion all seem equally foreign to its
> plan.[7]

Like the scientist, and like Katherine in *Night and Day,*
Virginia Woolf was fascinated by observable life, by experience, but also by what lay beyond observation. Leonard
Woolf in a preface to Mitchell A. Leaska's *Virginia Woolf's
Lighthouse* makes the sardonic statement, "What has always
surprised me is the extraordinary difference of opinion re-
garding (to put it crudely) what the novels are about." To
this basic problem the present study is primarily addressed.
The novels of Virginia Woolf are movements towards truth;
they are forms of thought, and by no means the repetition
of the same pattern of thought. We may start with the proposition that truth is relative and each life unique: "There will
be no form in the world unless Jacob makes one for himself."
As the form of *Jacob's Room* must be shaped from the
experience of Jacob, so must the form of *Mrs. Dalloway* be
found in Clarissa's. We do not find, as one critic suggests,
one novel written nine times, but nine novels. In the end
however Virginia Woolf has, in the exploration of novelistic
forms of truth, arrived at a position very different from the
one at which she began.

chapter 1

"Then comes the terror"

Virginia Woolf considered her novels as an adventuring, and in the adventure represented by each new novel something more radical was at stake than the achievement of an esthetic whole. The sense of risk, the need, as she put it, to "take her fences," did not come from the ego-anxiety of one desiring to be found acceptable to a sophisticated and exacting literary world; rather, it came from the difficulty of an expanding intention to master reality. Her sense of reality from the beginning is far from solipsistic, and the problems with which the external world confronted her are the very probably universal problems of loneliness, the need for relatedness, the knowledge of suffering, disillusion, danger, and confusion in all the ways that an individual meets the world. The traditional modes of thought did not provide her with the means to grasp reality and place individual experience in a credible design. At the beginning of her life as a writer, the forms of abstract thought, social, academic, and philosophic, had already proved inadequate, as shown in the cited passage from "The Mark on the Wall" and illustrated even earlier in *The Voyage Out*. The apprentice stage of the first two novels disclosed to her the further inadequacy of traditional realistic modes of thought in the novel. Subsequently, begin-

7

ning with "Kew Gardens" and *Jacob's Room,* Virginia Woolf
began to devise her own thought-structures for the form she
continued reluctantly to call "novel." Significantly, the discovery of new modes of thought occurred in the writing of
fiction, to be later given conventional argumentative form in
two manifestos published in 1924 and 1925, "Modern Fiction" and "Mr. Bennett and Mrs. Brown."[1] From the first
of these, a celebrated statement has been extracted and used
to define the esthetics, ethics, and metaphysics of Virginia
Woolf:

> Let us record the atoms as they fall upon the mind in the order
> in which they fall, let us trace the pattern, however disconnected
> and incoherent in appearance, which each sight or incident scores
> upon the consciousness.

Because of the frank challenge of the idea, it has been theoretically discussed by critics to the detriment of other suggestions in the same essay. Mitchell A. Leaska, for example,
writes:

> And from her fiction we know that her sense of reality originated
> in her belief that impressions—"the shower of innumerable atoms"
> —which bombard the nervous system from the inception of
> awareness to the end, are really all that one can ever know.[2]

Yet in the same essay, "Modern Fiction," Virginia Woolf
places her concept in a larger and less sensationalist context,
for she insistently opposes the materialistic art of the past
and calls for a recognition of spiritual reality, the artistic
pursuit of which requires not only talent and intellectual
boldness but also spiritual courage and authenticity. Moreover, Virginia Woolf refused to remain in any predetermined
position, even when that position had been established by
herself, and the manifestos of the early 1920s serve primarily
as an aid to the understanding of the middle period of her
work, encompassing *Jacob's Room, Mrs. Dalloway,* and *To
the Lighthouse.* Each of the novels following *To the Lighthouse* is a new form.

The formal evolution must be read in terms of the expression of meaning, and this in turn derives from the intellectual and emotional confrontation with the risks of existence, expressed in the most extreme states in the early novels *The Voyage Out* and *Night and Day* in the recurrence of terror. Subsequently, though the elemental problems remain, their meaning alters as a language is found to contain them adequately; each novel is a new configuration of meaning. The present chapter analyzes the sources of the terror, and its relation to the creative impetus. The history of the evolution of Woolf's thought remains, even in the late works, in highly charged symbolism which is partly a brief notation of reference to the experience of earlier novels. Because of the primary need at this stage for an outline of the initial conditions of Woolf's art, most of the references are to early fiction and to sketches in which the novelist herself performs the analytic function.

The alien earth

Fear of the earth itself is the most philosophic and the most generalized response; it is also more diffuse than the other fears, and might be called the underlying anxiety of existence. In the first period of her work, Virginia Woolf can imagine being a tree and can describe for us its sensations as an insect with cold feet climbs its bark, as in "The Mark on the Wall"; she can describe with serenity the dissolution of human forms in the general harmony of nature, as in "Kew Gardens"; in the final period, she can make Susan in *The Waves* an earth mother of the English countryside, caught with joy and solemnity into the cycle of terrestrial life. Behind these human acts of participation and submission to nonhuman nature lies a venerable assumption: the Judeo-Christian assumption that earth is man's garden. Even though Woolf cannot make the assumption which traditionally lies behind that attitude to nature—the assumption that there is a benevolent God—she begins her work as a novelist within a conception which places man in the garden of rational control. Nature is the English garden from which Rachel departs in *The Voyage Out*. It is domestic land, cultivated land, land which is bounded; fields of corn, hedgerows, rose gardens. This is nature where man has his home and has pressed his mark. Even the wild parkland has its place in a general human order, and is thus a safe place.

Fear first arises when, looking at the world, one sees that nature is not entirely bounded by man's reason and his desires. In *The Voyage Out* the other landscape appears.

. . . Here the view was one of infinite sun-dried earth, earth pointed in pinnacles, heaped in vast barriers, earth widening and spreading away and away like the immense floor of the sea, earth chequered by day and by night, and partitioned into different lands, where famous cities were founded, and the races of men changed from dark savages to white civilised men, and back to dark savages again. Perhaps their English blood made this prospect uncomfortably impersonal and hostile to them. . . .[3]

The sea everywhere seems primeval and measureless; that is the part it plays in the human system. It is not man's element and does not serve his need; or if it serves his need, it does so by its own laws or chances. The imagined view of earth like the sea widening in its own design, with barriers it erects rather than bounds that man has set, makes man's lodging on earth as uncertain as his tossing at sea. On this new earth, or this earth newly seen, man's acts are ephemeral and insignificant. One does not find the permanency of the English landscape, where the culture of a people is reflected on the face of the earth and makes nature show a human continuity, linking past, present, and future. It has entertained equally the savage and the civilized man, and, more troubling, has indifferently seen the savage return. So early in Virginia Woolf's life as a novelist, she shows an alien reality threatening the order of reality learned within the context of her own tradition. It is, as the novelist says, a "prospect uncomfortably impersonal and hostile"; it is the earth existing in its own right with its own laws or lawlessness which make human meanings irrelevant. Further, we note that because the earth is arid as well as boundless and forbidding, it is fearful. The sun itself, in the intensity of its presence, is not beneficent, and the landscape, sun-dried, is dead.

If we follow the explicit expression of this kind of fear chronologically, we arrive at a version which seems at first glance to be very different. In the essay "On Being Ill," first published in 1930, the earth again sees the vanishing of humanity and civilization, not in fire but in ice:

The wave of life flings itself out indefatigably. It is only the re-cumbent who know what, after all, Nature is at no pains to con-ceal—that she in the end will conquer; heat will leave the world; stiff with frost we shall cease to drag ourselves about the fields; ice will lie thick upon factory and engine; the sun will go out. Even so, when the whole earth is sheeted and slippery, some un-dulation, some irregularity of surface will mark the boundary of an ancient garden, and there, thrusting its head up undaunted in the starlight, the rose will flower, the crocus will burn. But with the hook of life still in us still we must wriggle. We cannot stiffen peaceably into glassy mounds.[4]

More explicitly than in the preceding passage, Woolf re-veals nature's hostility to life—that is, to life as we know it—and the threat that the human mind recognizes and the human body feels when its vitality ebbs. The fear of death in Virginia Woolf's work is always related to the imaginative or conceptual fear of the death of the world; the knowledge of death is the awareness of the failure of human continuity. In "On Being Ill" the gesture of affirmation is related to all of Woolf's novelistic strategies, for it confronts the problem of establishing a humanly meaningful design, without repudi-ating the threat or the evidence supporting it. In the passage cited, the threat is more fearsome than the spectacle of a sun-burnt land, for it refers not merely to the habit of self-importance in man but also to a relentless alien causality in the scientific theory of the cooling of the sun and the freezing of terrestrial life. The writer makes an affirmation which is virtually an act of will. The garden, which has become an esthetic rather than a vegetable form, bears a great burden of assertion. The rose and the crocus still belong to the garden that shows man's design and is faithful to his desire, and the writer herself points out the remnants of the boundaries man has set; but these flowers have a temper of assertion uncommon in flower-images, for they do not have the comfort of domestic familiarity, nor do they have the sensory opulence that gives such an erotic tone to some of the descriptions in *Jacob's Room*.

Instead, these images are charged with great metaphoric simplicity and hardness; they combine the thrust of esthetic form (hence, of civilization), the organic order of nature, and a new potency, the persistence of the life-force in conditions we cannot know and conditions which would demand the death of what we know: we would have to "stiffen peaceably into glassy mounds." Virginia Woolf was not prepared to do that. The basic challenge to Virginia Woolf is that of reconciling the cosmos to man, and of finding forms with the triple potency of the crocus in the passage cited.

This major challenge appears in a short essay which ends modestly by descending from the tragic vision to the comfortable and stable escape world of Augustus Hare's *The Story of Two Noble Lives*. Before we are left in that salutory irony, however, a double image of nature has registered. We have the garden, which may seem to be merely a delicious welter of color, sound, shape, movement, but is also the form of the natural world as tamed by man, and tamed not only for use, sustenance, and bodily pleasure but also for the ultimate pleasure, esthetic response. But there is in addition a nature which is not always present to the senses, and certainly not to control. Since these two bodies of nature need to be distinguished from one another, I use the terms "nature" and "chaos," the latter term including all the ways in which the external world may present itself without the human design called significant form.

The two passages cited offer, moreover, the pattern of imagery which is later, in the novels, to be extended to describe analogous conditions in the individual human being and in society: the fire of the sun which burns away organic life; on the other hand, the sheet of ice which would bury organic life under a sunless sky. The third condition that must be cited (and we note that this forms part of the second condition also) is the condition of colorlessness. "The Sun and the Fish" describes two experiences, the first of which is the eclipse of the sun:

This was the end. The flesh and blood of the world was dead; only the skeleton was left. It hung beneath us, a frail shell; brown; dead; withered. . . . The world became more and more solid; it became populous. . . . But still the memory endured that the earth we stand on is made of colour; colour can be blown out; and then we stand on a dead leaf; and we who tread the earth securely now have seen it dead.[5]

"The earth we stand on is made of colour." Even if Woolf merely meant "the earth of our habit," this statement would seem inaccurate, since the earth of the night is colorless. Night, we see, is another of the actions of denial the earth makes. In "The Moment," in which the meditation arises as night falls, Woolf says, "Then the sense of the light sinking back into darkness seems to be gently putting out with a damp sponge the colour of one's own eyes." As the essay progresses towards the expression of terror at the end, and just before the statement that forms the heading of this chapter, there is a passage showing the relationship between color, form, and consciousness:

The trees are growing heavier, blacker; no order is perceptible. . . . Nothing can be seen. We can only see ourselves as outlines, cadaverous, sculpturesque. And it is more difficult for the voice to carry through this dark. The dark has stripped the fledge from the arrow—the vibrations that rise red shiver as it passes through us.[6]

The skeleton of nature which remains when the sun is eclipsed, and the outlines of things and people seen when night falls, may have shape and design, but no order. That is, significant form and organic form in both senses are absent when detail and color are lost. Organic form is not outline; it arises from within and is the total being. It is the form the author confers when imagining the life of the tree in "The Mark on the Wall"; it is the form she confers when she sees the snail under the leaf as part of the organism of *Kew Gardens,* as a cell is part of the body. The outlines of things and people are abstractions. Reality is not an inert abstraction, but the sensory impact of voices, movement, three-dimensional flesh, with the red, blue, and green which are part of the living form and without which the form is a caricature. Literally, then, the earth we stand on, as intelligent beings, is made of color.

The earth may be alien because it does not reflect the structure of the civilization and history that Woolf knows, as is true of the world seen by Rachel from her pinnacle; it is true of the United States as Woolf conceived it after reading Sinclair Lewis, Sherwood Anderson, and Ring Lardner. The earth may, however, be more profoundly alien when it is seen to wheel in its own course, denying (not by any act but by its hostile being) man's conception of the garden. When it denies visual and intellectual form, Woolf finds it not merely alien but a promise of chaos.

Reasonless law like a snake

Aside from the fear of nature as something inherently *other,* something uncommitted to man's design, there is a recurring sense of an active principle in nature which is inimical and hidden. In contrast to the philosophic anxiety concerning the reality of man's garden, fear of the unreasoning force does not pass the threshold of the rational mind, and is therefore known obliquely. Again *The Voyage Out* provides the first approach.

The context of the following meditation by Helen Ambrose is the social intercourse of people taking tea and idly chattering:

Aimless, trivial, meaningless, oh no—what she had seen at tea made it impossible for her to believe that. The little jokes, the chatter, the inanities of the afternoon had shrivelled up before her eyes. Underneath the likings and spites, the comings together and partings, great things were happening—terrible things, because they were so great. Her sense of safety was shaken, as if beneath twigs and dead leaves she had seen the movement of a snake. It seemed to her that a moment's respite was allowed, a moment's make-believe, and then again the profound and reasonless law asserted itself, moulding them all to its liking, making and destroying.[7]

Just as Helen's intuition is unprepared for by anything in the preceding scene, so also the experience for the reader is a nasty and unexpected shock. Woolf has found a very accurate narrative device to convey the psychological revelation. The presence of the snake in *The Voyage Out* has mythic overtones which will be found later in *The Waves,* and a context to support the mythic reading is supplied more discursively. The snake is not the biblical one, but the world-snake which in Babylonian mythology was associated with the sea in a context which suggests a power contrary to the power man accepts: it was an emblem of chaos.[8] The association of the primordial snake with the powerful animal drive of sexuality is also very ancient; it obviously does not originate in Freud. However, in the work of Virginia Woolf, as suggested by the quotation above, both symbolic aspects are colored by the feeling of dread. The forces stirring suddenly beneath the routines of civility are ugly and vicious manifestations of the primordial irrational energies: hate and the will to destruction rather than sensuality or procreative desire. In a circular pattern of cause and effect, at the beginning of Woolf's venture, it is not easy to see whether the demonic force is destructive because it is repudiated by a rational and prudish society or whether society repudiates it because it is destructive. The problem here posed is the most intricate and perhaps the most basic to the sense of life evolving in the novels of Virginia Woolf, and the more complete study of its permutations is found in subsequent chapters. However, in its beginning it involves the sense of evil in the world and in man, manifesting itself first in Woolf's fiction in the male sex drive, which is perceived as unnatural. So long as Virginia Woolf adhered in any way to the nineteenth century morality of her father's house—that is, until she had wirtten *To the Lighthouse*—the snake is absent from her fiction, as if it did not belong to the natural world. It reappears, with emphasis, in *The Waves*.

A comparison of Victorian male and female attitudes to male sexuality, as found in a pair of repressed protagonists, is available in Woolf's contemporary Joyce. In *A Portrait of the Artist as a Young Man* Stephen Dedalus at one point (overwhelmed by the sense of sin) dissociates himself from his own genitalia, and thinks that his penis has a diabolic will of its own; but at least he recognizes the demon as attached to himself, belonging to him in some way. To the girl who is even more uninstructed, and who is discouraged from recognizing any corresponding symptoms in herself, the aggressive action of the male member is unnatural. However, both Stephen and Rachel are terrified by the force because it is counter to their moral instruction. In short, the entire civilized conception of man and nature is cast in doubt by the reasonless demonic action. Further elaboration of the problem from a girl's point of view is offered by Rachel's dream in *The Voyage Out*:

> She dreamt that she was walking down a long tunnel, which grew so narrow by degrees that she could touch the damp bricks on either side. At length the tunnel opened and became a vault; she found herself trapped in it, bricks meeting her wherever she turned, alone with a little deformed man who squatted on the floor gibbering, with long nails. His face was pitted and like the face of an animal. The wall behind him oozed with damp, which collected into drops and slid down. . . .
>
> . . . She felt herself pursued, so that she got up and actually locked her door. A voice moaned for her; eyes desired her. All night long barbarian men harassed the ship; they came scuffling down the passages, and stopped to snuffle at her door.[9]

Only once later, in *The Years,* does Virginia Woolf present the problem of sexual panic in a crude and explicit form, in the childhood experience of Rose, who is terrified by a man who exposes himself on the street corner one evening. Some of the details of the experience remind us of Rachel's dream: "It was a horrid face: white, peeled, pock-marked; he leered at her. He put out his arm as if to stop her." And a few paragraphs later: "As she passed he sucked his lips in and out. He made a mewing noise." Even if Rachel, like Rose, has had a childhood encounter with an exhibitionist, the hysterical response depends more on the context of meaning the child can provide than on the experience itself. In the careful ignorance provided for middle class girls before World War II, the male world could be as mysteriously terrible as the rites of a blood cult; Virginia Woolf is at pains to show Rachel's total ignorance and the graying of that innocence by a dread of unknown contamination. Woolf uses every device to tell the reader that Rachel's fear of sex is a fear of the monstrous. To say that the man of the dream is deformed and bestial is not enough; although he may resemble an animal, he is not an animal. He does not belong to normal experience, human or bestial, and is therefore a monster. Further, the monstrousness of female sexuality is suggested in the dream by the displacement of the congested wetness of the girl's own body to an external image.

Human nature proves to have a duality comparable to that of external nature. Just as the girl has had her experience of nature in a sheltered garden, so she has also had an experience (and an emphatic indoctrination) of man as a civil being, clean, rational, ethical, even august. Humanity has made a garden of itself, with boundaries and plots assigned to cultivation, and with designated patterns of relationship; it has made reasonable structures and ideal goals, and it progresses toward them even in the courtesies of social intercourse; the emotions that are acknowledged are Houyhnhnm emotions. In contrast, the child finds suddenly that there are forces at work, about to be loosed, which have no recognized place in the pattern and will indeed shatter the pattern.

The terror that results for the young girl is not simply a terror of the unknown maleness and its sexual instrument (though that is clearly present) but also a fear of an un-governed and irrational force. She feels the threat of chaos. The structures of civility that formed the inherited patterns of meaning are no more absolute and permanent than the garden that man makes, and in both man and nature the opposing forces are "reasonless."

The analysis of woman in relation to nature, to this point, illustrates the extreme emotional-intellectual dilemma of Vir-ginia Stephen, for it shows the contradictory demands of adherence to a learned system of ideas and the direct evi-dence of the experienced world. This aspect of the general problem of erecting structures of meaning is the most com-plicated and the least explicit, but the intricate relations of persons in Woolf's novels, in all kinds of relationships, touch upon it. The intensity of the struggle results in an ambivalent attitude to civility which is not present in Woolf's attitude to the garden. Peter Walsh may say in *Mrs. Dalloway*:

A splendid achievement in its own way, after all, London; the season; civilisation. . . . And the doctors and men of business and capable women all going about their business, punctual, alert, robust, seemed to him wholly admirable, good fellows, to whom one would entrust one's life, companions in the art of living. . . .[10]

But in *The Voyage Out, Night and Day, Jacob's Room,* and *A Room of One's Own* we find a trace of the rancor of deception resulting from the constrictions of social decorum, the falsity of conventional relationships, and the tyranny of man's institutions.

As a recoil from the inadequacy and the dishonesty of the official declarations of society, Woolf returns to the poten-tialities of the irrational. A tentative movement towards acceptance, a twinge of pleasurable excitement in what gives fear, is already found in *The Voyage Out,* with the recog-nition of erotic love. As the demonic force ceases to be purely external, the need to come to terms with it and its threat of submerging the reasonable and recognizable self becomes more urgent. A passage from *Night and Day* will serve to illustrate the extensions, in imagery and in meaning, of the basic oppositions, and to suggest the process of acceptance. Here Ralph sits to rest on the embankment, and an old derelict joins him:

It was a windy night, he said; times were hard; some long story of bad luck and injustice followed, told so often that the man seemed to be talking to himself. . . . The ancient story of failure, ill-luck, undeserved disaster, went down the wind, disconnected syllables flying past Ralph's ears. . . . The unhappy voice afflicted Ralph, but it also angered him. And when the elderly man refused to listen and mumbled on, an odd image came to his mind of a lighthouse besieged by the flying bodies of lost birds, who were dashed senseless, by the gale, against the glass. He had a strange sensation that he was both lighthouse and bird; he was steadfast and brilliant; and at the same time he was whirled, with all other things, senseless against the glass.[11]

The lighthouse has an almost automatic symbolic power, suggesting the traditional symbolism of light, reason, and civilization against darkness and barbarism. In Woolf's work it has the additional precision of the selective mind and imagination, which chooses what it wills from experience, and is therefore a symbol of control. We see Woolf experimenting with it on these terms in the sketch "The Searchlight," in which the light picks up certain details of experience and leaves the rest in darkness; and the more troubling or painful details are left in darkness. Yet it continues to be associated with the rational faculties, even when it represents some powers of imagination; hence, it belongs to nature as garden, whereas the wind belongs to imagery of nature as chaos. In the passage from *Night and Day*, Ralph recognizes the stability and control in himself, but also sees the destructive possibilities when they stand against the gale and whatever comes in the gale; the hard, unyielding tower may destroy not only "lost birds" like the old man but also something of himself. A part of him has the wind as its element, even when the wind is a gale. The lighthouse cannot stop the force, but only batter the beings caught in the force.

At this point, in *Night and Day,* there is only the power

of recognition; for the containment of the paradox in fiction, Virginia Woolf needed to evolve new concepts and new forms. A force which is outside the controlled human nature of society and intelligence has been released, and must be less uneasily included in the human concept. A progress of natural imagery reveals a change in feeling, and violent impulsion, often a rushing on the wind, becomes a means of conveying the modified terror which is mixed with exultation.

A rider on the random wind

If the source of terror is no longer an alien force in nature— cosmic or human—it is nonetheless still terror. When the boundaries between man and nature are breached, and man is no longer the master, the tamer, but a conductor of natural forces, a dependent, there are dangers as well as pleasures. The kind of pleasure offered him as compensation may be suggested by one of Woolf's digressions in the essay on Walter Sickert, in which she ruminates on the importance of color and the life-link between man and the world of color, imagining him at some primitive stage to have been like the exotic insects, "creatures drinking crimson until they became crimson," which die when the brilliant flowers fade. The compensation is a sensory ectasy. The danger is death. Woolf is aware of both at once, and the fear is the fear of the extinction of qualities we commonly call human—all dependent on the idea of man as rational—in a surrender to natural forces.

Surrender to sense impressions which are specific and limited and visual gives delight. Septimus Smith in the last minutes of his life is safe when his eyes are open and he perceives a screen, bananas, or Rezia playing with a child. "But directly he saw nothing the sounds of the game became fainter and stranger and sounded like the cries of people seeking and not finding. . . ." The purely receptive state is safe as long as there is light. In the darkness the alien earth reappears—that which is shape without form or color—and is internalized; the irrational force which has now been imaginatively accepted replaces the quiescent visual images of day with kinetic and auditory images. Whether pleasurable or not, these images are charged with barely withheld panic. The entire essay "The Moment" is a study of this process of departure from the visual and intelligent world of daylight to the extinction of rational identity in the dark, and the ultimate abandon to irrational forces; but I cite only the climactic passage:

> Then comes the terror, the exultation; the power to rush out unnoticed, alone; to be consumed; to be swept away to become a rider on the random wind; the tossing wind; the trampling and neighing wind; the horse with the blown-back mane; the tumbling, the foraging; he who gallops forever, nowhither travelling, indifferent; to be part of the eyeless dark, to be rippling and streaming, to feel the glory run molten up the spine, down the limbs, making the eyes glow, burning, bright, and penetrate the buffeting waves of the wind.[12]

When the irrational forces are essentially erotic, as in this passage, the experience is pleasurable. Although the familiar world is gone and the human creature has lost the form-giving faculty of vision, the surrender is not powerless, and there is no disintegration. She is consumed, swept away nowhere, but as a rider on the wind rather than a bird blown by it. In the kinetic images associated with the horse and in the fiery sensations of the body, a very powerful sexual drive is borne. Human impulse and cosmic force are at one, in rapture, ruthless, amoral. In addition, perhaps contingent on the erotic impulse and perhaps not, there is a will to power. "Trampling," "foraging," "streaming," "penetrate" are not passive, and only two of these words have strong sexual overtones; they reflect the active force of the human being who accepts the kinship of the cosmic forces, and are as undifferentiated.

The body of Virginia Woolf's work gives a wealth of evidence that Woolf could accept the sex drive, within certain esthetic limitations, but only when it was not predatory.

Sexuality, however, is very readily associated with the drive towards power. Although the erotic could be approved, the power drive had no place in the system of values Woolf's mind could accept. The problem of power has two aspects. The refusal of power as it operates in human relationships, which is seen in the treatment of characters like Doris Kilman and Sir William Bradshaw in *Mrs. Dalloway,* will be discussed in detail in chapter 3. But the sense of power in the self is also a source of anxiety, at least for women. While Jacob can accept the idea that he has unbridled appetite and a ruthless will to self-fulfillment, Clarissa cannot.

It rasped her, though, to have stirring about in her this brutal monster! to hear twigs cracking and feel hooves planted down in the depths of that leaf-encumbered forest, the soul; never to be content quite, or quite secure, for at any moment the brute would be stirring, this hatred, which, especially since her illness, had power to make her feel scraped, hurt in her spine; gave her physical pain, and made all pleasure in beauty, in friendship, in being well, in being loved and making her home delightful, rock, quiver, and bend as if indeed there were a monster grubbing at the roots, as if the whole panoply of content were nothing but self love![13]

The will to power, the will to fulfill the self and give it what it wants, is rejected, and Clarissa feels her thwarted will to power as hatred. The trampling hooves are unacceptable to her; the idea of self-love is unacceptable to her. The concept of womanliness will not permit the surge of this kind of power except in very highly evolved forms and in particular transformations. These several transformations will be discussed as they are significant in individual novels; here I will merely cite *Orlando,* which Virginia Woolf frankly admitted to writing with a great sense of release, with the license of fantasy. The transformation that permits the avowal of power and the desire to seize, have, and respond with the innocent ruthlessness of an animal is the simplest one of all, the transformation of sex. Since Orlando began life as a man, she can continue to respond with male gusto without penalty.

But the chaotic forces are not always internalized and felt as a union of power in which the human force can match the cosmic power. Perhaps more often we find the human creature helpless.

. . . If one wants to compare life to anything, one must liken it to being blown through the Tube at fifty miles an hour—landing at the other end without a single hairpin in one's hair! Shot out at the feet of God entirely naked! Tumbling head over heels in the asphodel meadows like brown paper parcels pitched down a shoot in the post office! With one's hair flying back like the tail of a race-horse. Yes, that seems to express the rapidity of life, the perpetual waste and repair; all so casual, all so haphazard...[14]

The incongruity of images and the lightness of tone encourage us to laugh and pass on. We are not concerned here with painful helplessness. It is a comic—and social—rather than a tragic powerlessness. Still, it conveys the contrast between the packaging of civilization and the random but irresistible impetus of other forces, which is the general theme of all the fears.

Ambivalence of attitude prevails in the early works, and though we may speculate, we do not find a close analysis of the threat of chaos to the self until *The Waves*. Release from the socially bound self into the free movement of the cosmos is sought; but when it is not a breaking outward of some inner force, sexual or generally vital, but a submission of the self to alien forces, the release always threatens to be disintegration.

"This mask from which peep two eyes has power to send me dashing like a moth from candle to candle"

The eyes of other people offer the same threat to the self that the alien forces of nature offer to the conceptual mind, and it is a threat which must be met continuously and not intermittently, as is true of the threat of nature. It is to determine Woolf's larger formal strategies in *Jacob's Room* and *Mrs. Dalloway*.

The problem is very close to that posed in Sartrean ethics.

The opulence of sensory experience in Woolf's fiction, and
the deliberate repudiation of logical structures as a means of
containing reality, should not blind us to the fact that conceptual forms are essential and very strong in Woolf's novels,
not only in the action of the novelist but also in the characters. Her characters are not merely sensory receptors of
variable sensitivity. They are creatures who are constantly
patterning the world and attempting to place themselves in
it as self-chosen images. Clearly, this is conceptual action
of the mind, no matter how illogical it may be. In the
process of ordering a world, the individual selects and arranges his own perceptions, and disposes objects. To a great
extent, other people are no more than objects in a scene, or
puppets with certain gestures to make. They play the parts
we assign them for a given occasion. So, as she is departing
for Spain, Virginia Woolf looks at the people on the street
and freezes them in a fragment of life:

Everywhere there is the same intensity, as if the moment instead
of moving lay suddenly still, because suddenly solemn, fixed the
passers-by in their most transient aspects eternally. They do not
know how important they have become. If they did, perhaps they
would cease to buy newspapers and scrub doorsteps.[15]

Such a casual reference reveals, even more tellingly than a
self-conscious confrontation would, the never-ending process
of reducing other people to fit one's own design. Most reduc-
tions of this kind are harmless, and indeed are unnoticed by
the victims. But since every person is at all times engaged
in the task of keeping his vision coherent and pleasurable,
and every person has his own vision, the existence of others
is a latent danger. No real problem arises until two people
face one another and one tries to impose on the other an
image that has no place in his world and is unacceptable
to him.

   Though she may make highly stylized patterns and treat
her characters at times symbolically, Woolf does not reduce
them to abstraction. Static symbolism is qualified by con-

trary images, humor, an ironic descent, or skepticism. But Woolf was aware of the power of an alien world-view as it manifested itself, not in vast abstractions or in political action but in the course of common life. Here perhaps the peculiar circumstances of being a woman in Edwardian England, with its confinement of feminine identity, has a bearing on Woolf's attitude and brings her in the end to a repudiation of power.

The pressures of alien human power which threaten to dissolve the self and its meaningful world vary in intensity and in the seriousness of the threat posed. The first kind, which is usually disagreeable and may give a sense of outrage, is the simple nullification of one's human meaning by seeing him as an object. This is the source of Katherine's unease, for example, in *Night and Day* when she sits under the curious eyes of the others at the meeting to listen to Ralph read his paper; and it is the source of the flutter of outrage in *Between the Acts* when the children carrying broken mirrors and tin cans reveal the audience in grotesque fragments.

Here a nose...There a skirt...Then trousers only...Now perhaps a face...Ourselves? But that's cruel. To snap us as we are, before we've had time to assume...And only, too, in parts... That's what's so distorting and upsetting and utterly unfair.[16]

Woolf's theoretical rejection of the realistic novel as written by Arnold Bennett—stated as a general literary theory in "Mr. Bennett and Mrs. Brown"—and the creation of a new mode in *Jacob's Room,* are a repudiation of the objective way of seeing and being seen. Woolf has been much criticized for not taking a more censorious attitude to characters such as Clarissa Dalloway; but, as *The Waves* will later warn us overtly, Woolf repudiates the role of judge. After *Night and Day* she does not permit her major characters to suffer that kind of reduction, simplification, or distortion.

A more outrageous extension of the habit of denial, and a source of anger as well as fear, is the judicial role of the

abstract mind, which evaluates by generalization and denies
another person an individual consciousness or individual
significance outside the abstract patterns. We see the attitude
exposed in the way that St. John Hirst looks at Rachel
Vinrace in *The Voyage Out:*

> "You see, the problem is, can one really talk to you? Have you
> got a mind, or are you like the rest of your sex? . . ."

> "About Gibbon," he continued. "D'you think you'll be able to
> appreciate him? He's the test, of course. It's awfully difficult to
> tell about women," he continued, "how much, I mean, is due to
> lack of training, and how much is native incapacity. . . ."

> Rachel looked round. She felt herself surrounded, like a child
> at a party, by the faces of strangers all hostile to her, with hooked
> noses and sneering, indifferent eyes.[17]

Although this kind of distortion occurs most pointedly when
it has to do with the relations of men and women, it is also
implicit in the prickly manner of her first two young women,
Rachel and Katherine, in judging others. At all times inadequacy of world-view, some fatal narrowness of being (most
often a failure of feeling or imagination, rather than of mind
or ego), leads to this distortion of reality. Its effect on the
other is shown not to be profound, because it is so obviously
a failure in the perceiver.

The last two threats posed to consciousness by a hostile eye
are more deadly. The first of these is found in relationships of
love, in which an image of the world and the self depends on
mutual action. Each of the two people has surrendered a part
of his vision. The eyes which look are not in the same head,
and they perceive vastly different things, so that the creative
act necessary to make a coherent image is exhausting. If one
grows weary or finds the image unsatisfactory, and refuses
to do his part, the entire structure gives way and chaos or
death comes. "Lappin and Lapinova," with all the force and
simplistic clarity of fairy tales, gives us the pattern of coopera-
tive creation and the result when one repudiates the creation.
The newlyweds, each with his own world, come together
strangely until they create a double identity. Here it is the

fancy of being the king of the rabbits and his consort. They make their private world, and "Without that world, how, Rosalind wondered, that winter could she have lived at all?" For much of the other reality of married life, in-laws and the life of rooms, is deadly constriction. But a day comes when the husband responds to rabbit-news with "What the deuce are you talking about?" and the mutual world collapses (as does the relationship). The effect, for the young wife, is a psychological death.

> She seemed to have lost something. She felt as if her body had shrunk. . . . The rooms also seemed to have shrunk. Large pieces of furniture jutted out at odd angles and she found herself knocking against them. . . . She went home and sat over the fire, without a light, and tried to imagine that she was out alone on a moor; and there was a stream rushing; and beyond the stream a dark wood. But she could get no further than the stream.[18]

And crouching there with her eyes glazed, she is shot by the husband who says, "Poor Lapinova, caught in a trap, killed." The story is different from other versions of the problem not only by its allegorical simplification but also by its suggestion that the world created by the newlyweds is less real than the world of family portraits and mahogany sideboards. In more complex situations, love poses the problem of a highly nuanced double existence in which entire constellations come together: in the stress on the self, some reorganization or disintegration of being, especially of the conceptual self, must occur. The young or ecstatic woman is particularly vulnerable. For this reason, the two novels dominated by women contain meditations on the terrors of love. Mrs. Dalloway at one time associates love with Miss Kilman, and sees it coupled with religion as a destroyer of "the privacy of the soul." In *To the Lighthouse* we find Mrs. Ramsay under continual assault by her husband to keep him steady in his world; even a lull in his conversation brings her to the alert with "an impulse of terror" to send out her forces to save the world.

Eroticism intensifies the danger:

> He turned on her cheek the heat of love, its horror, its cruelty, its unscrupulosity. It scorched her, and Lily, looking at Minta being

charming to Mr. Ramsay at the other end of the table, flinched for
her exposed to those fangs, and was thankful.[19]

If we compare Lily's terror of sexual ardor with Rachel's, we
find that the recoil is different, for Lily is afraid of being
devoured. The erotic always includes the danger of violation,
even later, in Jinny of *The Waves,* when the most happily
erotic woman has a vigor for combat: "Her ears were laid
back as if she might bite." Terror is part of the exhilaration of
the sexual experience.

Whether the fear of love is physical or spiritual in expression, it springs from a sense of the self's being overwhelmed,
overmastered, or breached so that unity and coherence of
being may decompose. It is like the fear of cosmic forces and
the sexual élan of the self in having potency both desired and
feared. The problem, as it finds expression in the early forms,
is to escape the dichotomy of the imprisoned self and the dis-
oriented self. In the process Woolf was to reexamine every
element of her world, in its ideas and in its affective evidence.
All the forces, in nature as well as in others, which inspire
desire as well as terror are not wholly alien; the self has similar power. They are forces which the imagination can grasp
as constructive or fecund.

However, just as there is correspondence between the fear
of great undomesticated forces of nature and the fear of the
other in relationships of sex or love, so there is correspondence between the fear of nature as an alien and sinister being
like a snake and the fear of people who mean to subjugate.
Although this last fear is the strongest, it is the simplest in
that the psychological response is single and consistent. The
other does not merely reduce one to an object in his own
design, or judge and reject, or require an effort of mutual
perception to construct a world for two; rather, he cannot
bear to live in a condition of relativity. Not only must he have
his absolutes, but, like weak humanity in the vision of Dosto-
evsky's Grand Inquisitor, he feels safe only in unanimity. So,
in spite of weakness he is the killer turned from action to

philosophy. "The Man Who Loved His Kind" is a sketch in black humor of the egotistical absolutism which must destroy all incompatible reality, the realities of others. Both the man and woman in this sketch show the spirit of negation.

> . . . Had he read some book? Again no, and then, putting her ice down, did he never read poetry?
> And Prickett Ellis feeling something rise within him which would decapitate this young woman, make a victim of her, massacre her, made her sit down there. . . .[20]

Except in *Mrs. Dalloway* Woolf never presents the type so crudely in a novel, or with such frank impulses of power and hate. However, the destroyers are usually characterized as flawed selves, with visible limitations. The bigots, haters, and converters are often ugly, poor, or inferior of caste, but this is not to say that all ugly or poor people have the desire to destroy others in order to impose their self-justifying image, or that the upper classes do not have such desires. The type finds its most terrifying embodiment in *Mrs. Dalloway;* Sir William Bradshaw is not given in terms of understandable aggression from weakness. Though nowhere as clearly and tragically apparent as in *Mrs. Dalloway,* this danger is a subtle threat in Virginia Woolf's work until the last works; it leads to anxiety about any explosion of power in the self, and revulsion from it, even when a repudiation hampers character by curbing spontaneity. For example, it causes a denial of power to strike, even in self-defense; to manipulate people directly, even in simple relations of leadership; or power to seize in the "unscrupulosity" of sexual desire. These are the most natural outbreaks of personal vitality and its assertion of its own power, but a long development was necessary for Woolf in order to allow them direct expression.

These terrors, which are in fact experienced philosophic problems, have been presented in simple terms in order to suggest the initial tendency of Virginia Woolf's mind. Long before she attempted a novel, her intention to be a writer announced itself as something more than egoism; although personal ambition and emulation provide one initial motive, her mind was essentially philosophic and exploratory, as shown by a comment in a letter of 1908: "I think a great deal of my future, & settle what books I am to write—how I shall re-form the novel & capture multitudes of things at present fugitive, enclose the whole, & shape infinite strange shapes. . . ."[21] Her first novel, on which she worked for seven years,[22] is a venture to command basic meanings.

chapter 2

From *The Voyage Out* to *Jacob's Room*

The progress from *The Voyage Out* through *Night and Day* to *Jacob's Room* is one from an incomplete experiment through a safe retrenchment to a successful experiment. Or perhaps one should say that the first novel is negatively successful in that it shows the problems which cannot be contained in old forms. Virginia Woolf herself in *A Writer's Diary* tells that she came to see herself, the author, as a gallant novice making a brave failure, but she does not analyze the nature of the failure. Josephine Schaefer sees it as a technical failure.[1] Though there are weaknesses of plot, characterization, and point of view, they seem to reflect philosophic problems, as for example in the crisis of the novel, which finds the protagonist in a state of unconsciousness.

But the technical, structural weaknesses appear obvious only when one recognizes that, morally, Virginia Woolf was attempting a new structure. A fairly explicit use of the key symbol of the ship indicates that Woolf did not intend to write a novel about "the preparation of a naive young girl for maturity," as Winifred Holtby suggests.[2] The title is an assertion of departure, not development. Development is what happens to Elizabeth in *Pride and Prejudice;* departure is what happens to Ishmael in *Moby Dick*. In the early passages of *The Voyage Out,* Woolf is at some pains to insist descriptively that the familiar world of England has become remote, mute, and unreal, and a new order of life must be claimed.

> The people in ships, however, took an equally singular view of England. Not only did it appear to them to be an island, and a very small island, but it was a shrinking island in which people were imprisoned. . . . Europe shrank, Asia shrank, Africa and America shrank, until it seemed doubtful whether the ship would ever run against any of those wrinkled little rocks again. But, on the other hand, an immense dignity had descended upon her; she was an inhabitant of the great world. . . . She was a bride going forth to her husband, a virgin unknown of men; in her vigour and purity she might be likened to all beautiful things, for as a ship she had a life of her own. (P. 29) [3]

It is clear that this passage states a major motif and a major intention. The girl Rachel is to leave the little island on which people are imprisoned—is in a sense to free herself in the great world—and like the ship is to move towards her own destiny. The analogies between Rachel and the ship are almost too obvious to mention, but "virgin unknown of men" applies to Rachel literally and to young womanhood figuratively. Finally, the assertion of "vigour and purity" in the ship which has "a life of her own" clearly forms a part of Woolf's thesis, to be found again in *Night and Day,* that women do in fact have a life of their own which has so far been unrecorded.

An early comment on Rachel's education, or lack of it, strengthens the analogy between the girl and the ship. Her ignorance is a kind of innocence or purity and implies freedom.

> Her mind was in the state of an intelligent man's in the beginning of the reign of Queen Elizabeth; she would believe practically anything she was told, invent reasons for anything she said. . . . But this system of education had one great advantage. It did not teach anything, but it put no obstacle in the way of any real talent that the pupil might chance to have. (P. 31)

Because *The Voyage Out* seems to be thoroughly conventional in style, form, and subject, many readers have quite naturally judged it by conventional standards, often with reference to Jane Austen. Certainly it does not offer a formal containment or resolution of the problems discussed in the preceding chapter, because it is largely an experiment in discovery. Woolf has undertaken a genre which has been strictly a male genre—the novel of youth's initiation and rebellion—and has tried to give it a feminine protagonist. Formerly novels with feminine protagonists had been social novels or picaresque novels. I can think of no novels—and Woolf apparently found no model—in which a girl could try out the world and successfully reject a good part of it, saying, "I will fly the nets of religion and country," as did Joyce's Dedalus. Yet the quoted passages from *The Voyage Out,* which show the proud departure from a shrunken known world, and the symbolic relationship of Rachel and the ship, indicate that Woolf did not intend to give Rachel a preparation for the familiar patterns of English life but a distance and a freedom which would allow her to test them. The style directs us to a criticism of English life from the first paragraph. This novel, then, prepares a trial of traditional patterns and traditional ideas, the judge to be a young woman free of the indoctrination of education. She has no facts, no ideas, no status (and therefore no stake in society), no necessity, and ought theoretically to be able to test society by innocent nature, her own authentic nature. As we will see, the original movement was checked by philosophic rather than technical difficulties. Though the novel seems to fall into the most banal category of novels about women, the love story, it is in reality a testing of the concept of love; it is not a novel in which all would have been resolved by mating had it not been for an unfortunate accident. The kind of novel that Woolf clearly began to write—and continued until chapter 14—is one in which the protagonist discloses the world and makes her own accommodation in it, with some rejection of the conventional and a corresponding assertion of the self.

From the beginning a great thematic burden, perhaps an excessive one, is placed on style. The first style may strike a reader as an imitative apprentice style full of awkwardness;

but its implications are so insistent on the first page of the
novel that Jean Guiguet objects:

Sometimes, as though the author were approaching her subject
from too far off, a scene may begin with generalizations which
introduce into this otherwise self-sufficient world a discordant alien
voice: that of the author herself.[4]

However, the first two paragraphs tell us a great deal about
the strategy of style in *The Voyage Out*.

As the streets that lead from the Strand to the Embankment are
very narrow, it is better not to walk down them arm-in-arm. If
you persist, lawyers' clerks will have to make flying leaps into the
mud; young lady typists will have to fidget behind you. In the
streets of London where beauty goes unregarded, eccentricity
must pay the penalty, and it is better not to be very tall, to wear
a long blue cloak, or to beat the air with your left hand.
One afternoon in the beginning of October when the traffic was
becoming brisk a tall man strode along the edge of the pavement
with a lady on his arm. Angry glances struck upon their backs.
The small, agitated figures—for in comparison with this couple
most people looked small—decorated with fountain pens, and
burdened with despatch-boxes, had appointments to keep, and
drew a weekly salary, so that there was some reason for the un-
friendly stare which was bestowed upon Mr. Ambrose's height
and upon Mrs. Ambrose's cloak. . . .

We are struck not only by the quaint sententiousness and the
eighteenth-century chattiness of the author's address to us but
also by the quality of this novel's realism, which persists when
the author disappears. The assumption of realism is that
reality or truth is known by faithful observation and record-
ing of external qualities, whether they be the semblance of
things or the actions of people; the eye is the key to truth. The
reader accepts the convention effortlessly because he tends to
believe that there is some residual truth in externals, no matter
how artfully selected and arranged. Virginia Woolf shows us
to what extent we are deceived. The eye may present images
devoid of experienced reality. In contrast to the strong kinetic
awareness of great realistic passages in *Ulysses,* for example,
or *Anna Karenina, The Voyage Out* is characterized by an
abstract realism. Whereas Tolstoy considers Kitty's ball-gown

worth an evocative page, and gives it nearly as much sensual life as he gives Vronsky's mare, Woolf tells us that Mrs. Ambrose wore a blue cloak. So the anonymous figures in the street become abstractions, identified and generalized from their fountain pens, their despatch-boxes, and their agitation. This detached and very cold style dominates the first half of the novel. The attitude it reflects is found also in subsequent, more detailed descriptions of people and in the more imaginative description of the receding land:

They had left London sitting on its mud. A very thin line of shadow tapered on the horizon, scarcely thick enough to stand the burden of Paris, which nevertheless rested upon it. (P. 23)

We see that the world—in this view of reality—is one from which the vitality has been bled. The general process of perception starts with the sensuous, but here the source has been lost or suppressed. What remains is intellectual and abstract.

When people are more individualized than in the street scene, they continue to be largely abstract; Rachel very early gives us the key word "symbol" for this state of abstract being. We see the abstract presence of people clearly in the first miniature society given, that aboard the *Euphrosyne*, not only in the stifling patterns of relationship (mistress and servant, father and daughter, husband and wife) but also through exposition of Rachel's past relationships. The most explicit indication is perhaps Rachel's memory of the way her middle class society deals with emotion: Rachel, in an effort to talk about feelings after the death of her mother, begins obliquely by asking one of her aunts how fond she is of the other aunt:

"I can't say I've ever thought 'how,'" said Miss Vinrace. "If one cares one doesn't think 'how,' Rachel," which was aimed at the niece who had never yet "come" to her aunts as cordially as they wished.
"But you know I care for you, don't you, dear, because you're your mother's daughter, if for no other reason, and there *are* plenty of other reasons." (P. 34)

The conclusion to which Rachel has come is that people are symbols, "featureless but dignified, symbols of age, of youth,

of motherhood, of learning"; and symbols do not speak to
one another. "To feel anything strongly was to create an abyss
between oneself and others." The sense of life to be had within
these abstract patterns is epitomized by Rachel's characterization of the scholarly Pepper as a fossilized fish.

All that can be known in these terms is very soon known,
and acceptable modes of social intercourse are narrowly limited. So Rachel's relationship with the servant Mrs. Chaily is
defined by an episode in which Mrs. Chaily makes a scene
about sheets simply because she wants a different cabin.
Rachel's response to the episode, afterwards, is in terms of
abstract roles: ". . . anger that a woman of fifty should behave
like a child and come cringing to a girl because she wanted to
sit where she had not leave to sit. . . ."

The dry and abstract style is hardly separable from society
itself. It implies that in society people respond to one another
according to a rapid process of abstraction which takes no
account of lively human qualities. Society—sketched on its
home ground in chapter 1 before the voyage begins—is one
of the major areas of exploration. Although England is not
only left behind physically but also rejected metaphorically as
a prison, the new world into which Rachel journeys is still
English. The people who belong to the exotic landscape are
scarcely seen. Helen and Rachel watch them briefly later, in
the evening promenade; Rachel dismisses them from her exploration of life after two comments: "They believe in God,"
and "We shall never understand." Whereupon they move on
to the hotel, back to English society.

The dry style and the social being it reflects are subjected
to an intermittent irony by glimpses of contrasting styles and
modes of being. In the beginning these glimpses are ambiguous. We are not sure, for example, that irony is intended when
Helen Ambrose dismisses Richard Dalloway as pompous and
sentimental after we have seen him behaving in a more complex and thoroughly manly fashion than anyone else on the
ship. But even before we are certain of the irony, we are

aware of the diminishing and dehumanizing tendency of the realistic style as Woolf uses it; it leads to a queer dissociation from experienced life. The passages in which the affective life erupts (Rachel's nightmare is the first of these departures) have a terrible intensity, partly because of the extreme contrast and partly because of the very fact that an eruption through a dead crust is necessary if life is to show itself.

After shipboard society the next version of society, that of the hotel, seems less constricted. It has more variety of persons and less fixity of relationships, and Rachel begins to show some eagerness to see what it has to offer. "We're going to see life. You promised," she says to Helen. The reader is taken into this world before Rachel is, and discovers in chapter 9 a dismal prospect for the venturing girl. The world of the hotel contains the aging Miss Allan, who is writing a primer of English literature; Mrs. Hughling Elliot, who is the wife of an Oxford don and whines about the emptiness of life; Susan Warrington, who is the poor relative of the invalid Mrs. Paley, and who notes in her diary, "How small the world is" and "Mem. ask about damp sheets." Finally there is St. John Hirst, who reads Gibbon into the night and, when interrupted by his talkative friend Hewet, makes sure that the time is not wasted, by paring his toenails.

The conversation between these two young men serves as a thematic pivot. Two views of society and its relationships are presented; Hirst's is the view that is relevant to the style of the novel and its people to this point. Hewet asks Hirst to describe the two women who were eavesdropping:

"You know I can't describe things!" said Hirst. "They were much like other women, I should think. They always are."
"No; that's where we differ," said Hewet. "I say everything's different. No two people are in the least the same. . . ."
"So I used to think once," said Hirst. "But now they're all types . . . Take this hotel. You could draw circles round the whole lot of them, and they'd never stray outside." (P. 123)

The narrative style supports Hirst completely in the beginning; after Rachel enters the world of the hotel, Hirst's view comes under intermittent attack; in the end it has been transformed. But this thematic development can be traced only after Rachel has been characterized.

The terms just used are in a way misleading, for Rachel is less a character than a consciousness, and the characters and styles of the novel reflect the siftings of this consciousness. It functions first abstractly, dutifully, and narrowly; it is dominated in turn by the father, by Helen, and by Hewet, and throws off the threatened dominance of Hirst and Evelyn Murgatroyd. These minds have the power of domination because they function according to a particular world-view and come to Rachel, aside from Hewet, on the level of ego. At the same time, Rachel struggles with what she has of her own, discovering what it is: in the beginning, nothing.

Rachel first presents herself as physically featureless (". . . Miss Rachel Vinrace, aged twenty-four, stood waiting . . .") and continues for many chapters to be as vague in body as in mind. Helen characterizes her face as weak, and Terence later notices that her woman's body is unformed. When she is not engrossed in her one passion, music, she is wrapped in cloudy dreams. She is so gauche that Helen feels desperate at being forced into the company of such an "unlicked girl." She is passive, and her desires are so undefined that she has the need to ask Richard Dalloway to tell her *everything*. She is uneducated and also ignorant, without being innocent. Her innocence is not a positive quality; it comes close to making her what Terence later calls Susan, a creature with no self. Far from having the spontaneous life of natural girlhood, her nature is clouded. She finds Dalloway fascinating, even though she does not agree with him about the importance of politics, until she is told that he is pompous and sentimental. She accepts the verdict without question. When Dalloway kisses her, she is excited, but her dream tells her that the kiss was bestial and loathsome, and she turns away from the erotic.

The fact is that the identification of Rachel with the ship, quoted in the beginning of this essay, is bitterly ironic. The girl does not have the vigor and purity of the ship, nor a life of her own, because her formation has been repressive in ways more devious than the ways of formal education. If we had nothing more than the previously cited passage recounting Rachel's discovery that strong feeling was to be repudiated, and that dutiful social gestures were to take its place, we would know that Rachel has indeed been indoctrinated in the rejection of natural life. Another piece of exposition shows that she has been almost totally ignorant of sexuality, but not sufficiently ignorant to be innocent:

> She was of course brought up with excessive care, which as a child was for her health; as a girl and a young woman was for what it seems almost crude to call her morals. Until quite lately she had been completely ignorant that for women such things existed. She groped for knowledge in old books, and found it in repulsive chunks. . . . (P. 32)

Her lack of innocence of mind is dramatically illustrated by her subconscious transformation of the pleasure of a kiss into a monstrous and nasty dream. With neither knowledge nor natural authenticity, she has nothing valid with which to test the conventional world. Hence, Rachel's consciousness is known through overt action and thought interpreted by others, and through an underground surge which cannot become overt before love brings a crisis. Only when an alien element enters her fixed world is it possible for Rachel's nonsymbolic potentialities to show themselves. In a sense, this first episode in Rachel's progress is traditional: the introduction of man in the role of mate displaces the known symbolic patterns in any young girl's story, and Woolf is merely bolder than Jane Austen in emphasizing the erotic shock. Perhaps she is also bolder in revealing the absence of being before that shock. A description of the *Euphrosyne* in a storm suggests the pattern for Rachel's responding to love. In the description of the storm, natural forces and human identity are entirely dissociated. The force of the storm gives some relief and pleasure in breaking up the old responses ("they had a perfect rest from their old emotions"), but there is no sense of similarity or even harmony between the human and the cosmic: people are helpless, like "potatoes in a sack on a galloping horse" or, with Rachel, a donkey or a wizened tree standing against the gale.

The violent shaking-up from external nature marks the first stage of Rachel's progress. Thereafter the deadly confinement of society is no longer felt to be inevitable. In the encounter with Richard Dalloway that follows, Rachel, like Evelyn M. later, reaches out for a psychological union but recoils from touch; but before the recoil she feels briefly the storm within rather than without: "She fell back in her chair, with tremendous beats of the heart, each of which sent black waves across her eyes." For the first time, we are aware that part of the search of the central consciousness is for a cosmic view, and that in the first stage of action Rachel has broken out of the lifeless but rational world of society into the violently alive but blind and anarchic forces of nature. The storm at sea and the body's sensations aroused by a kiss are of the same order. So, after the storm, and after her body has calmed, Rachel looks at the sea and the seabirds riding, and addresses nature: " 'You're peaceful,' she said. She became peaceful too, at the same time possessed with a strange exultation." At once the exultation is lost as from her dreaming mind another image, the image of tunnels and a monstrous bestial man, replaces the image of Richard Dalloway and the sea. The first stage of action very carefully prepares us for the last. The source of that vile image is as mysterious as the source of the illness that kills Rachel, and in both stages of unconsciousness the image of an oozing tunnel presents itself. Rachel may want to smash the routine world to atoms, as she later says, but there is a check and a recoil. For reasons that are to be clarified somewhat in the course of the novel, nature brings terror.

Woolf has the difficult task of revealing the evolution of consciousness from nothing. In the early chapters of the novel, much has to be conveyed by absence, and we have a hint of Woolf's awareness of the difficulty in Terence Hewet's thinking of a novel about silence. That beyond the bland exterior of Rachel there is a sentient and intelligent creature, inarticulate and semiconscious, is not revealed until her later confidences to Terence, in which she tells him of her fear of her father and her rage at the routine world of her aunts which she "wanted so vehemently to smash to atoms." And she expresses her sense of the freedom promised metaphorically by the ship:

> "A girl is more lonely than a boy. No one cares in the least what she does. Nothing's expected of her. . . . And that is what I like. . . . I like seeing things go on—as we saw you that night when you didn't see us—I love the freedom of it—it's like being the wind or the sea." (P. 261)

But this consciousness is repressed in the beginning. Furthermore, though she has analytic and articulate moments, Rachel is essentially as nonverbal as the music she loves, and her criticism of life is largely a criticism by action.

Thus the agon belongs to Rachel, but much of it, certainly in the beginning, needs to be verbalized by another. Woolf provides four characters who attempt to impose a world-view upon Rachel and who thereby serve as fragmentary reflectors of her consciousness: Helen and Terence as possibilities of affirmation, and Evelyn Murgatroyd and St. John Hirst as destructive forces.

Helen, who serves not only as a critic of society but also as a guide for the young girl, is realized very strongly and sharply. Her physical presence—her massive beauty, her posture and movement—is more vivid and specific than that of any other character except St. John. Her latent animal vitality, which shows itself at the dance, is opulent. She is vital, but she is not kind. The reader can sympathize even with the self-pitying Mrs. Elliot, who "left the villa half in tears, vowing never again to meet the cold and scornful woman." Though the narrator dismisses Mrs. Elliot's hurt, one finds Helen cold

and scornful with many people but oddly tender with St. John
Hirst, and one has a litle uneasiness about her judgment. Because of the combined powers of beauty, vitality, intelligence,
decisiveness (even ruthlessness), and the self-assurance that
makes her the only character to put St. John Hirst in awe, her
life-view imposes itself. She is magnificent but dark:

> She was not severe upon individuals so much as incredulous of
> the kindness of destiny, fate, what happens in the long run, and
> apt to insist that this was generally adverse to people in propor-
> tion as they deserved well. Even this theory she was ready to dis-
> card in favour of one which made chaos triumphant. . . . (P. 269)

Terence Hewet is the clear contrary power of consciousness, neither dark nor cold nor decisive, but kindly and con-
fused. Even physically he imposes himself less than Helen
does, for he is noticeably lacking in a virile power corresponding to Helen's female power. Though he knows more than
Rachel does and is more sophisticated, he is by no means
firmly committed to a vision of life. His kinship to Bernard in
The Waves is striking, and some of his metaphoric gropings
for a theory of human existence prepare for the entire experience of the later novel, as well as for Woolf's own belief, as
expressed in the literary manifesto of "Mr. Bennett and Mrs.
Brown":

> "The truth of it is that one never is alone, and one never is in
> company . . .
> . . . .
> . . . Bubbles—auras—what d'you call 'em? You can't see my bub;-
> ble; I can't see yours; all we see of each other is a speck, like the
> wick in the middle of that flame. The flame goes about with us
> everywhere; it's not ourselves exactly, but what we feel . . . (P. 125)

Terence, as a sensibility, has a different domain from that of
Helen. While she speaks of fatality, he speaks of human identity and relatedness. Although these are two aspects of
Rachel's search, the two views are far from being comple-
mentary. And it is no surprise that an undercurrent of hostility
runs through their relationship. Terence's view depends on
variety in human beings and human experiences, on penetra-

bility and flux. Helen's depends on attitudes that are simple, primitive, monolithic; though her ideas are not those reflected in social conventions, they are equally fixed and unresponsive to individuality. Terence's sensibility moves toward society, Helen's to nature. Because he has no firm, clear ideas (indeed, he sometimes makes judgments on people similar to Helen's), and even his theories are so vague and whimsical that he inspires, in general, indulgent affection but not respect, his consciousness has no chance of rivaling Helen's except through the power of love.

He serves for the testing of love in two ways. In his inner dialogue on the subject of love in marriage, he tests society in its great institutional provision for relatedness. When he reviews the married couples he knows and when he imagines scenes from married life, "he saw them always, walled up in a warm firelit room. When, on the other hand, he began to think of unmarried people, he saw them active in an unlimited world. . . ." Further, when he considers Rachel as a partner in marriage, he immediately begins to evaluate her according to conventional criteria which have nothing to do with his authentic response to her: he considers her punctuality, her conversational ability at a dinner party, her temper, her domesticity. He ends by throwing aside the institutional standards and preparing his proposal by making a repudiation: "I worship you, but I loathe marriage, I hate its smugness, its safety, its compromise, and the thought of you interfering in my work." Then he declares himself: "Oh, you're free! . . . and I'd keep you free. We'd be free together." (This passage suggests why no one takes Terence very seriously as a thinker.) In his judgment on society, Terence has spoken for Rachel; Woolf has been careful to show how Rachel feels about the stifling domesticity of her aunts. But it is not enough to speak for her. He shares in Rachel's active test of love itself as well as of society's provision for it.

Helen and Hewet provide the words and concepts that correspond to Rachel's wordless consciousness. To clarify the issues further, and to provide a strengthening contrast for the vague lovers, we have St. John Hirst and Evelyn Murgatroyd. Neither is a sympathetic figure, and both are very soon rejected by Rachel, but their attitudes are taken sufficiently seriously to be tested fully. Both are dissatisfied critics of society. Evelyn M., as the other characters think of her, is a young woman who is unfortunate by society's rules—she is an illegitimate child—but not therefore treated sentimentally; in her approaches to St. John, Terence, and Rachel, she is exposed and mocked more and more completely. She chafes against society in word and action, speaking against the dull routine of life, reaching out promiscuously for an intimacy which she wants to be an intimacy of the soul. She likes everyone; she rejects conventions and wants people to speak truly; she herself speaks glibly and at length; she is a feminist who longs to do great and romantic things, and finds most men dull because they are caught in the routine of business life. In action she shows herself to be a coquette who has no real sense of other people's feelings. Woolf's intention is obviously to show Evelyn's seemingly laudable breaking of social propriety in the name of warm relatedness to be spurious.

St. John Hirst is in contrast to Evelyn. While she has no legitimate relation to society, he is one of the inheritors. As he himself complacently admits, he is "one of the three, or is it five, most distinguished men in England." He is a fellow of King's at the age of twenty-four (Rachel's age). He belongs to a society within society, the intellectual aristocracy, and though he is highly individualized as a character, he is undoubtedly a spokesman for that world; the slight sketches of other intellectuals (Ambrose, Pepper, and Elliot) provide corroboration. He judges people not only in the sense of categorizing them and immobilizing them in their circles, but also in the sense of condemning, and his judgments have nothing to do with life. For example, Rachel "believed that her value as a human being was lessened because she did not happen to admire the style of Gibbon." He grasps people by intellectual concepts, as he grasps Helen's integrity of being by the large concept *woman* supported by the lesser concepts *wife* and *mother,* and avoids the evidence of specific reality. In fact, he interposes intellectual concepts and official titles between himself and experience wherein, as he indicates, he would be vulnerable:

> "Of course I am, disgustingly bitter, and it's a beastly thing to be. But the worst of me is that I'm so envious. I envy every one. I can't endure people who do things better than I do—perfectly absurd things too—waiters balancing piles of plates—even Arthur, because Susan's in love with him. I want people to like me, and they don't." (P. 243)

Although St. John is young and not yet fossilized, he is the first specimen of the abstract man who recurs frequently in Woolf's work, both polemic and fictional. In general, his consciousness is a negative one in that it shows intellectual systems as having been won at the cost of life. St. John is abstract and arrogant because of the inadequacy of self; his physical ugliness is almost emblematic.

These two ways for the young to respond to the world are negative because they are inauthentic. The stance, intellectual or romantic, is a response to motives other than the avowed beliefs, and the effect is a distorted and ugly life.

The first cycle of Rachel's experience has taken her from the dead safety of abstract social life (in which her role is that of "unlicked girl") to the terrifying unknown of nature, and back to social testing. In Santa Marina, her confidence restored, she begins to explore again. There is something of Jane Austen's briskness and clarity in the chapters introducing the second world that Rachel enters, and one has the impression that Rachel has her destiny in hand. We see the love story taking shape as Hirst and Hewet are introduced and as Hewet arranges an outing to the mountain. But this neat and familiar pattern, like the first one, goes ironically awry. The gaiety of the picnicking party is inane. Terence passes judgment on the view of life conveyed by that style,

and he speaks for Rachel also: "They are not satisfactory;
they are ignoble." In this second test, society fails to satisfy
the sense of life. But again, when nature presents itself,
Rachel retreats. Her second confrontation with nature, as an
observer of the erotic impulse of other people, deserves
citation:

> They saw a man and woman lying on the ground beneath them,
> rolling slightly this way and that as the embrace tightened and
> slackened. The man then sat upright and the woman, who now
> appeared to be Susan Warrington, lay back upon the ground, with
> her eyes shut and an absorbed look upon her face, as though she
> were not altogether conscious. Nor could you tell from her ex-
> pression whether she was happy, or had suffered something.
> When Arthur again turned to her, butting her as a lamb butts a
> ewe, Hewet and Rachel retreated without a word. (P. 163)

In the external realistic view, conveyed by the visual faculty
and the intelligence alone, we find sensuality made grotesque,
if not hideous as in Rachel's dream. It is the divestiture of
humanity. The bestial element is neither horrible nor terrible
but simply inappropriate. The visual faculty can tell nothing
of the human experience; it cannot discriminate between the
gesture of a lamb wanting to suckle and a man wanting to
caress, and indeed it cannot discriminate between pleasure
and pain. There is a hiatus between objective vision and experience, just as there has been a dissociation of understanding from physical sensation in Rachel's response to Dalloway's kiss.

Although the pattern is to be repeated, it is not quite a
circular pattern. The movement from society to nature and
back again becomes wider, the range of experience and meaning larger, the involvement of consciousness deeper. Only
once, however, is there harmony, a moment when society
ceases to be a collection of dead symbols—or, in Clarissa
Dalloway's terms, when the mind awakens from the dream
that great Greek letters are stalking about the room, and
recognizes real people. That is the episode of the dance,
which follows immediately after the excursion to the mountain. The dance begins with people in their previous brittle

association, like artifacts: "The couples struck off in different directions, leaving a thin row of elderly people stuck fast to the walls . . . The circles were broken up into separate pieces." "This is my idea of hell," is Rachel's consciousness. But in the sheer physical closeness and particularly in physical movement, life itself breaks through, and it is collective life as well as individual life. There is a release of individual sensuous being—a kinetic sense of life which shows itself in some incredible ways such as the Elliots' gallopade—and nothing opposes it. There is social harmony as complete as in the decorous actions of churchgoing, but in the dance the social form corresponds to and gives shape and sanction to the individual life-force. The release ends in serenity and certitude of being.

> "And so you've changed your view of life, Rachel?" said Helen.
> Rachel added another stone and yawned. "I don't remember," she said, "I feel like a fish at the bottom of the sea." She yawned again. None of these people possessed any power to frighten her. . . . (P. 198)

At the dance Rachel begins to live, and her sense of life is no longer interpreted entirely by Helen or Hewet. They continue to theorize and analyze, but the existential consciousness is Rachel's. The descriptive and narrative style immediately reflects the change. On the day after the dance, Rachel goes striding through the countryside, her head still sounding with the music of the night before. Though full of the joy of sound, she goes blindly through nature, or sees it only as masses of green or blue. She is brought out of the mind and its abstractions by a tree. "It was an ordinary tree, but to her it appeared so strange that it might have been the only tree in the world." For the first time, natural objects are seen and described. "Flowers and even pebbles in the earth had their own life." Even Gibbon arouses Rachel, in this birth of sensuous perception, and she thinks of Hirst and Hewet with "a kind of physical pleasure such as is caused by the contemplation of bright things hanging in the sun."

Although Rachel shows symptoms of the dazzled sensuous-

ness of people falling in love, she is far from being in love
with Hirst or Hewet, except as objects in the world. Rachel
feels delight in her own senses and in the world which stimu-
lates her senses. With the sanction of the conventional world
(dances are proper) and of the approved outlet for her
subjective being (music), Rachel's body has freed her. When
she can move to music, she begins not to fear the unfamiliar
beat of her own heart. The way opens to the sensuous and
passionate life, but when she poses the most natural of subsequent questions, "What is it to be in love?" she does so in a
mood of melancholy in contrast to the exultation she felt in
the awakening of her senses. She has discovered "a terrible
possibility in life."

It is an anti-love story. Aside from the long conversation of
chapter 16, in which Rachel and Terence approach one another psychologically with exquisite delicacy of sympathy
(but no erotic joy), the affair progresses with great confusion
and torment and is largely carried on in solitude, Terence
alone or Rachel alone. For Rachel, as Helen says, the effect
is that of "the sliding of a river, quick, quicker, quicker still,
as it races to a waterfall." We allow for Helen's somber view
of life, but the chaos of Rachel's consciousness as she begins
to feel the derangement we call young love, corroborates
Helen. There is a long tradition viewing love as frenzy and
madness, and the madness has been a fit subject for tragedy
as well as comedy. But Woolf is not writing either kind of
novel; Rachel is in search of a fruition of being and a
conception of life, and love threatens her with a loss of being
as great as that suffered in conventional society. It is certainly more exciting, but it promises nothing but the dull
routine of married life in the society Rachel sees, or the "terrible possibility" of being swept over the brink into chaos.

From the moment that she asks what love is until her death,
Rachel rushes more and more quickly toward the terrible
possibility. She seems to be caught in a dilemma she cannot
break. On the one side stands the prison of society, and on

the other the threat of nature. The continuing sense of the futility and sterility of social being is acted out in Rachel's exploration of the hotel, beginning with the chapel, where she sees the nurse as typical of social identity, "a limpet, with the sensitive side of her stuck to a rock, for ever dead to the rush of fresh and beautiful things past her."

She moves from cell to cell within the prison, visiting the rooms of Mrs. Flushing, Evelyn, Miss Allan, and watching the fierce decapitation of a chicken in the courtyard, and going to tea. Her sense of society leaves her first in depression and then in rebellion, which she vents by telling Helen that she is only half-alive.

It should be noted, however, that in these scenes in the hotel Woolf is no longer providing a perfect equivalence between reality and Rachel's sense of it. In these scenes Miss Allan and Evelyn are more than the comic caricatures Woolf provided earlier, but Rachel still responds to mechanisms. In this way a degree of detachment from Rachel is given, even when she is performing a criticism of life independent of Helen and Hewet. Ordinary people, like the ginger Miss Allan offers, are spit out by Rachel before she has really tasted. The reader's sympathy is subtly prepared for a shift in point of view long before it occurs.

Having repudiated society, Rachel turns to the river and tests nature. The journey inland on the river and the launching out on the swift current of love are one, or analogous, as Terence perceives the first night: "He was drawn on and on away from all he knew, slipping over barriers and past landmarks into unknown waters." By daylight nature is hardly more propitious: "The trees and the undergrowth seemed to be strangling each other." And when Hewet tries to read poetry,

> Whoever you are holding me now in your hand,
> Without one thing all will be useless,

the wild laugh of a bird and the "malicious question" of a monkey make him put away his book. The declaration of love made by Terence and Rachel is in this context. They walk into the deep forest and, to the churning sound of the river, make their trancelike statements, and they are as strange and terrible to themselves as the jungle is. Each speaks the other's name as reassurance; it is necessary, for they have lost their known identities.

Nothing could be clearer than the converging of all the points of view in a single consciousness of the jungle. The author's description, the lovers' emotional response, and Helen's thoughts find a desperate threat. The fragility of physical existence and the vulnerability of lovers are linked for Helen as she stands in the sunshine among the natives and foresees death.

She became acutely conscious of the little limbs, the thin veins, the delicate flesh of men and women, which breaks so easily and lets the life escape compared with these great trees and deep waters. A falling branch, a foot that slips, and the earth has crushed them or the water drowned them. Thus thinking, she kept her eyes anxiously fixed upon the lovers, as if by doing so she could protect them from their fate. (Pp. 349-350)

The jungle, the erotic drive, and death humble man and promise the extinction of the prize of his being, which begins to define itself in Rachel's struggle against love. The struggle commences as soon as the danger is made clear in these wilderness scenes. Love is not allied to nature as it awakened Rachel after the dance, making her see and feel, but rather it is allied to nature as it teems with senseless life and towers over man or falls indifferently upon him. Entering love is entering that wilderness. Terence gives a hint of this, thinking, when the lovers return to their companions, that existence is in two layers, one "the Flushings talking, talking somewhere high in the air above him, and he and Rachel had dropped to the bottom of the world together."

But in fact love exposes Rachel to the dangers of society as well as to the dangers of nature. The world has no place for the reality of lovers, and it puts them safely out of the way until they recover. So Rachel and Terence are left insistently alone until they feel isolated "as if, playing in a vast church, the door had been shut on them." Rachel rebels actively against the forms in which the world contains love as soon as conventional gestures begin to surround her experience again.

". . . I never fell in love, if falling in love is what people say it is, and it's the world that tells the lies and I tell the truth. Oh, what lies—what lies!"

She crumpled together a handful of letters. . . . It was strange, considering how very different these people were, that they used almost the same sentences when they wrote to congratulate her. . . . (P. 359)

But the battle between the lovers, and Rachel's battle with love itself, is joined because the self is threatened with subjugation and disintegration. There is a universal element in these fears, the fear that freedom will be limited by the other, and the fear that the integrity of the self may be damaged, but in Rachel the fear and resistance are extreme and total. Not only must the privacy of the soul be protected (even to the extent of placing her music beyond Terence's reach) but also the surface must be placed out of the way of violation. Caresses are noticeably lacking in the courtship; physical contact is limited to the lovers' wrestling like young boys. The more organic of the senses, and in particular the sense of touch, bear the threat of nature. A great and fatal dissociation of faculties in Rachel's response to Terence is reflected in her awareness of life at this time:

"Does it ever seem to you, Terence, that the world is composed entirely of vast blocks of matter, and that we're nothing but patches of light—" she looked at the soft spots of sun wavering over the carpet and up the wall—"like that?" (P. 358)

Terence's repudiation ("I feel solid") emphasizes the fragility of Rachel's being. Her body, being part of the vast blocks of matter of the world, is alien to the sensibility which is as inarticulate as music and as detached and ephemeral as visual perception. In short, the visceral response is totally lacking, or if it is present, Rachel will not consent to it.

It would seem that the battle ceases, and a coherent life has been won, at the last moment. Just before Rachel falls ill, an entire chapter is devoted to her resolution of the problem. The lovers have been invited to tea by Mrs. Thornbury, and in consenting to go, Rachel expressly makes peace with society, accepts her new role, and rests in her understanding with Terence. The appearance is deceptive. She has not reached any relationship with society; she has simply disarmed it, or reached a position where she is not afraid. People are no more real to her than in the beginning; they are further away: "And now the room was dim and quiet, and beautiful silent people passed through it, to whom you could go and say anything you liked. She felt herself amazingly secure. . . ." Similarly, she feels serene with Terence because the emotional life has stilled and the lover is placed at a safe distance:

Although they sat so close together, they had ceased to be little separate bodies; they had ceased to struggle and desire one another. There seemed to be peace between them. It might be love, but it was not the love of man for woman. (P. 385)

She goes on to declare her real life to be independent of Terence, and his of her. She is at peace because she has reduced both society and nature to shadows.

Terence eliminates the ambiguity in her statement by revealing, in his similar serenity as he sits at her deathbed, that the goal of their love is death. "They had now what they had always wanted to have, the union which had been impossible while they lived." For both lovers this union is an impossible idea, and the state of happiness reigns when the other is absent: Rachel experiences it while Terence is sleeping, Terence when Rachel is dead.

At this point in the novel, structural weakness accompanies thematic power. The crisis of Rachel's test of reality does not coincide with the crisis of the novel. The crucial actions for Rachel's test begin with the scene in chapel and end with her consent to a split life in which people and nature are held at an agreeable distance and her real life is hidden and independent. The nature of that true existence is not made explicit in her reverie just before the fatal fever comes, but throughout the novel imagery and action prepare us to recognize her desire as asocial, inarticulate (chaotic), and self-absorbed. At one moment in the lovers' wrestling, Terence states that Rachel would throw him into the sea if they stood on a rock together. Although she does not admit the hostility, her thoughts show that he is excluded from her joy: "To be flung into the sea, to be washed hither and thither, and driven about the roots of the world—the idea was incoherently delightful." Woolf has used the same metaphor for the love-trance and will use it for the sinking of consciousness before death, and all are prepared for by Rachel's serenity after the dance,[5] in which she describes herself pleasurably as a fish at the bottom of the sea at the same time that she builds herself a cairn of pebbles. Though she has wanted that sinking away from all the forms of human relatedness, she has felt terror when Terence was with her there. In dying she fulfills the desire that has been present from the beginning but has at times been obscured by details of active life. The sinking into the unconsciousness of death is a correspondence in action, then, to her essential sense of life and has a certain inevitability although it seems to be the result of fate or blind chance. At the point of Rachel's death, her destiny is fulfilled and her experiment concluded in a hard paradox: although brute nature and death (its manifestation) would seem to be the enemy of life, in Rachel's life there is complicity. What seems to be an assertion of the pure self, disembodied like sunlight, unrooted in earth or in society, is a denial of life. Freedom (Rachel's desire) is death. Rachel prepares for Rhoda, in *The Waves,* in whom these essential traits are found distilled.

The experiment has failed in a peculiar way: from the failure of Rachel's test of the world (and Terence fails also), a new possibility arises. Chapter 25 ends with the tragic cry of Terence. Chapter 26 begins with the darkness from which the lovers have disappeared. In this night there is nothing but

nature; but it is neither the nature of flowers and pebbles that
Rachel first saw with delight, nor the threatening nature of
the jungle. It is animistic nature.

> In this profound silence one sound only was audible, the sound
> of a slight but continuous breathing which never ceased, although
> it never rose and never fell. It continued after the birds had begun
> to flutter from branch to branch, and could be heard behind the
> first thin notes of their voices . . . but when the sun rose it ceased,
> and gave place to other sounds. (P. 433)

Although the appeal is ostensibly auditory, it is not sound
of the same order as the previous sounds of birds and monkeys. The sound of the night breathing brings with it a kinetic
sense of a gigantic body, and it is in this order that a new
nature enters the novel and makes possible an active sympathy
between human nature and cosmic nature. There are no
longer inert blocks of matter played upon by a fitful light. Life
is in matter itself, in the body, breathing, throbbing with the
beating of the heart; people reach out to one another with
hands of flesh. After the long night's breathing, the human
world awakens again and people resume their roles; but roles
and gestures are no longer mechanical. Society knows the
pain and the splendor, and heroically makes its gestures, in
defiance of cosmic nature and in sympathy with cosmic
nature, but always asserting an active mastery of life.

The new consciousness is unrelated to any of the preceding
voices—the author's, Helen's, Rachel's, or Terence's—and it
imposes a startling structural break. All the barriers and con-
flicts of the novel are broken up by the vitality and authority
of this new voice: the opposition of society to nature, the
conflict between social identity and authentic existence, the
walls between people (and Hirst's resting at peace in the hum-
drum world he formerly disdained is the most striking example). Although the one person who is most significant in
this end-action, Mrs. Flushing, weeps rebelliously for Rachel's
death, goes out to face the storm but calls it splendid, and
shortly turns to an ardent debate about life on Mars, the new
consciousness avoids deep immersion in any self. The self as
an exclusive consciousness is insufficient, even deadly, and the

feminine self has proved to be a narrower box than the masculine. The last two chapters of *The Voyage Out* represent a
tentative movement towards total consciousness. But by its
very nature in avoiding the intense inner experience of any
person, it is a diffuse consciousness and inhospitable to a
novelistic focusing of action.

In her next novel, Virginia Woolf does not pursue the possibility of total consciousness glimpsed in the conclusion of *The
Voyage Out,* but turns to one aspect of the final affirmation—
the reconciliation with society—and returns to a feminine
protagonist, attemping to find the girl's destiny within conventional society freshly and more richly seen. The author's
own attitude to the second novel, as revealed in her diaries,
was that *Night and Day* was "more mature and finished and
satisfactory"[6] than *The Voyage Out,* and in spite of E. M.
Forster's preference for *The Voyage Out,* she reasserted her
belief that *Night and Day* had "less brilliance on the surface"
but more depth.[7] Only as the conception of *Jacob's Room*
began to take shape in 1920, did Woolf revise her estimate
and find her first novel a "more gallant and inspiring spectacle."[8] *Night and Day* is less gallant—and throws less light
on the existential problem—because it is less candid. In spite
of the copiousness and discursiveness of thought as well as of
scene and action, the psychological problems are thoroughly
rationalized, so that the emotional depths are merely hinted
and left unresolved.

The title is not made clear until two-thirds of the novel is
done.

Why, she reflected, should there be this perpetual disparity between the thought and the action, between the life of solitude and
the life of society, this astonishing precipice on one side of which
the soul was active and in broad daylight, on the other side of
which it was contemplative and dark as night? (P. 358)[9]

The competence that Woolf felt so proudly on finishing
Night and Day is to be found in *Day* rather than in *Night.*
Having made a reaffirmation of society in the first test, Woolf
returns to it exhaustively, wedging her heroine tightly into a

social structure and loading her with the routine duties and relationships of middle class life. Some of the vigor and warmth of the last pages of *The Voyage Out* are to be found in the realization of characters (particularly women) and interior scenes in *Night and Day*. One has only to compare the characterizations of Evelyn Murgatroyd and Mary Datchet to see that surface realism has been replaced by a sympathetic realism; and a comment of Katherine's, when her aunt repeats the current gossip about her, provides authorial comment on the photographic image of reality: "The indecent spectacle was her own action beheld for the first time from the outside; her aunt's words made her realize how infinitely repulsive the body of life is without the soul."

The life of society includes literature, politics, domesticity; family relations, worldly ambition, courtship, crusading; fine dress, bag-lunches, the zoo, the underground. It includes, in the beginning, everything but the heart's desire. As Katherine thinks (resuming the thematic problem where *The Voyage Out* left it), life is "an affair of four walls, whose objects existed only within the range of lights and fires, beyond which lay nothing, or nothing more than darkness."

Yet it would seem that the terrors of *The Voyage Out* have been mastered, if we judge by Katherine's actions and introspection. She is mistress of every situation: she manages the household in practical fashion; she presides over the tea table; in helping her mother write a biography of her famous grandfather, she is the only efficient and disciplined agent; she has an imperious, even arrogant, mastery of all relations, and awes her peers; she becomes engaged to a man who worships her. The *other*, it would seem, holds no terrors for her. Similarly, she is undismayed by the cosmos. She is not terrified by the engulfing of human history in the cosmic process. She is exalted.

. . . The stars did their usual work upon the mind, froze to cinders the whole of our short human history, and reduced the human body to an ape-like, furry form, crouching amid the brushwood of a barbarous clod of mud. This stage was soon succeeded by another, in which there was nothing in the universe save stars and the light of stars; as she looked up the pupils of her eyes so dilated with starlight that the whole of her seemed dissolved in silver and spilt over the ledges of the stars for ever and ever indefinitely through space. Somehow simultaneously, though incongruously, she was riding with the magnanimous hero upon the shore or under forest trees. . . . (P. 205)

She allies herself secretly with the forces of negation, and is hostile to life; her fulfillment is in dissolution of human identity, whether it be in social terms, in terms of civilization, or in relatedness. For this reason, we find her entire social life to be dead and deadly. She goes through the mechanical motions of showing the little museum of her grandfather, the poet, but she hates poetry and repudiates it at every opportunity; she presides at the tea table with grace and beauty and propriety, but makes the young newcomer Ralph Denham feel miserably out in the cold; she allows herself to become engaged to William Rodney, but shows him in every word and gesture that she despises him. Without the scant clues to her dark world, Katherine's daylight self would be incomprehensible or repellent. The two clues are Katherine's dream of the magnanimous hero, and Ralph's divination that her darkness is a repressed ardor which does not find "uncalculating passion and instinctive freedom" with Rodney. "It was in her loneliness that Katherine was unreserved." The four walls of the Hilberys' drawing room have no place for Katherine's desires, repressed or unrepressed; and her erotic urge as well as her intellectual desire (for mathematics) have become associated with the unpeopled dark.

Katherine's spontaneous emotional responses are so far in exile that she cannot distinguish between the emotions of love and pity, and is baffled when people find her unsympathetic after she has behaved with cruel coldness. She gazes in wonder and delight upon Mary, who can say "I love him" and make no mistake. Although the entire novel is an assault on the fortification of the numb and solitary self, the final breach by

the power of love is a melancholy one, as Leonard Woolf
commented upon reading the novel for the first time. Katherine places her discovery of love at the moment of discovering fear. She recognizes love by the nightmare anxiety she
experiences on the night when she fails to find Ralph at his
office. She wanders in the dark like a lost child. Her efficiency
is gone, and also the cold splendor of her solitude. Chaos
comes. She approaches the condition of Ralph when, much
earlier, he finds himself vulnerable in love.

> He felt himself now, as he had often fancied other people, adrift
> on the stream, and far removed from control of it, a man with no
> grasp upon circumstances any longer. Old battered men loafing at
> the doors of public-houses now seemed to be his fellows. . . .
> They, too, saw things very thin and shadowy, and were wafted
> about by the lightest breath of wind. For the substantial world . . .
> had slipped from him . . . there was no limit to the flood of dam-
> age; not one of his possessions was safe now. (P. 162)

This is like the terror of love in *The Voyage Out,* but here less
intense. The river on which the lover finds himself adrift does
not threaten to end in a waterfall, but the fear of being out of
control persists. In the end the loss of control is accepted by
Katherine to the extent that she allows herself to move in
someone else's dream. But the fear does not end, and the
imagery of winds and waters continues. The love-fear is en-
durable because it is finally contained in a tenuous conception.
The conception is as transient as the moment in which the
lovers stand on the threshold between the literal dark and
lamplight, and depends on Katherine's being able to step over
the threshold into the light: that is, to move away from the
chaos of love into the containment of the civilized four walls.

The containment is worked out extensively in the studies of
Ralph, for he is in every way freer and more complex than
Katherine, not only in relationships with the world but also
in introspection. He provides the language of imagination
necessary to escape the dichotomy Katherine finds between
self and society, action and dream. As Woolf states, Katherine
is simple, and her distinctions are clear and monolithic: if she

steps outside the four walls, there is only darkness. Ralph, who thinks figuratively and therefore suggestively, sees links and the possibility of simultaneity, which would be paradoxical to Katherine's rigidly controlled mind. For Ralph no condition is exclusive. When he is adrift on the water or blown by the gale, he is in human company; when he is alone in the dark with his dream of love, the light from her dwelling falls upon him; his dream of love and beauty are bound to the daylight world in the person of Katherine. Ralph has his own dichotomy and his own chaotic darkness: "He had a strange sensation that he was both lighthouse and bird; he was steadfast and brilliant; and at the same time he was whirled, with all other things, senseless against the glass." Yet he provides the great symbolic transformations that modify the opposition of night to day. In lamplight, which Katherine has seemed to consider as artificially prolonged daylight obeying daylight rules, Ralph sees a third order of being, again comparable to the lighthouse, that of "a general glory of something that might, perhaps, be called civilization; at any rate, all dryness, all safety, all that stood up above the surge and preserved a consciousness of its own." The dream of civilization and the dream of love are one for Ralph, and both have their value in shining out into the complex dark. The dark, as previously indicated, is social and philosophic as well as instinctual, and the Hilberys give him light at all the levels of his being. It is a real light, and a steady one.

He also gives Katherine her image of reconciliation, but it is less integral to the novel and less efficacious in reconciling society and the self. The symbol, one doodled by Ralph while trying to compose a love letter, is a blot fringed with flame. Katherine first accepts it as a figure for the universe, as Ralph has intended; it is similar to Terence's "aura," a halo for certain objects of life, and this meaning is in keeping with Ralph's symbolic use of the lamplight of the Hilberys. Katherine, however, makes the image her own, and sees in it a flame burning through its smoke. She identifies it as Ralph, and sees it as a source of life. This is, in the end, the strange collaboration, communion, or oblique communication: each unintentionally provides the other with a light for his darkness—allows himself to be transformed into a necessary light —and yet each remains essentially alone in his darkness.

> Moments, fragments, a second of vision, and then the flying waters, the winds dissipating and dissolving; then, too, the recollection from chaos, the return of security, the earth firm, superb and brilliant in the sun. From the heart of his darkness he spoke his thanksgiving; from a region as far, as hidden, she answered him. (Pp. 537-538)

For Katherine in particular, the resolution is won from chaos for a brief moment by the power of imagination, and it slips back into chaos. Unlike Ralph's light, it is made, not given. "The problem had been solved; she held in her hands for one brief moment the globe which we spend our lives in trying to shape, round, whole, and entire from the confusion of chaos." The power and beauty of the image are great, yet the imagination in its moment of whole vision contains very little of what the novel offers. True, it encompasses a harmony of Ralph and Katherine and their relationship to chaotic natural forces. For that moment, all other people and other situations must disappear. But it is a precarious and partial containment, necessarily brief, and the novel itself must find a different resolution. The Katherine who steps back into the lighted world, thus suggesting an acceptance of both worlds, but a permanent commitment to society, is still a young woman who feels outraged by others' impinging upon her. The fact that she comes to disclose a part of her privacy of being to one other in no way alters her characteristic movement of repudiation and self-containment. Nor does the sympathetic study of other individual characters in isolation alter the isolation, though it disguises it. The omniscient author, having the power to enter the private mind of anyone, may give the reader a total—or almost total—view of character, but the realistic action still shows people presenting sharp edges to one another, with the exception of Mrs. Hilbery and Cassandra. *Night and Day* is a retrenchment after the boldness of *The Voyage Out,* and solves none of the problems found in that novel except the problem of love, and that solution is ambiguous. Katherine finds love neither so fearsome nor so desirable as the first pair of lovers thought, because the danger of total invasion of the self is nullified. Romantic union is not possible. As the lovers walk by the river, Ralph may be possessed by his romantic dream, but it is the invasion by an idea, not by Katherine herself. "She might speak to him, but with that strange tremor in his voice, those eyes blindly adoring, whom did he answer?" Katherine's own dream does not have Ralph, even an imaginary Ralph, as an object of ardor, and the sweep of his passion moves safely because it moves on the periphery, and the center of being is still inviolate. Shakespeare has provided the image (in a passage quoted early in the novel) for the final relationship between Ralph and Katherine:

> To be imprison'd in the viewless winds,
> And blown with restless violence round about
> The pendant world . . .

Night and Day is a formal retreat and a slight thematic advance; the containment is a forced containment. In thinking about *Jacob's Room,* Virginia Woolf comments indirectly on the unsatisfactory aspects of her second novel by suggesting that the new form will "give the looseness and lightness I want," "get closer," and "enclose everything, everything." And she warns herself that "the danger is the damned egotistical self" as in Joyce and Richardson.[10] Two of these suggestions are most significant for the present analysis. The Katherine of *Night and Day* reveals in a very clear, concrete form the dangers of the egotistical self, though these dangers are also to be found more subtly and insidiously in style and method. Woolf warns herself against the authorial egotism found in the aggressive pyrotechnics of *Ulysses,* which is (she thinks) Joyce's underbred self-display. If that were all, it would be a strictly craftsmanlike discipline Woolf demanded of herself.[11]

However, the warning also constitutes a philosophic proposition. Although she makes no comments relating authorial egotism and narrowness to character conception, it is legitimate to make the connection when the "new form" she has found constitutes not only a revolutionary change in structure, style, and point of view but also a mutation in the concept of character long before Woolf justified it in the famous essay "Mr. Bennett and Mrs. Brown."

Katherine, who is called an egoist by Mary Datchet, is the last character of her kind in Woolf's work, except in unsympathetic roles. In spite of her womanly beauty, grace, and good breeding, she is more like Ridley Ambrose than the women in the center of later novels. Both withdraw literally from human society in order to be closeted in the pursuit of intellectual abstraction and immutability; both live in an emotional, physical, and intellectual world so narrow that anyone else would suffer claustrophobia; and both reject instantly any person or any style of life at variance with their conceptions. Virginia Woolf herself, like most other people, recognized a tendency to throw up screens between herself and anything that disturbed her conception of the world.[12] But the egotistical self—a Katherine—is not merely narrow and exclusive. It is tyrannical, and would impose its conception on the other. For this reason Katherine must be judged in the society of *Night and Day* to be deadly. She withdraws from the world and imposes on it a grotesque image which destroys (as we see in Rodney) its own real life. The self is a jealous god and recognizes no other.

An inclusive and harmonious world is not possible as long as the self is a Katherine. When one rejects the self as a bounded being, a conceptual entity that judges and rejects or accepts in terms of its own integrity, then fear of the *other* ceases. However, the danger of the tyrannical self is averted in a love relationship only at the risk of a new danger, replacing a rigid self (which has control by a denial of life) with a being so open that it can be invaded by chaotic forces, as

Katherine's frozen empty night may be invaded by Ralph's night with birds blown by a gale. The compromise and the harmony at the end of Katherine's story, effected largely by the power of language and image—by a contemplative vision —are not translated into action. Woolf's next movement was to alter her sense of personality.

Jacob's Room is the first attempt, then, to write a novel in which a conception of being is not dependent on a conception of self. Nearly every reader from Leonard Woolf on has commented on the shadowy sense of character in *Jacob's Room,* and many see that the effect is intentional; yet Woolf is criticized for succeeding in doing what she meant to do, and she is judged in terms of a contrary conception. In the inception of this novel, the form came first, and the quality of life the form was to embody. The subject came later. "I'm planning to begin *Jacob's Room* next week with luck," Virginia Woolf writes in her diary on April 10, 1920. "It's the spring I have in mind to describe. . . ."

By discarding the narrow and despotic self, Woolf attempts to achieve total consciousness—returning to a possibility in *The Voyage Out*—given order by sensibility rather than ideas. She intends to capture the heart of the world in a particular mood: we might take her suggestion and say, for the sake of brevity, that it is the mood of spring. It is at once apparent that perfect harmony exists between Virginia Woolf's first intuition of the "new form" ("Suppose one thing should open out of another") and the process of green nature in spring. If the metaphor is extended to include the unfolding of human personality in childhood and youth, the organic wholeness of *Jacob's Room* is suggested. The springtime spontaneity is not achieved by excluding winter; but storm and desolation are not the condition of life.

The conception of human personality implicit in the new form is that appearance corresponds to reality, and that the world is in harmony with man. Distinctions of inner and outer being are merely distinctions of visibility, not of kind, and the artist can make the inner being visible by finding its correspondent in the physical world. Philosophic concepts and moral codes form no part of the structure or consciousness of this novel, because they are unnatural. Experience and abstract thought are not naturally related in the way that the material world and sensibility are related, because for most people abstract thought has its source in someone else's experience; the experience has been not a reflection of reality but an artificial substitute for it. The author enters *Jacob's Room* to make a comment that cannot be made by any of the natural creatures of the novel: ". . . It must come as a shock about the age of twenty—the world of the elderly—thrown up in such black outline upon what we are; upon the reality."[13] Although Jacob is an intellectual who reads Plato and has heated debates with his friends, and also has a degree of intellectual intolerance, abstract thought is not the stuff of his life. After he has marched through the *Phaedrus,*

Plato's argument is stowed away in Jacob's mind, and for five minutes Jacob's mind continues alone, onwards, into the darkness. Then, getting up, he parted the curtains, and saw, with astonishing clearness, how the Springetts opposite had gone to bed; how it rained. . . . (P. 109)

And in an intellectual argument with Bonamy which ends in a scuffle, the scuffle—rolling on the floor—bares the reality veiled by abstract argument. If one were to suggest a philosophic explanation that Virginia Woolf herself, remaining faithful to the attitude of the novel, could not formulate, one might begin by inverting the allegory of the cave so that the shadows seen by the world's slaves are ideas, and release into the sunlight is release into authentic experience. Division of the self from the world and from others is the work of the conceptual mind.

If, then, the imposed forms are repudiated and the novel and life evolve naturally, one ought to have an authentic form which does no violence to experienced reality. Within the limitations, which are poetic rather than conceptual or temporal, of the world-consciousness that accompanied her intuition of form, Virginia Woolf succeeded completely. In the end, however, the novel achieves an abstract form as well as an organic form. The unity that Katherine in *Night and Day* saw for a brief moment only and set apart from the process of existence and the form of the novel, becomes an emblem of the entire form of *Jacob's Room:* the globe. The novel has no sharp angles, not even an end. Josephine Schaefer has noted that Woolf uses various devices to link beginning to end, past to eternal present. She goes on to suggest that the novel could well begin where it concludes; but such a reversal would destroy the primary form of the novel, which is organic and has its analogy in the growth of a tree, emphasized by Woolf herself on the final page as Jacob is evoked when "all the leaves seemed to raise themselves." The circle as a form is descriptive not because of its reversibility but because the circle is a symbol of wholeness, and the continuous movement is in stasis; the form is completed in Jacob's world, simultaneously retraced for the author, retraced for the reader. It is present as well as past. Many of the intrusions of the author are devices to emphasize this eternal recurrence.

And what I should like would be to get out among the fields, sit down and hear the grasshoppers, and take up a handful of earth— Italian earth, as this is Italian dust upon my shoes.
Jacob heard them crying strange names. . . . (P. 135)

If we consider what happens to human character in this new form, we find that it is radically changed by relationship —by dispersion—yet no violence is done to the conventions of character delineation Virginia Woolf had inherited from the Edwardians. "Characters" are not radically different from those in *The Voyage Out*. Though she avoids stiff descriptive paragraphs, Woolf delineates character by physical appearance, and by dialogue and action, as in *The Voyage Out*. In reality the characters are not shadowy, even though they are not essentially pictorial.

By extracting details scattered throughout the novel, we can give an objective characterization and situate Jacob accurately in his society. He is tall, heavy, handsome, Grecian in his view of life and in his aspect, yet "barbaric" as Bonamy says, in his desires. That seems to mean obscure and irrational. Jacob has a romantic idea of love, and feels contempt for women who are approachable. He is a second son, not the favored one, of a widow; he is relatively poor. He is admired by his peers and loved by women. He is a Cambridge man with a fairly well-defined set of snobberies. He enters the business world, where he is bored but driven by a continuing intellectual ambition. These facts are conventional and convenient, just as it is convenient to be able to say of a movement in nature that there is a light breeze. But personality itself is as invisible as the wind, and like the wind is known by its touch and by what it moves. Therefore it is a distortion to say in abstraction from context, "Jacob is handsome." We discover that Jacob is handsome when the dancers on Guy Fawkes day wreathe him with flowers for being "the most beautiful man" ever seen. We discover that Jacob is handsome when Sandra Wentworth Williams sees his head on a level with the head of Hermes, and Hermes suffers by comparison. The objective scene and the sensibility of Sandra are part of the reality which cannot be captured by a vaguely descriptive label such as "handsome". The physical characteristics of people are part of a larger physical context, and the sensibility of people works upon the physical reality as the wind acts upon a tree to change its shape. Between mind and matter there is reciprocal and harmonious action. So we find Jacob "regal and pompous" in the British Museum, and cannot with certainty say whether this aspect of his personality is an aspect of the British Museum, or whether the British Museum is an objective manifestation of qualities in Jacob. However, the title, as well as the emotional focus, supports the second explanation, and a comment Virginia Woolf later made on Turgenev seems so much more telling as a key to *Jacob's Room* than to

Turgenev's novels that it deserves consideration here. Woolf states that Turgenev plots not by a series of events but by a series of emotions; and, more significantly even, she finds that personality has a mysterious ordering power:

A Bazarov, a Harlov seen in the flesh, perhaps, once in the corner of a railway carriage, becomes of paramount importance and acts as a magnet which has the power to draw things mysteriously belonging, though apparently incongruous, together.[14]

In *Jacob's Room* Woolf notes that all the incongruous details of life have "for centre, for magnet, a young man alone in his room," but the comment on Turgenev is far more explicit and illuminating.

The power Woolf tries to mimic is a power residing in something other than mind or will or indeed action of any kind. It is a power residing in *being*. Whenever Woolf tried to define it discursively, the result was the kind of helplessness she recalls in Roger Fry, who in the course of a public lecture came to a painting by Cézanne, and lapsed into silence: "When reason could penetrate no further, broke off; but was convinced, and convinced others, that what he saw was there."[15] The mysterious radiance of personality is glimpsed in *The Voyage Out* and again in *Night and Day,* but in images which might serve a contemplative vision without having any apparent manifestation in action. Terence's fumbling speculation on the flame which is "not ourselves exactly, but what we feel" has already been discussed. Ralph in *Night and Day* carries the analysis somewhat farther. He sketches the blot surrounded by flame during a reverie which arrives at a mystical conclusion for the lovers' relationship in transcendental sharing. Fortunately, he does not remain in sterile romanticism but comes to earth, again in terms of the blot and flames. The image is Katherine herself, but also "all those states of mind that had clustered around her" and

that encircling glow which for him surrounded, inexplicably, so many of the objects of life, softening their sharp outline, so that he could see certain streets, books, and situations wearing a halo almost perceptible to the physical eye.

Ralph's analysis stops short of finding the source; he does not know whether the halo is the virtue of the object or of the perceiver. However, Woolf's cited comment on Turgenev makes the passive active and suggests a collaboration that *Jacob's Room* confirms. If we consider, for example, the apparently purposeless encounter of Jacob with Mrs. Norman in the train, we find that Mrs. Norman, who is a middle class mother with the conventional attitudes of her type, begins by responding to Jacob in terms of fixed attitudes ("Men are dangerous"), and ends by placing him safely in a proper pigeonhole, yet feels the stirring of an authentic response to personality. "Grave, unconscious . . . now he looked up, past her . . . he seemed so out of place, somehow, alone with an elderly lady. . . ." The power is in Jacob's being, not in the elderly lady; he calls out her response. Characters who are glimpsed and gone, like Mrs. Norman, play a part much larger and more creative than that of being reflectors or of establishing one of Jacob's social identities. They are fragments of total consciousness; in seeing and being seen, however briefly, they open a part of Jacob's reality to the reader's knowledge, and they modify it and are modified by it. Because there is a response to personality, Jacob's world can be enlarged by whatever Mrs. Norman's world contains that is true to Jacob's world. Specifically, Mrs. Norman adds a consciousness of life that is colored by the nostalgia of the elderly for the bloom and vigor of youth, and the sweet humility of nineteenth-century woman before man. In the two pages concerned with Mrs. Norman, an entire world of old-fashioned relationships is suggested, not in the repressive but in the affirmative manifestations. The bigoted and repressive elements are sketched, made ridiculous, and left behind when Mrs. Norman's world is bridged by Jacob's world. This is a general pattern of relationship, and it depends on the "bubble" or the "halo" of Woolf's earlier intuitions: it is an intangible bridge between two beings, or beings and objects, and it depends on the life of both. It permits harmony of incongruities (Mrs. Norman and Florinda can belong to the same world) and is partially independent of Jacob's specific attitude, although it is related to the general complex of his feeling. Without the aura, elements of existence fall apart, become strange and inert, as happens twice in this novel. For the Plumers, dutifully entertaining young men at luncheon, Jacob is a faceless undergraduate who arrives late. For Jinny and Cruttendon, in their Paris Bohemia, Jacob is a bourgeois. Neither sterile conventionality nor sterile unconventionality responds to Jacob's magnetism, the emotional tone falters, and a momentary break in coherence results.

Every character who touches Jacob has some negative or destructive quality which is filtered out by the aura of Jacob's being, but the deadly, sterile, or ugly qualities are not ignored. Even Jacob's mother, who is warm and vivid and who establishes the tone of sensuous bucolic ease for Jacob's childhood, has a very fundamentally negative attitude which leaves Jacob unharmed. Betty Flanders' sentimentality about her dead husband and the word "love" are charming masks for a rejection of male sexuality, as we find when she gloats over poor old Topaz, who was once the kitten of her suitor Mr. Floyd: "She smiled, thinking how she had had him gelded, and how she did not like red hair in men."

The continuity and the process of opening out depend on sympathetic links, not on similarity of life, temperament, or ideas. The continuity between persons and nature is similar. The sympathy between man and nature is far from naive; it does not depend on the child's image of the meadow in the sun, even when Jacob is a child. There are reciprocity and the enlarging of consciousness, as in relationships with people. The wild horse in Jacob, for example, is dormant until he is out of England and among sharp, bare hills on the way to Olympia; the religious sense is unknown until he sees the Scilly Isles "pointed at by a golden finger issuing from a cloud." From the fall of the great tree in the forest, the child learns something about the inexplicable collapse of great, imposing things; chapel at Cambridge recalls this melancholy lesson. In general, human personality is in an active rather than passive relationship with nature, and in the collaboration man has the task of conferring order and meaning. At the very beginning, Woolf makes clear this relationship, and also the elliptical method by which continuity between sensibility and the external world will be established. Betty Flanders' pen blots, her eyes fill with tears, and the world alters: "The entire bay quivered; the lighthouse wobbled. . . ." A wink dispels the tear, and the world is in order again. It is not necessary to follow Betty Flanders in a rambling interior monologue in order to see the movement of her personality; further, the swiftly altering images reflect more accurately the brevity and lightness of the spiritual clouding. Finally, the immersion in the self involved in introspection is avoided completely, and this last point is crucial in *Jacob's Room*. In this novel people do not shut themselves in a private room to think. Jacob's room, unlike Rachel's room or Ridley's or Katherine's, is not a means of seclusion from the world but is the world itself. When Jacob is physically in his lodgings, he is reading Plato, wrestling with Bonamy, going to bed with Florinda, writing a letter, considering politics. When his mind moves into the dark after reading Plato, it is for only five minutes; then he goes to the window to look at life. When he muses during chapel at Cambridge, his thoughts are related to the outer world. He is completely nonintrospective, even at the moment of life when he loses his aura and the characteristic quality of his consciousness—the tone of the novel—alters. We may take this central episode as a test of the success of Woolf's method and the entire strategy she has attempted.

Jacob's affair with Florinda ends when he sees her on another man's arm. Woolf tells his sensation ("as if the switchback railway, having swooped to the depths, fell, fell, fell"), but she disclaims knowing his mind. He returns to his rooms; we leave him there, for episodes outside his room, with the help of nature, are to convey his state of mind.

"Life is wicked—life is detestable," cries Rose Shaw. That is the line that begins the next incident, the account of the frozen relationship of two beautiful people. Then the eye of consciousness roams Soho in the dark, finding externally the hostile and brutal impulses of human chaos. "The lamps of London uphold the dark as upon the points of burning bayonets." The passage continues through Soho, with raw meat, raw voices, contemptuous eyes, babies with purple eyelids, and a sad man fingering the raw meat. Next we return to Jacob, who is still alone in his room reading the *Globe* and severely subjecting himself to the wasteland of politics. An almost unpeopled scene follows; it is the only winter scene of the novel. "Spaces of complete immobility separated each of these movements. The land seemed to lie dead. . . ." Jacob goes to bed. The next chapter begins with Jacob gossiping with the Countess of Rocksbier over lunch; then it finds Jacob at the hunt, and recounts the sensations of the action.

Hedges and sky swoop in a semicircle. Then as if your own body ran into the horse's body and it was your own forelegs grown with his that sprang, rushing through the air you go, the ground resilient, bodies a mass of muscles, yet you have command too, upright stillness, eyes accurately judging. (P. 99)

Between the falling of the railway and the leap of the horse, there is an interval of alienation, even though the literary method is the same and the links between people and between man and nature still bind. An alternate view of the world is epitomized by the scenes presented to the reader in the one evening when Jacob sits alone. In that other world, the vital links of sympathy are missing, and people, whether they are graceful figurines or raw flesh, are as empty of human value as the newspaper Jacob reads, recounting "a strike, a murder, football, bodies found." Frigidity, hostility, butchered flesh, and a cosmic context which is frozen, inhospitable to life, unresilient, and incoherent: "Spaces of complete immobility separated each of these movements. . . . Stiffly and painfully the frozen earth was trodden under and gave beneath pressure like a treadmill."

It is a death of the spirit, chaos, "chasms in the continuity

of our ways," and it defines very clearly the difference between the consciousness of the world magnetized by Jacob
and that of Woolf's first novel, uncontrolled by Rachel, who
saw herself washed this way and that by the primeval forces.
The magnet of Jacob's consciousness has a force of its own.
Jacob's force is not based on intellect or will—though there
is harmony between will and energy—but it is the timeless
surge of the life force, beyond the domain of reason. Movement and continuity—space, time, flesh, and spirit—resume
in the thrust of the jumping horse, placing us in Jacob's
world once again. The presence of the life-force, and its
lapse, are not explained, because they are inexplicable, but
the context indicates that Virginia Woolf was at least con-
fronting the problem of eros, and recognized the union of
desire and will as the source of energy.

Woolf does not convey Jacob's crisis by introspection,
because inward-turning is not characteristic of Jacob's sensibility. If he is thwarted, he does not retire to a solitary
darkness, but looks out to others in the dark; if the body
seems reduced to disjoined and salable flesh, the outer world
reveals it. Relatedness is Jacob's mode of being. Dream likewise has no place in his world. Instead, for Jacob there is
a reverie in which all the elements of relatedness achieve a
synthesis, and time and space are breached, not in a mystic
vision but in a world-consciousness which is made in finite
relationships. Jacob's love affair with the sophisticated Mrs.
Williams come to a crisis which in the final pages of chapter 12 serves the same function as a recognition scene in
Greek tragedy. The passage is not a narrative climax, because nothing happens. Woolf leaves Jacob and the beautiful amorous lady just at the moment which would be most
interesting from the standpoint of action. No doubt they
become lovers; Woolf gives the reader not the action but the
recognition; and the totality, Jacob's world-synthesis, comes
in a concentrated moment. Jacob has walked to the Acropolis at night with Sandra Wentworth Williams. He feels him-

self to be in a Mediterranean land where the wind rushes across dry places, makes the cypresses creak, and swirls Sandra's veils. He gives her a volume of Donne's poetry.

> Now the agitation of the air uncovered a racing star. Now it was dark. Now one after another lights were extinguished. Now great towns — Paris — Constantinople — London — were black as strewn rocks. Waterways might be distinguished. In England the trees were heavy in leaf. Here perhaps in some southern wood an old man lit dry ferns and the birds were startled. The sheep coughed; one flower bent slightly towards another. The English sky is softer, milkier than the Eastern. Something gentle has passed into it from the grass-rounded hills, something damp. The salt gale blew in at Betty Flanders's bedroom window, and the widow lady, raising herself slightly on her elbow, sighed like one who realizes, but would fain ward off a little longer—oh, a little longer!—the oppression of eternity. (P. 160)

Here are the boldly inclusive leaps which make consciousness total in time, space, and disparate minds, a totality which has been prepared for discreetly by all the oblique links between minds and matter in preceding episodes of the novel. The space between London and Constantinople is Jacob's earthly scope, but that space includes time past and time future; for Jacob, at this time present on the Acropolis, has not yet gone to Constantinople. It evokes the tender nature of the English landscape—the garden—which is consonant with the mood of spring and suggests Jacob's bucolic childhood, at the same time that he stands in the "trampling energy of mood" of the rising wind on the Acropolis. It encompasses the loves of Jacob, from the tenderness of mother and child to the overmastering but idealized eroticism of the man and woman in Athens, and correspondence between spirit and matter in the equivalence of scene and mood. Finally, in the present moment which links Jacob in Athens and his mother in Scarborough, the wind blows into her window with a different meaning from that of the Mediterranean wind, so that a different world opens out, and though it is seen but briefly, its hint becomes a part of the consciousness of Jacob's world. The intimation of death that Betty

Flanders has is partly the mother's forewarning of her son's death, partly the mother's sense of doom in her son's eroticism taking him to another woman; but it is also a hint—and there are others like it—that the total and perfect consciousness magnetized by Jacob would have been mortal even if Jacob had not been killed in the war, for it is the consciousness of youth.

Previously it was suggested that this novel does not include either introspection or dream. Although Jacob is not a dreamer, and neither are his peers or the people who are linked to him, in the end his world comes to its completion when he is drawn to another world, that of Sandra Wentworth Williams; and Mrs. Williams is indeed a dreamer, making gorgeous dreams in which she rises like Venus from the sea, but also making life a dream, vague and cloudy like her language:

". . . And everything is soft and vague and very sad. . . . But everything has meaning." . . . "One must love everything."
. . . .
The tragedy of Greece was the tragedy of all high souls. . . . She seemed to have grasped something. She would write it down. (Pp. 140-141)

Sandra has both Clarissa Dalloway and Septimus Smith in her language, and all three are fundamentally alien to Jacob's world (yet Sandra has a magnetism as strong as Jacob's) in their imaginative creation of a world from dream rather than from sensation. In the joining of these two worlds in Athens, Jacob's own world comes to its fullness, but also to its end in the sense that completion is conclusion.

The concentrated vision of chapter 12 is the climax of the novel; after Jacob returns to London, there is a breaking of links, dispersal of people, fading of vision, and disappearance of Jacob, all to return only when Bonamy's memory, magnetized by the room just as Bonamy has been by Jacob himself, evokes that wholeness in the name *Jacob,* and the leaves rise. Just as the consciousness of Jacob has been present for people when Jacob was in exotic lands, so it can be present when Jacob is dead. There is no end, except for Betty Flanders, for whom the rich variety of Jacob's life becomes "confusion," and she holds out a pair of old shoes.

Passing references have already been made to the power of Virginia Woolf's new form to encompass characters, attitudes, and experiences which do not properly fall within Jacob's range. In analyzing character we have found that the sympathetic aura of Jacob gives him a link with others and opens entire lives which only touch his in passing; in looking for Woolf's method of revealing Jacob's despair, we have found that his mood is conveyed by externals, in society and nature. The method used to bridge all the chasms of personality, space, time, and experience is essentially the same. To introduce ideas which are not Jacob's, Woolf finds a link, like the sympathy Mrs. Norman feels for the young man, to lead into the un-Jacobean idea. Sometimes the links are physical, as in the commentary on the Italian landscape, which might almost be Jacob's view of it as he rides on the train. Sometimes they are associations of mood, as in the passage following Jacob's exultant departure from a good party, in which the excitement of the phrase "drums and trumpets" leads from Jacob's sense of a "magnificent world" to a sketch of the less magnificent joys of the humble, the shabby, and the drunken. Sometimes a character inspires general comments, as the brief essay on beauty in women follows from a specific view of Fanny Elmer.

The links are associations in time, intended to show Jacob's action, a past action, moving in the present. Two revealing sentences, already quoted in another context, disclose Virginia Woolf's whole intention in the shifting of verb tenses: "Plato's argument is stowed away in Jacob's mind, and for five minutes Jacob's mind continues alone, onwards, into the darkness. Then, getting up, he parted the curtains. . . ." The past tense may be taken to be the literal action and the literal scene which are the solid base of

Jacob's world, and the present tense may be considered the
timeless action of consciousness, linked to Jacob and consistent with his being, but not bound to his finite existence.
So it is that the great university professors, the chapel at
Cambridge, the London streets, the British Museum, the
sufferings of passion, the joys of passion, the classic dream,
and the pseudointellectuality which stifles thought, existed
in the past and in the present, and were much the same for
Jacob as for us. However, the present tense often introduces
a sensibility very different from Jacob's. One of the most
significant passages to illustrate the difference occurs as
Jacob and his friend Timmy Durant sail toward the Cornish
coast during holidays at Cambridge.

> But imperceptibly the cottage smoke droops, has the look of a
> mourning emblem, a flag floating its caress over a grave. The gulls,
> making their broad flight and then riding at peace, seem to mark
> the grave.
> . . . .
> And what can this sorrow be?
> It is brewed by the earth itself. It comes from the houses on
> the coast. We start transparent, and then the cloud thickens. All
> history backs our pane of glass. To escape is vain.
> But whether this is the right interpretation of Jacob's gloom as
> he sat naked, in the sun, looking at the Land's End, it is impos-
> sible to say. . . . (Pp. 47-48)

The sorrow inspired by beauty, rising from the earth, its
dwellings, and all history, is the narrator's sorrow, and it is
a sorrow related to Jacob not merely by the contemplation
of Land's End but also by the narrator's seeing Jacob as
already in his grave, seeing the process by which all youth
is clouded and each window of life is blocked by history.
However, the narrator's view of life is not only foreign to
Jacob but also antithetical to his view. The sense of trans-
parency and of the ethereal, while it recurs, is not characteristic of Jacob, though a number of critics have been more
concerned with it than with Jacob's own sensibility. Through
the alien consciousness linked to Jacob's and shaped by it,
the novel gains not only an expansion in time and experi-

ence but also an incursion of the terrors which Jacob's world does not naturally inspire. In the passage just quoted, the other consciousness is the tragic sense of life, in which the sight of sunlight, beauty, spontaneity instantly bring premonitions of storm, death, and necessity. For it the life-matter brews a meaning other than itself, and a fatality in nature and society blocks the true expression of individual being. Jacob, on the other hand, has no tendency towards transcendental meaning, even though he reads Shelley. " 'What for? What for?' Jacob never asked himself any such questions, to judge by the way he laced his boots; shaved himself. . . ."

Through the consciousness which finds expression in the present tense, then, the two terrors associated with the separate self are allowed fragmentary expression, but not enough to disturb the harmony of form. The dark foreboding of death and frustration in the passage above is cryptic; and it is rapidly qualified by reality—Jacob naked in the sunlight. In precisely the same way, the terror that comes when the self is cut adrift from the tangible and visible world is introduced and comes under the control of Jacob's form. For example, in "For if the exaltation lasted we should be blown like foam into the air. The stars would shine through us," the images of helplessness and insubstantiality are not characteristic of Jacob's sense of life and not intended to be understood as his. Jacob is fundamentally earthy: his exaltation, the surge of his vital force, is in the symbol of the jumping horse; his awareness of death, in the sheep's skull and the fallen tree; his love of beauty, in the collection of butterflies. He is never more ethereal than that; he is not blown, insubstantial, into air. If he is gloomy, he traces its source to "respectability and evening parties where one has to dress, and wretched slums at the back of Gray's Inn— something solid, immovable, and grotesque." Because of this solidity, the images of dispersal are limited. In short, Jacob's life and Jacob's consciousness set safe bounds for the formless impulses, whether the impetuous and flyaway spirits are part of his action (in the person of Fanny Elmer, for example) or in the fluid consciousness of the narrator. The effect for the novel as a whole is to render harmless a threat of chaos in the imagination by making it an insert, as it were, a momentary impulse of exaltation in Jacob's mind.

In general, the other fears are managed in the same way. The fear of sexuality, and more generally the fear of the powerful emotions and desires, is nearly vanquished for this novel by the fact that the protagonist is a man. It is not unseemly for Jacob to recognize his elemental urges and to let the wild horse in him gallop. When he goes into his bedroom with Florinda, however, he leaves outside his door, in the form of a letter from his mother, the mind which would think, "Behind the door was the obscene thing, the alarming presence, and terror would come over her as at death, or the birth of a child."

Still, the attitude is rendered harmless in Jacob's world: Jacob emerges from the bedroom "amiable, authoritative, beautifully healthy, like a baby after an airing." The narrator's voice, in the present, points out the contrast between Jacob's world and the continuing, life-denying other consciousness. The facts of sexuality, it says, are

concealed and the evenings for most of us pass reputably, or with only the sort of tremor that a snake makes sliding through the grass. . . . If Florinda had had a mind, she might have read with clearer eyes than we can. She and her sort have solved the question by turning it to a trifle of washing the hands nightly before going to bed, the only difficulty being whether you prefer your water hot or cold, which being settled, the mind can go about its business unassailed. (P. 78)

Jacob's Room gives the first affirmation of sexuality in Virginia Woolf's work, but it is a rather therapeutic one, and it is sharply distinguished from love. One can scarcely speak of it as eroticism, since it has none of the esthetic qualities of sexual love. Though Jacob may briefly see Florinda's body as beautiful in the beginning, he thinks of her as a little prostitute decorating her lips. With her he tends the needs of his body; he likes her well enough, and is sufficiently touched in his vanity to be jealous and disillusioned when he sees her with someone else. The narrator's own comment, though it allows the possibility that Florinda's attitude is the right one, qualifies her broadmindedness in such a way that the entire comment seems acrid. Sexual experience as a natural function of the body might be more appropriately compared to something other than washing the hands; and to transfix the proponents of such attitudes in a phrase such as "she and her sort" is to make the narrator's ambivalent feelings obvious. We have come some way from Betty Flanders' sense that sexuality is an obscene thing, but only so far as to consider it a base function to be performed largely in order to clear the mind of distractions.

However, in the course of the novel one notes most the wrongness of social patterns rather than a danger in sexuality itself. A number of things are wrong: in weighing Florinda, who is promiscuously generous but vulgar, and Laurette, who is rather elegant and intelligent but paid, Jacob's judgment boggles; and, more serious, desire cannot touch the young woman whom Jacob thinks he respects, because laws of class make Clara Durrant as different from Florinda as teacups from monkeys. The young man begins sexual life with a divorce between appetite and affection, and the respectable young woman begins and ends "a virgin chained to a rock."

Sex, then, is unproblematic, natural, and devoid of both enchantment and terror. Love, on the other hand, is still a problem for everyone but Jacob. Others who grapple with love—Bonamy, Clara Durrant, and most notably Fanny Elmer—suffer for it, yearn fruitlessly, and undergo the usual obsessive narrowing of sensibility of frustrated aspiration. Clara Durrant's love is the most melancholy, but Fanny Elmer's the most enlightening. For Fanny, Jacob plays the same role that Sandra Wentworth Williams plays for Jacob, a focus of desire for an ideal *otherness*. Jacob is *Tom Jones,* knowledge in general, the sensory sweetness of nature, beauty, respectable society, power, adventure; he is almost the entire fabric of civilization for her. She can give him nothing but an absurd and childish moment of play. More significantly, he is not merely the focus of desire; he holds the key to desire, and Fanny needs him in order to have any object of desire. Though the sketches of Fanny are full of charm and sympathy, Fanny's kind of love is necessarily hopeless in its dependency, and it is in contrast with the subsequent study of Jacob's love.

In Jacob's love Virginia Woolf finds a solution to the problem of the *other* in solving the problem of love. Fulfillment of love does not require reciprocity. For Sandra, Jacob is a handsome young man who appeals to her, as young men frequently do, and she will put his volume of Donne on her shelf beside the ten or twelve other volumes reminding her of a moment that "mattered for ever," but she will think of him objectively and see the relationship as comparable to that of Alceste and Elimène in *The Misanthrope*. The solution does not involve action. We do not know what word or act Sandra obscurely felt was required on the Acropolis, and we do not know what took place; perhaps nothing at all occurred. The solution does not involve possession of another person (the familiar convention of a young man's initiation by an older, and married, woman serves Woolf well here), nor does it rely on vicarious experience of the other person's life. Jacob can no more possess Sandra Wentworth Williams or her experience than he can possess Pentelicus; in fact, Jacob's response to the woman and the foreign scene is the same, at the time the novel approaches its climax: "If it goes on much longer I shan't be able to cope with it." Coping is not submitting, nor is it rejecting. In loneliness, the bare hills of Italy, Athens, the "illusion," as Woolf calls it, of classic Greece, the dreamy sophistication of Sandra Wentworth Williams, and the rolling wind of life so unlike the gentle breeze at home, Jacob confronts a world totally and magnificently different from his own. It has its own aura, and in the reciprocal magnetism, Jacob's coping must be in the heightening and perfect ordering of his own sense of life.

This is of course one commonly accepted result of love; the episode in *Jacob's Room* is unusual only in showing the process reflected in a total consciousness of life rather than in tracing its physiological or psychological effects. The power of eros is seen in the sweeping wind which brings together all experience, at the same time charging each object of experience with vitality, "the indescribable agitation of life." One has only to compare the description of dawn coming to London, at the end of chapter 12, with a previous scene of the London street at the beginning of chapter 5, to see how complete the transfiguration has been. From "the red and blue beads . . . run together on the string" of the buses, in the earlier passage, we go to "a whir of wings as the suburban trains rush."

Even in the vulnerability of love, there is no danger of shattering the order that sensibility has created. Although Sandra Wentworth Williams is beautiful, sophisticated, mysterious, and skilled, she serves merely as a focus for Jacob's diffuse feelings and perception of life without sharing them. The situation is rather like that of Katherine walking beside Ralph's ecstatic darkness in *Night and Day*. There Katherine felt excluded from Ralph's dream of life, saddened, critical; but here the experience itself is captured, not seen from the outside as an unreality and not opposed by another who seeks a shared vision. Terence in *The Voyage Out* was not convincing when he cried, "You'll be free," and Rachel was not credible when she claimed that she and Terence would have their independent lives; but Jacob and Sandra, without making any claims, prove the possibility of freedom and integrity without isolation or repudiation. Each has a complete world. What Sandra takes of Jacob to add to her world he never misses, and indeed never knows; nor does Jacob ever fully know Sandra's reality.

This culminating episode, as well as the opening episode, clarifies the limitations of the novel. The reader of realism is likely to object to this view of love because it is obviously not a love which bears daily repetition or responsibility. The entire novel is lacking in responsible love, an absence even more striking in the relationships of the Flanders family. The relations of sons to mother or of brothers to one another are as uncommitted as the relations of strangers in a train. Jacob's brothers are indeed no more than ghosts. The threat of the Other is eliminated partly by the absence of the demands made upon one another by people who are socially bound together. In *Jacob's Room* there is no binding. This is not to say, however, that these omissions and these limitations imply weakness in the world-view or in the novel. The completeness, vitality, and harmonious sweep of consciousness which I have called "total" constitutes after all the completeness of spring-time, a young life, not negated by other complete and true visions.

Death, finally, the great threat to existential meaning, enters as a motif in chapter 1, and emerges briefly into consciousness again at significant moments in Jacob's evolution. For Jacob himself death holds no terrors; the sheep's skull interests him, as any other fact of life interests him. For the rest, death's meaning is the subject of meditation by the voice of the present. The melancholy premonition of the end of youth and beauty in the process of nature, which is more somber than Jacob's (inspired by the coast of Cornwall in the passage already cited), is the thought of the narrator. The destruction of war, again action in the present, is described so mechanically that it has no persuasion of reality: it seems to have no bearing on the real life of a Jacob or a Bonamy, and to hold no dangers of destroying Jacob's human meaning.

Like blocks of tin soldiers the army covers the cornfield, moves up the hillside, stops, reels slightly this way and that, and falls flat, save that, through field-glasses, it can be seen that one or two pieces still agitate up and down like fragments of broken matchstick. (P. 155)

This is the stylistic method of the early passages of *The Voyage Out,* deliberately exaggerated to convince the reader that this action is disconnected from the order of life. We have no sense of tragic destiny in the suggested warning that Jacob's life is to end in precisely that way, and the disconnection is made possible by the subliminal insistence on life as consciousness, not as flesh. Jacob's death, to be tragic or even terrible, would have to imply the extinction of his meaning in a return to chaos, but Woolf is careful to show that his life survives, even though he has physically disappeared. In part, the new form suggests a symbolic containment in the circle of action: as the winter of desolation, in this novel, is surrounded by spring, so the threat of death is surrounded by life, and the seasonal impermanence of death lends its symbolism to the death of persons. A double conquest of death is won: the conquest in nature, in which green life springs from the dead, and the conquest that is the power of the human mind alone, in which life springs invisibly in memory. In drawing parallels between the life of man and the other life of the world at the novel's climax, however, Woolf insists on this distinction: "Only here—in Lombard Street and Fetter Lane and Bedford Square—each insect carries a globe of the world in his head. . . ." Jacob's aura, his personal power of meaning, does not disappear, because it has altered the minds of others. In the globe of the mind, Jacob continues, and the entire world of his sensibility goes on; he is more present for Bonamy, who sees the leaves raise themselves and calls "Jacob," than he was in the beginning for Archer, who ran down the beach calling his invisible little brother.

There are obvious parallels between *The Voyage Out* and *Jacob's Room* in the confrontation between the unformed personality and the world, and even in the completion of destiny by death. But every problem that proved insurmountable in *The Voyage Out* has been mastered in *Jacob's Room,* and it seems that escape from the terrors as well as the constrictions of life had to be accomplished by a male protagonist. (We note that the respectable young girl in *Jacob's Room* is

still as immobile as Rachel was in the beginning of her story.)
The young man is not shown in dutiful relationship to a family
nor dominated by a parent. He is, it seems, free of all compul-
sions and restraints; if he should be bound by the patterns of
"the world of the elderly," it would be by his own choice. With
this male freedom, Woolf can perform the creative test that
was apparently not possible in *The Voyage Out*. Even with a
greater mastery of style in 1920, and with a lively idea of a
new form, Woolf could no more have made Clara Durrant its
embodiment than she could Rachel. The terrors of a Rachel
or the submission of a Clara are of course not strictly feminine;
men, as even *Jacob's Room* shows, are not often free. But the
possibility of freedom was conceivable in a man, and Woolf
first worked out the problems of an existential valuation and
meaning for life where it was most possible imaginatively.
This is undoubtedly the import of Woolf's comment that
"*Jacob* was a necessary step, for me, in working free."[16]
Having learned where lay freedom-in-relatedness and authen-
ticity-in-society, Woolf returns to women as central figures and
returns to a male mind again only in *The Waves*. Having
defined the terrors of nature and the abyss, and having found
a method of mastery which involves a harmony of consciousness and literary method, she moves to more complex and
more difficult lives.

chapter 3

Mrs. Dalloway and To the Lighthouse

The formal principle Virginia Woolf discovered in *Jacob's Room* found complete fruition only in *Mrs. Dalloway*: " 'I am what I am, and intend to be it,' for which there will be no form in the world unless Jacob makes one for himself." Mrs. Dalloway is Woolf's only novel to evolve from a character,[1] and the composition of Clarissa's character brings Woolf "more close to the fact" than Jacob did, as she desired, because Clarissa brings society.

Preliminary sketches of Clarissa Dalloway and her world are to be found in *Jacob's Room* as well as in *The Voyage Out*. Clarissa brings from *The Voyage Out* a nature defined as feminine by conventions of society at a certain time and place, in contrast to Helen, who is female by nature; the former's quality expresses itself in scents, jewels, lovely gowns, charm, intuition, sympathy, worldly ease, practical inadequacy, and movement within fashionable society and the Establishment. But Sandra Wentworth Williams, who forms a psychological link between *Jacob's Room* and *Mrs. Dalloway,* is significant at a depth which cannot be defined in a phrase or two; she is significant out of proportion to her place in *Jacob's Room.*

85

As Jacob lives by nature, Sandra lives by art and imagination. She is in touch with the material world as a dragonfly is in touch with the stream. When the evening wind moving the dirty curtains of her hotel window is accurately registered but gives rise to a reverie of love for the peasants, we see that the primary sense impression has been divorced from its context and made to serve a symbolic function in a totally unrelated context of sensibility. We see further that her sense of beauty and her sense of harmonious meaning rest in artifice, taking her own person and human relations as the esthetic field.

Sandra Wentworth Williams, ranging the world before breakfast in quest of adventure or a point of view, all in white, not so very tall perhaps, but uncommonly upright . . . got Jacob's head exactly on a level with the head of the Hermes. . . .

Still, a lady of fashion travels with more than one dress, and if white suits the morning hour, perhaps sandy yellow with purple spots on it, a black hat, and a volume of Balzac, suit the evening. Thus she was arranged on the terrace when Jacob came in. (P. 144)

'Arranged' in the last sentence gives the key to Mrs. Williams. Her sense of her own beauty, her upright bearing, her quest of adventure in relatedness (and not merely with young men), her trophies of successful moments of creation, her very deliberate charging of every small encounter and passing perception with esthetic significance, reflect the action of the creative imagination when it is housed in a patrician woman who works upon the stuff of life rather than upon other matter in an imitation of life. In this sense, Sandra Wentworth Williams is clearly a sketch for Mrs. Dalloway. However, the weakness in Sandra's creative process is that it cannot deal faithfully with ugliness and destruction, but tends to glance off incompatible reality and rest in its own esthetic vision: the dirty curtains become an idea of love for the poor. Woolf is meticulous in showing the danger of sentimentality as well as the more serious danger of alienation from reality which I have already pointed out in citing passages of Sandra's reverie which could have come from Septimus Smith. Sandra is a preliminary sketch, then, for the two extreme positions in *Mrs. Dalloway,* the sane and the insane, Clarissa and Septimus.

Although this kind of feminine creative sensibility interested Virginia Woolf from the beginning of her life as a writer, there are also from the beginning very clear and explicit authorial reservations about the character. In *The Voyage Out* these are expressed not only by Helen's contemptuous shattering of the glamorous image Rachel has of Clarissa, but also in the frailty of the woman herself, her dependence on the equipment of civility to the extent that the disorder of her cabin, while she is seasick during the storm, reduces her to a kind of chaos. In *Jacob's Room* the ironic distance at which Woolf holds Sandra Wentworth Williams reveals her reservations as clearly as explicit statement could. Woolf's misgivings about Clarissa in *Mrs. Dalloway*—found in the *Diary* rather than in the novel itself—are ambiguous. The tinselly effect that Woolf worries about even as she is concluding the novel is only in part an authentic literary concern. A certain glitter is part of the aura of Clarissa in both the novels in which she appears, and there is the real danger of glamour showing itself to be tinsel, as of style becoming manner, inherent in the subject.[2] It presents a very delicate problem in taste; one can never argue with a writer who is working from nature (as Woolf worked in *Jacob's Room*), but in art and manners taste has no objective verification. However, Woolf's uneasiness has another motive, related to her fear of criticism: that is, the desire to work within the expectations of her society, and the conflict between its judgment and her sense of the reality in a Clarissa Dalloway. The problem is complicated by an inconsistency in the judgment of her society, for a Clarissa in life as in art performs the defined rites of femininity acceptable to her society but is disparaged for doing so.

The problem Clarissa poses, by her conceived nature, is two-edged: it is essentially the problem of Rachel caught between the sterile forms and symbols of society and the unfixed and alienated self, but in *Mrs. Dalloway* Woolf arrives

at thematic resolution which is a celebration of the mystery
of the inviolate self as well as of civilization. In writing *Mrs.
Dalloway* Woolf undertook again the task of finding valid
form within the confines of society, for civilization cannot be
celebrated in the abstract. Peter Walsh states the theme which
is implicit from the moment the novel opens upon Clarissa
Dalloway making her way to Bond Street:

A splendid achievement in its own way, after all, London; the
season; civilisation . . . there were moments when civilisation,
even of this sort, seemed dear to him as a personal possession;
moments of pride in England; in butlers; chow dogs; girls in their
security. Ridiculous enough, still there it is, he thought. (Pp. 61-
62)[3]

Like all societies, the one which contains Clarissa Dalloway
is not only seriously flawed but also full of clutter, triviality,
and folly. The germ of the novel was "Mrs. Dalloway in
Bond Street," and in the first or Bond Street movement of the
novel in present time we are caught in the stream of cosmo-
politan humanity, with emergent figures and realistic detail
to capture the social and cultural quality of London and
English society in 1922. The shops, the shopkeepers, the
gentleman with the job at court, a veteran of the war, the
newly arrived provincial, ladies shopping for gloves, omni-
buses, skywriting; and through the miscellany the larger and
more abstract structuring of the strokes of Big Ben, and the
motorcar containing perhaps royalty, moving through the
flux like musical themes. Mrs. Dalloway is in civilization,
both in its concreteness and in its generality. In thorough
contrast to Rachel Vinrace and Katherine Hilbery, she is
committed to her social identity and focuses her life on
creative acts of civility, "doing her part," as Peter says. As
Peter also suggests, Clarissa's commitment is far from naive.

Considered in isolation, abstracted from the specific aura
of the novel, Clarissa's society is far from charming. It can be
seen magnetized by class and religious symbols representing
what T. S. Eliot wanted when he became a British subject:
monarchy, Toryism, and Anglo-Catholicism. The characters

who live within Clarissa's apparent world—aside from casual contact in the street or shops—are people of the privileged class; their roles and relationships are as rigid as those seen aboard the *Euphrosyne* in *The Voyage Out,* and the people are equally antipathetic. Hugh Whitbread, as he appears early in the novel, is stuffy, overmeticulous, falsely gallant. Sir William Bradshaw, a physician to the wealthy, makes "a fine figurehead" at best. Lady Bruton, "a strong martial woman," entertains gentlemen at lunch very elegantly, but is moved by an appetite for power. Lady Bexborough, who opened a bazaar after receiving news of her son's death, is socially admirable (for her stoic manner protects society from her suffering) but hardly human.

The tendency of society, as we have seen in *The Voyage Out* and *Night and Day,* is to make life abstract, to reduce persons to images or symbols, and in the action of *Mrs. Dalloway* which occurs in present time the process of abstraction is very evident. When others see Clarissa, the mental action is the reverse of the viewers' response to Jacob: where Jacob might be an expansive or poetic symbol, Clarissa is a restrictive or public symbol. Scrope Purvis takes note of her comfortably as one of his class symbols; for Miss Pym too, Clarissa defines class relationships, for Miss Pym "owed her help," and for this relationship it suffices that Clarissa is kind. As a class symbol, Clarissa evokes the opposite response in Miss Kilman, but the symbol remains the same. So it is with other social relationships, and we see social patterns and social identities acting upon life to make it static, definite, and safe. People present themselves by those very images, as Clarissa now at fifty judges herself by the image she presents: the absurd pink face she thinks she presents to the world hangs before her own eyes. Even more definitively, she feels, when called upon to draw herself together as a self, an "imperceptible contraction. She pursed her lips when she looked in the glass. It was to give her face point. That was her self—pointed; dart-like; definite."

Society—the abundance of other eyes—makes this call

upon the person and causes this reduction. Even the encounter of old friends, old lovers, involves a sharp contraction
of each. Peter Walsh, coming upon the physical presence of
the woman whose idea provides much of the radiance of his
life, feels the contraction as embarrassment; and he defends
himself by taking out his pocketknife. Whether we look at
passing encounters or at the bonded relationship of man and
wife, we find the patterned maintenance of distance, guarded
preservation of amenities, and stylized images. A sophisticated and silken hardness of relations is one of the conditions
of Clarissa's life and one of the polar tensions of Woolf's
novel. It is not an obvious condition, perhaps, until Septimus
Smith encounters Sir William Bradshaw; at that time all the
destructive potentiality of the formal hardness of Clarissa's
society finds expression. Yet in the opening episode, Clarissa's
reverie tells us how it denies personality: ". . . only this astonishing and rather solemn progress with the rest of them, up
Bond Street, this being Mrs. Richard Dalloway; not even
Clarissa any more; this being Mrs. Richard Dalloway."

Thus, in addition to the external signs of the structure of
English society, there is the constant inner confrontation with
the intransigencies of being a woman in that society. *Mrs.
Dalloway* in its entirety, and *To the Lighthouse* in part, are
expressive forms for the recognition of gender as a social
limitation of being. *Mrs. Dalloway* strikes some critics as
being a minor work essentially because it is a realization of
one gender only, in this sense as limited as *A Portrait of the
Artist as a Young Man* in the Joyce oeuvre.

Affirming woman within a social role (as was not done in
The Voyage Out or *Night and Day,* but only indicated as a
task to be done) poses a double problem for artistic integrity,
for Woolf was already keenly aware of personal falsifications
in femininity and also of the danger of proposing society
exclusively from a female point of view, since society is most
restrictive from that point of view. In *Mrs. Dalloway* these
limitations are avoided partly by the technical devices which
serve to draw other minds into Clarissa's consciousness,

partly by placing Clarissa at an age past some of the reefs of sexuality.

Yet the essential pattern remains feminine and obeys a decorum of acceptance, passivity, with creative acts occurring in the insubstantial terrain of perception and of social arts as ephemeral as those of Indian sand painting. On the one hand, in terms of media there is the inert substance in the background: the leaden sound of Big Ben, the unyielding world of names (Mrs. Dalloway, Lady Bruton, the prime minister) from which only Peter Walsh is partially free. At the other extreme fly the loose atoms of passing experience from which the creative patterns must be made. But in the middle—and it is a most dangerous middle ground—are the opulent patterns of memory, the sentimental libido of a time of illusion. The lyricism of a woman's youth requires more reticence than that of a man (as in *Jacob's Room*); frank avowal of erotic vulnerability is repellent.[4] The dispersal of the energies of being in sentimentality, as well as their concentration in aggression, is a danger always on the edge of the consciousness and of the formal containment of *Mrs. Dalloway*.

Although sentimentality usually involves the evocation of feeling by an inadequate object in external reality, the sentimentality of a young girl's memory in *Mrs. Dalloway,* and also in *Jacob's Room,* involves a censored response and a vocabulary revealing stereotyped response: "Then came the most exquite moment of her whole life passing a stone urn with flowers in it. Sally stopped; picked a flower; kissed her on the lips. The whole world might have turned upside down!"

The self-avowed male sentimentalist, on the other hand, remembering the crisis of love, recalls more fully his own reactions. Peter Walsh, going back to the moment of Clarissa's rejection, finds memories of physical intensity:

She did not move. "Tell me the truth, tell me the truth," he kept on saying. He felt as if his forehead would burst. She seemed contracted, petrified. She did not move. "Tell me the truth," he repeated, when suddenly that old man Breitkopf popped his head in carrying the *Times;* stared at them; gaped; and went away. They neither of them moved. "Tell me the truth," he repeated. He felt that he was grinding against something physically hard; she was unyielding. (Pp. 71-72)

Although Clarissa in the present does not live on dream, as Peter Walsh clearly does, the selective agent of memory has filtered out the elemental kinetic and sensuous elements of experience, leaving something as volatile as the air balls which are associated with her place of youth, Bourton. As a result, the "caves" of memory, the technical discovery which made possible the form of *Mrs. Dalloway,* are capacious and complex only as total memory, wherein the kinetically known life of Doris Kilman and the lustiness of the old street singer can complete the ideal memory of Clarissa. Such evasions of sensual memory in Woolf's women will continue until the issue is met in *The Waves* and *Flush.*

Clarissa fears love nearly as much as she fears hate, and for much the same reason. "Love destroyed too. Everything that was fine, everything that was true went. Take Peter Walsh now." And she has already informed us tersely that Peter's love "was intolerable, and when it came to that scene in the little garden by the fountain, she had to break with him or they would have been destroyed. . . ." The insistence of ancient love in Peter Walsh joins oddly with the Proportion and Conversion of Sir William Bradshaw and the love and religion of Doris Kilman ("The cruellest things in the world . . . clumsy, hot, domineering, hypocritical, eavesdropping, jealous . . .") to anatomize the emotional threat of *Mrs. Dalloway* and to explain the quality of Clarissa's memory and her amorousness. Clarissa defines her adolescent feeling for Sally Seton as "disinterested," and it seems clear that her failure of Richard at Clieveden and Constantinople is related to her aversion for any hot, domineering, jealous love. Frigidity, "the contraction of this cold spirit," is the negative element in disinterestedness and benevolence. So it is that her awareness of erotic love as "something warm which broke up surfaces and rippled the cold contact of man and woman" comes in the most intangible ways, and in the safest context, empathy with another woman:

It was a sudden revelation, a tinge like a blush which one tried to check and then, as it spread, one yielded to its expansion, and rushed to the farthest verge and there quivered and felt the world come closer, swollen with some astonishing significance, some pressure of rapture, which split its thin skin and gushed and poured with an extraordinary alleviation over the cracks and sores. Then, for that moment, she had seen an illumination; a match burning in a crocus; an inner meaning almost expressed. (P. 36)

The sensuality of the metamorphic statement about the world in this passage may lead one to read more serious Sapphic implications in *Mrs. Dalloway* than would be implied by Clarissa's early crush on Sally Seton. Yet such an interpretation would be misleading, for the sensuality evoked is perfectly in keeping with the more generalized but equally notable diffusion of being described earlier:

. . . Somehow in the streets of London, on the ebb and flow of things, here, there, she survived, Peter survived, lived in each other, she being part, she was positive, of the trees at home . . . part of people she had never met; being laid out like a mist between the people she knew best, who lifted her on their branches as she had seen the trees lift the mist, but it spread ever so far, her life, herself. (Pp. 11-12)

Although both passages suggest an erasing of the edges of self, the former involves a paradoxical openness of being, for the world is not diffused but remains a closed circle. The kindling of life is an inner experience, whereas in the imagery of mist of the second passage the self flows outward. Eroticism, instead of providing the way to physical intimacy with others, informs the private self and ultimately the creative imagination. The image can be compared to the experience of Katherine in *Night and Day* when at the end "she held in her hands for one brief moment the globe which we spend our lives in trying to shape, round, whole, and entire from the confusion of chaos." That globe too is one of trans-

figured eroticism, perhaps even more self-contained than that
of Mrs. Dalloway.

The control and the sublimation of erotic feeling are entirely consistent with the life-art of Clarissa Dalloway; the
corresponding control of the anarchy of communal relatedness is in the social art of the party which concludes the novel.
Both acts of form giving, however, are limited. Both Clarissa
and Virginia Woolf recognize and state the danger incurred
in the closing of the powerful and threatening drives of desire.
"Cold, heartless, a prude [Peter] called her," and Clarissa
recognizes that the nunlike seclusion of her narrow bed in the
present represents a contraction of being that began many
years previously, in her failure of Richard: "She could not
dispel a virginity preserved through childbirth, which clung to
her like a sheet." At a certain moment, it is necessary for her
to allow entry to the powerful impulses which are threatening
or destructive, and which in her daytime life she has intermittently mastered. At her party, in the moment of social
triumph (for the prime minister has come), she retreats from
her position of social approval and safety:

. . . But after all it was what other people felt, that; for, though
she loved it and felt it tingle and sting, still these semblances, these
triumphs . . . had a hollowness . . . and suddenly, as she saw the
Prime Minister go down the stairs, the gilt rim of the Sir Joshua
picture of the little girl with a muff brought back Kilman with a
rush; Kilman her enemy. That was satisfying; that was real. Ah,
how she hated her—hot, hypocritical, corrupt; with all that power;
Elizabeth's seducer; the woman who had crept in to steal and
defile. . . . She hated her; she loved her. (Pp. 191-192)

The party is the outward show of the form found for life,
and within its narrow range of time and space contains the
affective past, the past of English society, crime, madness,
despair, and death; it is necessary for Clarissa to preserve her
essential detachment then, and particularly to preserve it in
facing those who are nameless save for the name of their
power—here, the prime minister. At such a moment the inward source of power, hot and crude as it may be, is needed.

Even at the brief instant of affirmation, however, the impulse of power and desire is recognized as immoral, and it must be accepted in its inherent corruptness.

In this novel no manifestation of power or eroticism is found which is either esthetically or morally pleasing. In her radically esthetic sense of life, Clarissa must always be threatened from within and without. In a sense, the aridities and artifices of her society reflect on a communal level a similar need for control; but the level is an inferior one, partly because it is without awareness. The closed car, Big Ben, Hugh Whitbread, Lady Bruton exist in a world in which hate, carnivorous desire, and the Spirit of Conversion have been disguised but not transformed, and aridity is the result of empty forms: the world-globe above without a fluent rupture. So it is that Big Ben, which structures the day of *Mrs. Dalloway,* marks time with a sound that is leaden. The inert power of that sound is constantly dispelled, as Clarissa dispels the oppressive power of the prime minister, by admitting the chaotic elements.

Septimus Warren Smith, and in part his wife Lucrezia, demonstrate the dangers the life of Clarissa Dalloway is designed to disarm. The destruction of self possible in human relationships is most evident, in this novel, in Lucrezia's desolation and loss of identity when the role central to her life is not confirmed by her husband. Her definition of herself as Mrs. Septimus Smith is the only public identity she has in the foreign land of England; she clings to it as to a ledge, in contrast to Clarissa, who feels her identity as Mrs. Richard Dalloway as a state of invisibility.

The danger for consciousness embodied in Septimus, since it is more dramatic and extended, has received much more attention, and the parallels and links between the minds of Septimus and Clarissa are clearly central to the novel. The terror which her life contains is overt and uncontrolled in Septimus; the entire range of fears initially analyzed is in fact demonstrated in the destruction of Septimus; the fear of the cosmos, the fear of the unknown forces in the self, and most notably the fear of others. The last-named fear is found in all its nuances. The alien gaze of others constantly threatens his tenuously constructed world; the words as well as the gaze of the doctors, the men of power, unequivocally aim to deny his existence, his perception of the world; his wife Lucrezia, though she promises some safety in the simple warmth of her domesticity, is also a constant reminder of another image of being to which he cannot attain.

The terror of the cosmos, like the fear of the self, is a mixed fear. "The world has raised its whip; where will it descend?" is answered by a joy so intense that Septimus weeps when he sees the signals in the sky. The terror of the forces within him is manifest in ways that reproduce the source of cosmic fear as discussed in the first chapter. In particular, the need of the visual sense to confer order, the feeling that the world and the self distintegrate when one's eyes are closed, and the identity of color and life are found in Septimus' consciousness at his crisis, just before the entrance of Dr. Holmes:

> Going and coming, beckoning, signalling, so the light and shadow, which now made the wall grey, now the bananas bright yellow, now made the Strand grey, now made the omnibuses bright yellow, seemed to Septimus Warren Smith lying on the sofa in the sitting-room; watching the watery gold glow and fade with the astonishing sensibility of some live creature on the roses, on the wall-paper. (P. 153)

The auditory and kinetic senses are the ones which feel the threat to personal order, as Septimus knows: "But directly he saw nothing the sounds of the game became fainter and stranger and sounded like the cries of people seeking and not finding, and passing further and further away." Or we may find both the threat and the compensatory joy in one of the earliest incursions into the consciousness of Septimus:

> He would shut his eyes; he would see no more.
> But they beckoned; leaves were alive; trees were alive. And the leaves being connected by millions of fibres with his own body,

there on the seat, fanned it up and down; when the branch stretched he, too, made that statement. . . . Sounds made harmonies with premeditation; the spaces between them were as significant as the sounds. . . . All taken together meant the birth of a new religion. . . . (P. 26)

The failure of Septimus, usually analyzed in terms of insanity, is presented by Woolf in terms that repudiate the clinical approach and draw no sharp boundaries between normal and abnormal. Neither is his fate to be placed at the safe distance of social protest, though certainly he is used as an argument against political power and the use made of it to destroy lives, or maim them, in wars. Dominantly, the analysis of Septimus' mind is philosophic in its intent, similar to the preparation for existential psychoanalysis in Jean-Paul Sartre's *Nausea*. The world-ordering faculty depends on the authority of sight which distinguishes otherness and keeps things sharply distanced; the poetic faculty—imagination—depends on the impinging of one thing upon another, the loss of fixed boundaries. As Septimus feels himself to be bereft of body, leaving only nerve fibers "spread like a veil upon a rock," so Clarissa imagines an attenuated presence "laid out like a mist." Creative minds, literary minds, must resolve a seeming paradox. Septimus, the aspiring poet, the worshiper of Keats and Shakespeare, has not found the resolution, and he approaches it only briefly before his death, when he comes most near to Clarissa's mind, in the conclusion of the paragraph cited above:

Outside the trees dragged their leaves like nets through the depths of the air; the sound of water was in the room, and through the waves came the voices of birds singing. Every power poured its treasures on his head, and his hand lay there on the back of the sofa, as he had seen his hand lie when he was bathing, floating, on the top of the waves, while far away on shore he heard dogs barking and barking far away. Fear no more, says the heart in the body; fear no more. (Pp. 153-154)

This ease in the life of the body, including the auditory and kinetic, comes only when the visual authority has been established. The self does not disintegrate in the sea, because it is no longer a "veil upon a rock" as previously but a solid object easily distinguished from other objects such as hats, buses, and trees.

The moment in which the world is given form (and therefore safety) by Septimus is linked to Clarissa in several ways. The grateful dependence on the other is described in similar terms, whether the other is Rezia or Richard. "Hat, child, Brighton, needle. She built it up; first one thing, then another, she built it up, sewing." Clarissa, hearing at her party of Septimus' death, thinks,

Even now, quite often if Richard had not been there reading the *Times,* so that she could crouch like a bird and gradually revive, send roaring up that immeasurable delight, rubbing stick to stick, one thing with another, she must have perished. (P. 203)

The delicate meshing of the necessary forces—the world (the *other*), the dynamo within, and the mind creating order— occurs for Clarissa, but not for Septimus except in one brief interval. Woolf is not exploring the reasons for the failure so much as exposing (and respecting) the failure. The creative dynamo of Clarissa is partly compromise: "She had schemed; she had pilfered. She was never wholly admirable. She had wanted success." This difference, and the difference in the way that the Shakespearean line is understood, will return us to the major thematic line of the novel. "Fear no more the heat o' th' sun" is Septimus's line only in its most limited reference to the elegy from *Cymbeline,* and it is Septimus's line of liberation: "Fear no more the frown o' th' great,/ Thou art past the tyrant's stroke." However, the line is in its largest application Clarissa's line; and the play *Cymbeline,* in which the song functions as an elegy for a seeming death, is a triumph of artistic form over matter of tyranny, injustice, spleen, and destructive lust. *Cymbeline* is filled with the stirring of the "brutal monster" which Clarissa Dalloway defines early in the novel. Septimus, when he returns to Shakespeare after the war, sees only the track of that monster:

How Shakespeare loathed humanity—the putting on of clothes, the getting of children, the sordidity of the mouth and the belly!

This was now revealed to Septimus; the message hidden in the beauty of words. The secret signal which one generation passes, under disguise, to the next is loathing, hatred, despair. (P. 98)

For Clarissa, on the contrary, the Shakespearean line serves as a liberation from the immediacy of the flesh, the ego, and others, each time it comes to mind. It frees her from Hatchards' shop window, releases her to memory of beauty, an "image of white dawn in the country," and almost simultaneously allows her to be reconciled to the fact that "This late age of the world's experience had bred in them all, men and women, a well of tears." The Shakespearean lines and the creative act of Shakespeare are in a sense one: the mind's triumph over corruptness without excluding it. The other triumph, that of the inviolate soul (as understood by Clarissa), is that of Septimus; by death he refuses corruption:

A thing there was that mattered; a thing, wreathed about with chatter, defaced, obscured in her own life, let drop every day in corruption, lies, chatter. This he had preserved. Death was defiance. Death was an attempt to communicate, people feeling the impossibility of reaching the centre which, mystically, evaded them; closeness drew apart; rapture faded; one was alone. There was an embrace in death. (P. 202)

Two of Clarissa's desires are symbolically satisfied by Septimus's act: first, the desire to be free of the limitations of the body and to be laid out like a mist over the garden of the world; and second, to be totally free of others, tyrants and lovers alike. "A thing that mattered" or a "centre"—Woolf refrains from using the word "soul"—is inevitably tainted by circumstance and can be shown perhaps only in a state we call madness, wherein it is freed from contingent reality. Thus Woolf affirms it, Septimus's death with the "treasure" intact. The final act of Septimus is presented not as a social indictment or a tragic waste of life but as a choice.

But the novel does not affirm such a choice. Rather, it surrounds Septimus as *Cymbeline* surrounds the moments of death in Imogen. The final echo of "Fear no more the heat o' th' sun" marks a stage onward from that, for the death of Septimus and the old lady's putting out the light excite

Clarissa to creative action. She will return to her party, and the leaden circles of the clock will continue to dissolve.

For the alternative to Septimus's way is the way of art, and the forms of *Mrs. Dalloway* imitates the form-giving of Mrs. Dalloway. The basic rhythm of the novel is not that established by the hours of Big Ben but that created by the tempo of three streams of consciousness: those of Clarissa, Septimus, and Peter Walsh. Each consciousness is associated with a pattern of images and a temporal definition. If these were described in verb tenses, they would be present perfect, present, and present progressive. They can also be differentiated in kinds of consciousness, though there is a danger in applying stock terms, even Jungian terms.

The narrative tense used by Woolf is consistently the past tense; nevertheless, there are perceptible shifts in psychological time. In the beginning Clarissa Dalloway is very uncertainly in present time, though she walks in Bond Street assaulted by the sensations of a moving city. Even though we might expect her mind to be focused on the future because of the coming party, the physical experience of life is immediately translated into memory. The impression a reader has in this episode, of richly sensory flux is due to the momentary sharing of impressions by many virtually anonymous minds—a new position of the omniscient narrator.

The impression is intensified by the counterpoint of Septimus's consciousness, which the external world constantly threatens to breach and overwhelm, and which translates the past (e.g., the death of Evans) into present anxiety on the perceptual level: "The world wavered and quivered and threatened to burst into flame."

The rhythm of the first movement of the novel is established by these two extremes of consciousness playing upon the same external facts and on the same themes: the almost overwhelming sense of ephemeral beauty, the current of fear, and the withholding from others. In both personalities there has been an interruption of feeling, if "feeling" is defined as

a flow of being outward to another. For Septimus the interruption is a chasm: "Far away he heard her sobbing; he heard
it accurately, he noticed it distinctly; he compared it to a
piston thumping. But he felt nothing." Clarissa, on the other
hand, has a gift for people, for "knowing" people; yet there
is an interruption of the emotional flow.

Only with the entrance of Peter Walsh—with his egoism,
sentimentality, and love of the world of social action—can the
total consciousness of *Mrs. Dalloway* be complete. Peter
Walsh is vulgar. His esthetic sense, if he has one, does not
censor his responses as he walks through London claiming it
in its materialistic chauvinism, able to doze and dream safely
on a park bench, surrounded by its babies, its madness, and
its amours. He touches, though not deeply, the life of street
flirtations, bourgeois hotels, and imperialistic power. Yet he
is one of the roots of Clarissa's life, and she must share his
consciousness. The obverse is that Clarissa must be accepted
by Peter. On a more abstract level bearing upon the form of
the novel, Clarissa's art needs Peter's recognition because
Peter is the world. Art in a vacuum is not art; it must touch
the world.

The peculiar contribution of Peter, in addition, is in his
power to feel, to express, and to respect eroticism. The emotional potency of women is acknowledged, paradoxically, in
Peter Walsh's subconscious and externalized in the figure of
the old street singer with her inarticulate song of love.
Whereas Richard Dalloway later sees her as a social devia-
tion, "stretched on her elbow (as if she had flung herself on
the earth, rid of all ties, to observe curiously, to speculate
boldly . . . impudent, loose-lipped, humourous)," Peter Walsh
sees her as a spring:

. . . Still, though it issued from so rude a mouth, a mere hole in
the earth, muddy too, matted with root fibres and tangled grasses,
still the old bubbling burbling song, soaking through the knotted
roots of infinite ages . . . streamed away in rivulets over the pavement . . . fertilising, leaving a damp stain. (P. 91)

In Peter Walsh's mind, the images of woman come together: the great mother, the object of courtly love, the prey,
and the earth spirit. However, he gives figurative form to what
has already been found symbolically in Clarissa's reverie, completing the analysis of love suggested by her world "which
split its thin skin and gushed and poured with an extraordinary alleviation." The unseemly, asexual, pantheistic spirit of
love is yet sexual; fertile and primeval, it breaks the forms of
civilized life in the human being and in his creation the city.
The shattering of convention and inert matter contrasts with
the pent and raging eroticism of Doris Kilman, and also with
the sterile formalism, proportion, of Sir William Bradshaw. It
completes Clarissa's alternate symbol of amorous form as a
burning blossom by showing its roots, and complements it by
showing them crude, deprived of elegant form.

The figure of the singer without sex, social identity, or
beauty is central to *Mrs. Dalloway,* which is concerned with
beauty in a sexual social identity; it contributes its strength
to the final synthesis of Clarissa and to her altered consciousness. Elaborations of this figure, and the varied readings of
her meaning, provide one key to the evolution of Woolf's
forms. However, in *Mrs. Dalloway* she serves merely as a
powerful central image, and with the dream-woman who
arises from Peter's subconscious as he dozes on a park bench,
a nature-compound that liberates the human mind from society while permitting the human being to remain within it.
The transcendent mother is described in terms of the key imagery of the consciousness of both Clarissa and Septimus:

. . . This figure, made of sky and branches as it is, had arisen
from the troubled sea . . . as a shape might be sucked up out of
the waves to shower down from her magnificent hands, compas-
sion, comprehension, absolution. (P. 64)

As the amorous singer is the gnarled root of life and a
spring welling from the ground, the divine mother is branches
meeting sky; thus the two mythic images complete the Tree
of Life. The permanence and incontrovertibility of the mythic

identity again emphasize the incompleteness of Septimus, who perceives trees to be alive, but as if the branches were not rooted and as if their mysterious life were a threat to his.

On a realistic or logical level, one cannot say that Clarissa participates in the mythic visions of Peter, or that her life demonstrates the completeness of the Tree of Life. To a large extent, that completeness is the work of the novel rather than the character, and is perceived more clearly by the reader than by Clarissa or Peter. However, despite reason, Clarissa acquires in the course of the novel a fullness of consciousness that she does not have in the beginning. Specifically, she has an intuitive knowledge of Septimus Warren Smith, a man she has never met, and of the ancient singer, whom she has never seen. In the moments of solitude when Clarissa withdraws from her party after learning of Septimus' death, she recognizes explicitly the terror against which her art and her rationality have defended her. In part, the terror is defined as a fear of physical death, and the participation in Septimus's suicide brings her to a recognition and conquest of the terror at a more radical level than that given shortly before, in one of the thematic keys which Peter Walsh provides:

So that to know her, or any one, one must seek out the people who completed them; even the places. Odd affinities she had with people she had never spoken to. . . . It ended in a transcendental theory which, with her horror of death, allowed her to believe . . . that since our apparitions, the part of us which appears, are so momentary compared with the other, the unseen part of us, which spreads wide, the unseen might survive, be recovered somehow attached to this person or that. . . . (P. 168)

The experience of Clarissa proves to be less comfortable than the theory, for she not only sees the suicide, in imagination, but also feels "a thud, thud, thud in his brain, and then a suffocation of blackness." Beyond the agony and horror of physical destruction, as she thinks in solitude of Septimus Clarissa begins to enumerate the fears and to make them kinetic rather than metaphoric. There is the terror of human evil, "some indescribable outrage—forcing your soul,

that was it. . . ." There is the terror of the life-imperative of
society: "the overwhelming incapacity, one's parents giving
it into one's hands, this life, to be lived to the end, to be
walked with serenely," and retribution in terms of the forces
of chaos, "her punishment to see sink and disappear here
a man, there a woman, in this profound darkness. . . ."

The confrontation with fear ends in a triumph over darkness; for as she sees the old lady in the room opposite quietly
putting out the light while Clarissa's party continues brightly
lighted, she accepts the rhythms of being, and death as part
of the rhythm: "The young man had killed himself; but she
did not pity him; with the clock striking the hour, one, two,
three, she did not pity him, with all this going on."

In these affirmations, which have their share of the hardy
and unlovely affirmation of the old singer, Clarissa has removed herself from the growing narrowness of her nun's bed
and from the limitation of her ardor to a sublimated response
to floral beauty. The sky, darkness, old age, and death have
made her free. Terror is transformed. In the end the terror
of life and of relatedness is equated by Peter to ecstasy.

In the party which provides the final and integrating episode in the novel, Clarissa stands between present and future,
though the past is contained as well, and she has found a
reconciliation of the solitary treasure of being and the public
assembling of forms. Civilization has also lost the narrowness of 1920 patrician English mores, and has become
archetypal. Woolf has incisively cleared away the prime min-
isters and Sir Williams to make clear the distinction between
civilization and power structures. What is left is a harmonious movement of contrary individuals within a ceremonious
form, dependent nevertheless on a solitary imperative of
choice.

To the Lighthouse may strike one at first reading as a
companion piece to *Mrs. Dalloway* in that both novels are
dominated by a feminine figure and capture woman's order,

in which one of the fundamental principles is that the women act within the conventional limitations of the married woman, who must derive some of her order from her husband. However important this similarity is, we find that Woolf is not concerned with the feminine order as hub of being in *To the Lighthouse.* On the very simple level of novelistic structure, Clarissa Dalloway is in the center of her novel; she is present in the beginning and the end, and the novel's themes come together and are resolved in her person and her mind. Mrs. Ramsay, on the other hand, dominates the first section of the novel, dies parenthetically in the second, and is revived as an idea in the end, in the imagination of the artist Lily Briscoe, and as an unconscious presence in the actions and attitudes of her family. Her final presence merely as an ideal force, elusive, intermittent, and ambiguously restorative to those who are touched by it, makes it impossible for her to triumph as Clarissa triumphed, in her own person. In the end, indeed, another order triumphs, or at least holds Mrs. Ramsay's order in balance.

Like Helen Ambrose in *The Voyage Out,* and in contrast to Clarissa Dalloway, Mrs. Ramsay in *To the Lighthouse* is womanly rather than feminine, in the order of nature rather than that of art or society. A very clear comparison is suggested, for example, by the difference between the dinner parties of which the two women make much. At Clarissa's party conversation, social position, and visible elegance of person and scene are important elements of the form; at Mrs. Ramsay's dinner party, natural fecundity firmly holds the center—in the *boeuf en daube,* the sumptuous fruit, and the excitement of the late-arriving lovers. In no other novel by Woolf—not even *The Waves*—is nature such a compelling presence. "Yes, of course, if it's fine to-morrow," Mrs. Ramsay says in the first line of the novel; they might go to the lighthouse if the weather was fine, and Mr. Ramsay said it would not be fine. The casual and realistic introduction of nature's power is strengthened by a wide range of realistic

detail: the scene itself, in which one looks out upon garden
and sea; the insistence of sea and wind, always present to
the senses, even indoors, but also enforcing modifications of
the routine of life, as a daily companion does; the emphasis
placed on the body, the animal nature of man, in its range
from appetite to dissolution; the maternal fecundity of Mrs.
Ramsay herself, whose eight children bound through the
scenes and who is seen by her son rising "in a rosy-flowered
fruit tree . . . into which the beak of brass . . . plunged."

Although Mrs. Ramsay may seem to be identified with
nature, in her beauty and fecundity and in her awareness of
all the sensuous reality that her husband does not perceive,
she is fundamentally at enmity with nature. She feels that
she is in a state of siege, threatened by a vague force called
"life," and she would net if she could all the blossoms in
her garden to make them safe in her order of emotional
permanence rather than in nature's system of flux: ". . . She
went up to say good-night to them, and found them netted
in their cots like birds among cherries. . . . Never will they
be so happy again." The sound of the surf is the signal of
danger; the doors must be closed against the sea wind; the
weather must be willed to be fine for the journey to the lighthouse. The tree, firmly rooted though flourishing, is her emblem. Mrs. Ramsay is to be linked, in fact, with the dream-
woman of the preceding novel, a giant figure made of sky,
branches, and twilight, a figure tempting men to quietude:

So, he thinks, may I never go back to the lamplight; to the sitting-
room; never finish my book; never knock out my pipe; never ring
for Mrs. Turner to clear away; rather let me walk straight on to
this great figure, who will, with a toss of her head, mount me on
her streamers and let me blow to nothingness with the rest.[5]

Although Mrs. Ramsay does not offer the possibility of
nothingness, she offers the temptation of quiescence in moments of beauty. In *To the Lighthouse* the feast comes to
that sort of moment:

. . . Just now she had reached security; she hovered like a hawk
suspended; like a flag floated in an element of joy which filled

every nerve of her body fully and sweetly, not noisily, solemnly rather, for it arose, she thought, looking at them all eating there, from husband and chlidren and friends; all of which rising in this profound stillness . . . seemed now for no special reason to stay there like a smoke, like a fume rising upwards, holding them safe together . . . something, she meant, is immune from change, and shines out . . . in the face of the flowing, the fleeting, the spectral, like a ruby. . . . This would remain. (Pp. 162-163)[6]

The dish of fruit, with the objects of nature cut from the natural order and placed in the order of art, serves to concentrate the meaning of her relations in life—relations with her husband, her children, her guests: "Indeed she had been keeping guard over the dish of fruit (without realising it) jealously, hoping that nobody would touch it."

The intensity of the emotional aura which surrounds her, and the sensuous immediacy of the pages in which she is present ("The Window"), are due in part to her awareness that life is at every moment in danger of disintegration, and to her offering a fierce energy of human meaning to net it; in part it is due to a brilliant awareness of an order of life which has no need of effort and is indeed antithetical to the content of her life as Mrs. Ramsay. These moments of awareness cast doubt on the entire struggle and on the thematic struggle of the novel, and contribute to the pessimism of the pattern traced in *To the Lighthouse*. The contrary awareness is conveyed in images of fish and light, two radical images for Woolf's mind, and they are in opposition not only to the fountain of energy Mrs. Ramsay pours on those about her, but also to the title symbol of the lighthouse.

. . . At the moment her eyes were so clear that they seemed to go round the table . . . without effort like a light stealing under water so that its ripples and the reeds in it and the minnows balancing themselves, and the sudden silent trout are all lit up hanging, trembling . . . and the whole is held together. . . . (P. 165)

This state of harmony and ease, clearly in contrast to the decisive stroke of the lighthouse across darkness, is one merely glimpsed and lost. It is a miracle in which the human

eye is unnaturally and unreasonably present in a unity of
fish, water, and light. It is a state of unity that cannot occur
in the action of human life. More naturalistic is the conjunction of energy and death, or light and dark, in Mrs.
Ramsay. In Lily Briscoe's painting, as she explains her
abstraction of Mrs. Ramsay, "a light here required a shadow
there," and in Mrs. Ramsay's view of herself, the long, steady
stroke of the light from the lighthouse is her stroke; yet she
is essentially a wedge of darkness.

The effort, "all the being and the doing, expansive, glittering, vocal," is thus not in true opposition to all that is represented by Mr. Ramsay, as one might suppose. They are the
male and female of the conquering mind. Mrs. Ramsay
orders her forces against the chaos of nature, as Mr. Ramsay
confronts the desolation of nature: "It was his fate . . . to
come out thus on a spit of land which the sea is slowly
eating away, and there to stand, like a desolate sea-bird,
alone." In the realistic world, the lighthouse represents the
difficult reality of the mind, and the discipline imposed on
desire and sense. Such is the lighthouse seen by day, near
at hand, whether by Mrs. Ramsay, James, or Cam.

For how would you like to be shut up for a whole month at a
time, and possibly more in stormy weather, upon a rock the size
of a tennis lawn? she would ask; and to have no letters or newspapers, and to see nobody . . . and then a dreadful storm coming,
and the windows covered with spray, and birds dashed against the
lamp, and the whole place rocking, and not be able to put your
nose out of doors for fear of being swept into the sea? (P. 14)

Although Woolf here uses some of the same lighthouse images
first occurring in *Night and Day,* the stress is no longer
heroic. It is made even less heroic by the inevitable association with Mr. Ramsay, whose mind is constantly identified
with desolation, and whose marriage, we learn, tends to be
stormy.

He would start from the table in a temper. He would whizz his
plate through the window. Then all through the house there
would be a sense of doors slamming and blinds fluttering as if a

gusty wind were blowing and people scudded about trying in a hasty way to fasten hatches and make things shipshape. (Pp. 305-306)

By night, when it is perceived not as a place but as a power, the lighthouse means something quite different to Mrs. Ramsay, something that excludes her husband. Its true significance for the woman is secret, for it calls upon the contemplative and religious mind. As Mrs. Ramsay looks at the lighthouse in the early evening when the light begins to move, she associates it with "losing personality," that is, losing her identity as wife and mother and entering into empathy "until she became the thing she looked at." But this mood of contemplation progresses almost at once into religious affirmation and thence to ecstasy:

(She woke in the night and saw it bent across their bed, stroking the floor), but for all that she thought, watching it with fascination, hypnotised, as if it were stroking with its silver fingers some sealed vessel in her brain whose bursting would flood her with delight, she had known happiness, exquisite happiness, intense happiness, and it silvered the rough waves a little more brightly, as daylight faded, and the blue went out of the sea and it rolled in waves of pure lemon which curved and swelled and broke upon the beach and the ecstasy burst in her eyes and waves of pure delight raced over the floor of her mind and she felt, It is enough! It is enough! (Pp. 103-104)

This power of the lighthouse, which requires darkness, is thus the power of Mrs. Ramsay, but it is also a mysterious power which transcends her. It is related to another ambiguous symbol, that of the match burning in the crocus in *Mrs. Dalloway,* because of the similar release of joy. The liquid gush of pleasure in both passages is highly erotic, but removed from the arena of sexual act. In both novels this experience of the woman is not related to marriage and is unknown to the husband. In *To the Lighthouse* it relates Mrs. Ramsay to her children James and Cam, who remember this power in their mother as they sail disconsolately to the lighthouse, and can endure partly because that delight still runs in their memories: "The Lighthouse was then a silvery, misty-looking tower with a yellow eye that opened suddenly and softly in the evening. Now . . ." The enchantment of the lighthouse in James's memory, and Mrs. Ramsay's enchantment, are the power of imagination, at a great expense of energy, to offer an alternate truth to that of Mr. Ramsay; it is able to create for the child Cam a fairy garden of a nightmarish pig's skull, and it is able to sustain Mr. Ramsay in the illusion of love. This fructifying imagination relates her also to Lily Briscoe, who feels the coming of creative power "as if some juice necessary for the lubrication of her faculties were spontaneously squirted," and the fertility of the act is again associated with loss of personality and of the consciousness which relates her to the world of Mr. Ramsay.

Yet the novel is a disciplinary act upon that kind of truth and fecundity. The sterility of Mr. Ramsay's vision is established as truth from the beginning, and the author's intention, as indicated by the first *Diary* reference to *To the Lighthouse,* was clearly to place her father in a dominant position: on May 14, 1925, she writes, "But the centre is father's character, sitting in a boat, reciting We perished, each alone, while he crushes a dying mackerel."[7]

In part, the ascendancy of the arid rational mind has historical and sociological reference (Lily's muttered refrain, "Women can't write, women can't paint," or Mr. Ramsay's indulgent acceptance of the vague minds of women, passed on in Cam's agreement never to know the points of the compass), but Woolf penetrates to the sources of motive, and her analysis is without sociological optimism. The pattern in *To the Lighthouse* has the inevitability of tragedy. Although the opposition between the night and the day, between Mrs. Ramsay's imagination and Mr. Ramsay's reason, is a true dichotomy, the novel progresses in terms of triads of reality attempting unity. The major structural triad is the division into sections, "The Window," "Time Passes," and "The Lighthouse," written in three distinct styles reflecting three psychological realities and revealing three conceptions of nature. The second triad, less immediately evident but ultimately the one offering thematic resolution, is that of Mrs. Ramsay, Mr. Ramsay, and Lily Briscoe. The final triad in terms of the resolution of social forms is that of father, son, and daughter sailing to the lighthouse.

"The Window," which captures Mrs. Ramsay's nature in its style, actions, and points of view, also indicates in its title another definition of Mrs. Ramsay: that is, a creature circumscribed by a house, looking out upon a world limited by a narrow window. The window is a household eye meeting the visionary eye of the lighthouse. Although Mrs. Ramsay makes excursions into the town, they are domestic excursions which do not significantly enlarge her vision. Framed by the window, the players of the world appear. Her household domain is a microcosm in which she is by no means protected from the threatening forces of the greater world; even her errands indicate her awareness of loneliness, suffering, and death, but she need not move from her window to see these realities. Her husband, her son, Charles Tansley, Lily Briscoe, and Augustus Carmichael provide her with this news. Her domestic action in "The Window"—managing a household, feeding it, keeping it amused and hopeful—is an effort to design social forms which make life possible for people. The forms she offers are simple: a journey to the lighthouse for James, a mating expedition for Paul and Minta, a feast for everyone, a game of gender definition for little Rose. These domestic acts are rituals of defense against Life.

And Rose would grow up; and Rose would suffer, she supposed, with these deep feelings, and she said she was ready now, and they would go down, and Jasper, because he was the gentleman, should give her his arm, and Rose, as she was the lady, should carry her handkerchief. . . . Choose me a shawl, she said, for that would please Rose, who was bound to suffer so. (Pp. 127-128)

For Mrs. Ramsay, domestic beauty, beauty of manners, is the only articulate and active response to a world order which is tragic; beyond these gestures there are only secret, inarticulate feeling and unsystematic musing.

Though limited by a Victorian world and a rational husband who defends himself from life by refusing to see it and charges through the garden reciting "The Charge of the Light Brigade," Mrs. Ramsay's mind in silence is in harmony with the Elizabethans, and for her as for Mrs. Dalloway there is a Shakespearean summation:

> Yet seem'd it winter still, and, you away,
> As with your shadow I with these did play.

These lines, and the entire pattern of secret sensibility in Mrs. Ramsay, are related to loss and danger of a very complex order. In spite of her great strength and beauty, Mrs. Ramsay is a creature immobilized. Her symbols, the tree, the light-house, and the window, emphasize the fixity of her destiny. Rooted like a tree, she relates the sensuous, mythic, and metaphysical awareness of solitude, death, and dissolution to her own physical existence. Death is not an idea before which her ego can stand heroically; death like the surf eats away the land on which the ego stands, at every moment. Mrs. Ramsay's intensity of pleasure in ephemeral moments is, like that of Renaissance poets, a response to the presence of death. So also her anxious protection of her husband, sending him waves of life-giving illusion, is due to her knowledge that he is heroically, in the mind, defying death.

The fear of nature as it exists outside the cultivated garden is not merely a fear of the natural cycle of mortality and of the perishing of human effort at the edge of an unmastered sea; it is also a fear of moral disintegration of which the first and most generalized implication is the loss of meaning. As we have seen, the human instrument of meaning for Woolf is the eye rather than the mind. The extreme visual keenness of Mrs. Ramsay herself, her identification of her own meaning in terms of the eye of the lighthouse, and the effort throughout the novel to find meaning through the painter's art emphasize the dependence on an interplay between perceived object and perceiving subject, rather than on abstract and absolute intellectual formulations. In *To the Lighthouse* the full definition of vision occurs at the end, for Lily Briscoe's last words, "I have had my vision," reflect the entire range of meaning from perceptual ordering to intuition and creative imagination and finally religious revelation.

One of the arcane reaches of Mrs. Ramsay's sensibility, and of *To the Lighthouse,* is the religious experience echoed in Lily Briscoe's summation. The complete experience does not occur in "The Window," but the root is in Mrs. Ramsay's response to the light, to the dinner party, and to Shakespeare's sonnet. An original garden, an original joy, an archetypal communal harmony exist in the reaches of memory, and Mrs. Ramsay attempts to recover Eden, knowing that before her is only the shadow of it. If the reality comes, it is only for a moment, in duration as long perhaps as the third stroke of the lighthouse beam. Permanence of such reality is alien to human life, although it is a desire of the mind. The aspiration of the visionary mind is made most explicit in "Time Passes":

In those mirrors, the minds of men, in those pools of uneasy water, in which clouds for ever turn and shadows form, dreams persisted, and it was impossible to resist the strange intimation which every gull, flower, tree, man and woman, and the white earth itself seemed to declare . . . or to resist the extraordinary stimulus to range hither and thither in search of some absolute good, some crystal of intensity, remote from the known pleasures and familiar virtues, something alien to the processes of domestic life, single, hard, bright, like a diamond in the sand, which would render the possessor secure. (Pp. 204-205)

The natural world, even in the garden, contains always a threat of the denial of that range of human meaning. So, with Mrs. Ramsay gone, nature is eerie:

Violets came and daffodils. But the stillness and the brightness of the day were as strange as the chaos and tumult of night, with the trees standing there, and the flowers standing there, looking before them, looking up, yet beholding nothing, eyeless, and thus terrible. (P. 209)

The religious experience, the vision, occurs only when eye, object, and mind are aspects of a larger unity; but in the world of the Ramsays, the world of biological and cultural continuity, objects are ultimately alien and do not serve man. The eye of Mrs. Ramsay and the mind of Mr. Ramsay compose a world which is constantly threatened by independent burgeoning of life—vegetable, mineral, and animal.

As the eye is primary in defining meaning, the abstract mind being more subject to error, so Ramsay is dependent upon his wife. Yet he is offered, from the beginning, as the voice of truth. His truth is verifiable and verified in the accuracy of his first statement, "But it won't be fine."

Similarly, the virtues he thinks he embodies are the virtues needed for life, i.e., for the journey to the lighthouse. For the lighthouse is life's illusion. At least as visioned in "The Window," it is the imagination.

> . . . Life is difficult; facts uncompromising; and the passage to that fabled land where our brightest hopes are extinguished, our frail barks founder in darkness (here Mr. Ramsay would straighten his back and narrow his little blue eyes upon the horizon), one that needs, above all, courage, truth, and the power to endure. (P. 13)

Mrs. Ramsay, in adhering to imagination, is telling lies: "Now she flew in the face of facts, made the children hope what was utterly out of the question, in effect, told lies."

Certainly the qualities to be demonstrated in the final journey to the lighthouse are precisely those claimed by Mr. Ramsay: courage and the power to endure. Mrs. Ramsay does not endure. Mrs. Ramsay dies, as the reader knows she must. Rather, she cannot live, because she is too constantly the food of life for those around her. Even at the moment of unity at the dinner in which everything comes together harmoniously (appetite, art, love, marriage), there is the sense of weariness, this moment having come only after great expense of vitality.

The curious groundnote of depletion which sounds even when Mrs. Ramsay is most opulent as a 'rosy-flowered fruit tree' can be understood only by following the novelist behind the decorous furnishings of reason, discovering the emotional dangers and deprivations which accompany the Victorian morality of the Ramsay world. A highly symbolic, even mythic, vehicle is used by Woolf to suggest the emotional charge sustaining the Ramsay morality; but the means of revelation is so oblique that it serves to conceal almost as much as it reveals.

The central portion of "The Window" finds Mrs. Ramsay reading a fairy tale to her son James, while outside Lily Briscoe stands at her easel talking to William Bankes and attempting to find the right forms for her painting (i.e., trying to understand Mrs. Ramsay). The fairy tale is the accompaniment to thematic statements about art, marriage, mortality, and illusion, and it introduces problems which are suppressed in the conscious thought of the major characters. For example, we know that the slightest hint of doubt about male supremacy fills Mrs. Ramsay with anxiety, but the fairy tale "The Fisherman and His Wife" is primarily concerned with the testing of that idea. "I do not want to be king," says the Fisherman. The Wife replies, "If you won't be king, I will; go to the Flounder, for I will be King." And in his subsequent rhyming complaint to the Flounder, the Fisherman says,

> For my wife, good Ilsabil,
> Wills not as I'd have her will. (P. 90)

Although the tale is incomplete, with a major hiatus in the middle, there is an evident causal relation between wifely insubordination and terrestrial chaos. Within the safe confines of art and myth, the terror of chaos can be suggested and its prerational force indicated. The self-will of the Fisherman's Wife somehow results in a corruption of natural force and of the great element of life and death, the sea. In Woolf's work the sea may be a destroyer, or it may be the element in which life moves, or it may be life itself, as a force; in any case, it is clean. Yet here the sea first becomes "grey and thick," then "dark grey, and the water heaved up from below, and smelt putrid," and finally breaks with a rage of destruction, reducing nature to chaos and crushing society.

No rational explanation is given; it is not possible to understand in any sane way why the sea should go rotten. Hence, it is an equivalent of the childish madness (or mythic consciousness) of James as well as of the religious dread which neutralizes the power of Mrs. Ramsay. The social forms and roles which so limit and cripple intelligent people like the Ramsays, Lily Briscoe, and Mr. Carmichael are no longer seen as comic and grotesque, the result of silliness, as they tended to be in *The Voyage Out*. They are a terrible necessity, a painful salvation from the disorder and pollution of human feeling. People must marry, thinks Mrs. Ramsay, "whatever she might feel about her own transaction."

The tacit lie or repression which undermines Mrs. Ramsay's world is her need to create illusion because she will not acknowledge certain aspects of reality. Mrs. Ramsay's truth must be fairy tale, for "she did in her own heart infinitely prefer boobies to clever men who wrote dissertations" but could not live by her spontaneous feeling. Her true emotional life is hidden in the wedge of darkness to which she retires, and the outflowing of life to others, even her family, is as intermittent and secondary as the flashing eye of the lighthouse. Sexuality is, of course, in the wedge of darkness.

Although Virginia Woolf uses images of the universal unconscious mind to convey the sexual dread, aspects of it are also explicit in the musing of Lily Briscoe and in the analysis of the relationship of Minta Doyle and Paul Rayley. Lily's dread of the vital force, and the moral justification of it, are very clear and central; the instinctive recoil occurs in "The Window," and the moral placement of it in "The Lighthouse":

He turned on her cheek the heat of love, its horror, its cruelty, its unscrupulosity. (Pp. 158-159)

(Suddenly, as suddenly as a star slides in the sky, a reddish light seemed to burn in her mind, covering Paul Rayley, issuing from him. It rose like a fire sent up in token of some celebration by savages on a distant beach. . . . And the roar and the crackle repelled her with fear and disgust, as if while she saw its splendour

and power she saw too how it fed on the treasure of the house. . . .)
(Pp. 270-271)

The significance of Minta Doyle is less explicit. She is treated by Lily with fastidious aversion. If impotence is the great sexual fear of men, pollution is surely that of women. In myth and tradition, woman needs to fear being cast out as unclean. The putrid sea of the fairy tale clearly reflects this fear. The eventual collapse of the marriage of Paul and Minta (a marriage so central to Mrs. Ramsay's creative efforts) is the result of Minta's having become unclean, i.e., having rebelled against the discipline of marriage, broken the forms, and mocked the safety. At a level never explicitly discussed, social forms in general and the institution of marriage in particular are a purification of life.

Although at the end of "The Window" Mrs. Ramsay has triumphed, completing the domestic rituals and achieving at last a peace with her husband, in which her truth and his truth come together and are modified in a moment of visionary happiness, "Time Passes" shows the fragility of her triumph, and its inconsequence in the order of nature. After her triumph by light and vision come the forces of darkness and dissolution. As the Ramsays have always feared, a "profusion of darkness" floods the house like a sea. The discipline of human order disappears, and wanton forces explore forbidden places. Carnations bloom among cabbages; the house accepts rats and butterflies equally. The house reverts to modes of rudimentary life which intrude, "snuffing, rubbing." Mrs. McNab, old and simple, is the only sustainer of human meaning. Yet the image of Mrs. Ramsay as light is still present to the old cleaning woman:

She could see her now, stooping over her flowers; (and faint and flickering, like a yellow beam or the circle at the end of a telescope, a lady in a grey cloak, stooping over her flowers, went wandering over the bedroom wall . . .). (P. 211)

And the beam of the lighthouse "sent its sudden stare over bed and wall in the darkness of winter, looked with equan-

imity at the thistle and the swallow, the rat and the straw."
The process of nature, seen in this chapter as "fertility" and
"insensibility," is arrested by the memory of human meaning,
that is, of Mrs. Ramsay. In this context, human meaning and
human survival are seen dependent on memory, for indeed
the Ramsays represent here cultural continuity, survival of
civilization, rather than the glory and suffering of individual
lives. The house must be restored, the rats evicted, the grass
mowed, in order that a human future, based on a human past,
may be possible. In the process of human continuity something must be sacrificed: the harmony with nature which
might permit humanity to be as much at ease as the fish in
water, but would obliterate the strife and the tragic consciousness of the Ramsays.

Messages of peace breathed from the sea to the shore. Never to
break its sleep any more, to lull it rather more deeply to rest and
whatever the dreamers dreamt holily, dreamt wisely, to confirm . . .
   Indeed the voice might resume, as the curtains of dark wrapped
themselves over the house . . . why not accept this, be content
with this, acquiesce and resign? The sigh of all the seas breaking
in measure round the isles soothed them; the night wrapped
them. . . . (Pp. 219-220)

But that peace is a dream from which one awakes; even in
dream it is felt as a temptation, for it is a betrayal of an idea
of order which cannot merely be identified with the Victorian
age. It is the Western intellectual tradition. Cosmic harmony,
the great chain of being and reason lie behind the charms of
Mrs. Ramsay's decaying house. Without human reason there
is chaos. "Did Nature supplement what man advanced?" the
narrator inquires. The answer, which deprives man of happiness, is that nature is not his ally but is indifferent. Nature
alone becomes "gigantic chaos" with forces playing "idiot
games"; even its beauty is "terrible."
   So far, the significance of "Time Passes" has been discussed
in terms of its function as a link between the past of "The
Window" and the present of "The Lighthouse." Further implications of this chapter for Virginia Woolf will be dis-

cussed later, for in these passages there is an evident separation of conscious and unconscious motives. As planned and discussed in the *Diary,* Woolf thought of the middle section as a technical challenge: "and then this impersonal thing, which I'm dared to do by my friends, the flight of time and the consequent break of unity in my design",[7] but the actual writing and the final meaning of the passage go far beyond technical virtuosity and the Ramsay design.

The thematic center of *To the Lighthouse* (in terms of human action in time) is made explicit at last in "The Lighthouse," even though it was explicit in Woolf's own notes from the beginning. The significant moment is the journey between the visionary world and the rational world, committing and accepting an act of death. Yet the journey resurrects the world of Mrs. Ramsay in a modified form. The essential unity of Mr. and Mrs. Ramsay, as well as of *To the Lighthouse,* is present in structure and plot as well as idea, for Mr. Ramsay completes in fact the voyage that Mrs. Ramsay promised in fairy tale. But the lighthouse to which they sail is not the lighthouse seen from their island.

For James and Cam, the dreams of childhood are resurrected only to be laid aside in memory, and the lighthouse of the mother must be reduced to the "stark tower" to which the father leads them. The island of their childhood must be reduced to a distant and unreal shape. The journey must be made in stress, as a duty. Because we are led by Mr. Ramsay, who does not see things, the readers have no sensuous enticements on the way but are pressed to the goal. Lily Briscoe too is to depart from Mrs. Ramsay, and to see her beauty as a quality too easy and final: "Beauty had this penalty—it came too readily, came too completely. It stilled life—froze it."

On the one hand, "The Lighthouse" reveals the limitation of Mr. Ramsay's truth; on the other, it affirms his dominance. The price of the heroic and arctic purity of Mr. Ramsay's reason is that it cannot reach its destination with life whole.

In "The Window" we learned that Mr. Ramsay, in the expeditions of the mind, could not move past Q. Mr. Ramsay's books are about "Subject and Object and the Nature of Reality," and the symbol of his abstract problem is a kitchen table.

And with a painful effort of concentration, she focused her mind, not upon the silver-bossed bark of the tree, or upon its fish-shaped leaves, but upon a phantom kitchen table, one of those scrubbed board tables, grained and knotted, whose virtue seems to have been laid bare by years of muscular integrity, which stuck there, its four legs in air. (P. 41)

The comic image of Mr. Ramsay in his bare and helpless integrity has great charm and justifies some of the affection shown him. But the shift in authorial attitude, as well as in the conceptions of Lily Briscoe, has its sign in the beauty later found in dedication to so ludicrous an abstraction:

The kitchen table was something visionary, austere; something bare, hard, not ornamental. There was no colour to it; it was all edges and angles; it was uncompromisingly plain. But Mr. Ramsay kept always his eyes fixed upon it, never allowed himself to be distracted or deluded, until his face became worn too and ascetic and partook of this unornamented beauty which so deeply impressed her. (Pp. 240-241)

Trivial and homely as the symbolic object may be, devoid of any of the truth of fairy tale, it signifies a stoic determination to bring the mind to a merciless confrontation with the reality which has troubled Virginia Woolf from the beginning: the Aristotelian reality of verbal structures and also that of impenetrable otherness. One implication of such a view of reality—for life, as for the novel—is that people are known as objects and social roles. Against that view Virginia Woolf protested in "Mr. Bennett and Mrs. Brown"; Rachel Vinrace chafed against it in *The Voyage Out*. Clarissa Dalloway complained of it when she noted a loss of identity in becoming Mrs. Dalloway; but Mrs. Ramsay is beyond complaint, for she has no given name, even in the beginning.

To the Lighthouse is a voyage of acceptance of such limitations of being. Symbolic actions in the final section, re-informing the Fisherman pattern, provide a dramatic focus. While Lily on shore is invoking the presence of Mrs. Ramsay for her painting, Woolf breaks off to interpolate: "[Macalister's boy took one of the fish and cut a square out of its side to bait his hook with. The mutilated body (it was alive still) was thrown back into the sea.]" The fish has a quasi-religious symbolic function in Virginia Woolf's ordering of the world, and the elegance of its elemental harmony with its world reminds man of his alienation. Whereas Mrs. Ramsay has recognized the ease and harmony of the fish as beautiful, desirable, and mysterious, the men in the boat going to the lighthouse recognize the fish only as something to be caught, used, and discarded. So the unease and the effort of the journey, like Mr. Ramsay's straining of the mind, is a measure of the distance from elemental harmony. The hope of a diamond-like permanence becomes the acceptance of "some old stone lying in the sand" and the recognition of loneliness as truth.

Yet that treatment of nature and being is accepted, for the reality, or truth, of Mr. Ramsay is a place of safety, perhaps the only one, in a world of flux. It is a defense against mystery; it is a protection against death, promising as it does to be the "diamond in the sand" of human permanence; and it is a salvation from chaos. Further, it is a security for women similar to the security the idea of God offers to men. Cam reveals this aspect as she takes a parcel of food from her father:

This is right, this is it, Cam kept feeling, as she peeled her hard-boiled egg. Now she felt as she did in the study when the old men were reading *The Times*. Now I can go on thinking whatever I like, and I shan't fall over a precipice or be drowned, for there he is, keeping his eye on me, she thought. (P. 314)

Similarly, Lily Briscoe finds that she can save herself from great demands of human sympathy in Mr. Ramsay's world by saying, "What beautiful boots!"

Yet Mr. Ramsay's truth is not mere evasion of complexity,

and much of its power derives from the fact that it is so radically connected to the tragic beauty of Mrs. Ramsay's truth. For both James and Cam, the intensity of a nearly forgotten childhood is recovered by its association with an autocratic father; and through hate love is remembered. For Lily Briscoe the past vision returns in the garden harassed by Mr. Ramsay. Even so, much is lost, for the central tree (with its "fish-shaped leaves") resolving her original structure now becomes a stark, abstract central line.

The only relief from the austertiy of Mr. Ramsay's rational and egocentric world and the stress of will needed to preserve it is in the involuntary memory. Providing an analogue to the human condition, a force in inhuman nature releases the voyagers from the oppressive dominance of the father. At a certain moment the journey gains some of the ease of the fish, but by a power outside the command of human will. Suddenly the little boat is caught by the wind. By the spontaneous movement of nature, Mr. Ramsay, Cam, and James are saved from a welter of frustration and hate, dominated by a past in which Ramsay injured the spontaneous life of his children:

> At last he [James] ceased to think; there he sat with his hand on the tiller in the sun, staring at the Lighthouse, powerless to move, powerless to flick off these grains of misery which settled on his mind one after another. A rope seemed to bind him there, and his father had knotted it and he could only escape by taking a knife and plunging it... But at that moment the sail swung slowly round, filled slowly out, the boat seemed to shake herself, and then to move off half conscious in her sleep, and then she woke and shot through the waves. The relief was extraordinary. They all seemed to fall away from each other again and to be at their ease. ... (P. 288)

In the end as in the beginning of the novel, there is a contrast between the order which is unconscious and natural and the order which is imposed by an effort of the will and imagination. The first is miraculously given, and the second is born of a union which can be called marriage, since the elemental pattern of man-woman mating is the most obvious analogy. It is an adequate analogy, however, only in terms of sexual stereotypes such as that introduced by James, in which the male symbol is a destructive artifact and the female symbol is an object of natural abundance. In *To the Lighthouse* Woolf's psychology is clearly close to that of Freud in its definition of sexuality. The male order, with its cult of reason and its sacrifice of unconscious life, triumphs. Even art, the form of human expression least subject to the definitions of Mr. Ramsay's world, is dependent on them. Mr. Ramsay is acknowledged as the presiding intelligence by all of them, even though the sense of loss is not dispelled.

Mrs. Dalloway and *To the Lighthouse,* though radically different in structure, style, and theme, have significant similarities which place them together in the larger configuration of Woolf's work. They represent the major and final effort of the novelist to define and affirm the experience of women in a traditional realistic context and to find in the narrow confines of the house the full expression of the human dilemma. These two novels in which woman is seen as *Mrs.* mark the poles of euphoria and stoicism characteristic of Woolf's novels. They end upon a definition of art—expressed in Lily Briscoe's life as well as her painting—which depends upon a degree of monastic deprivation and tightly disciplined form, and appeals to a highly refined symbolic sense. In short, the view of life to which we are taken by *To the Lighthouse* overcomes one danger only to fall into another. Chaos is mastered, but sterility presents itself.

We recall that one threat of the cosmos is that it may freeze life; the ice age may descend. The Ramsays, for all their great charm, their children, their flowers, their goodness, also represent this power—or this negation of power—which is antithetical to life. The characteristic posture of Mr. Ramsay, in his mind, is that of the leader of a hopeless polar expedition; his theme is, "We perish, each alone"; and his amorous stance is that of a famished wolf in the snow. Mrs. Ramsay's beauty may, even Lily supposes, freeze life;

and certainly her daughters feel her censorship everywhere. But the most important objection to the Ramsays may be (because of the thematic structuring, concluding with Lily's painterly vision) that the order of *To the Lighthouse* would immobilize art.

However, *Mrs. Dalloway* and *To the Lighthouse* also trace the discovery of a new possibility; it is not a technical breakthrough as in *Jacob's Room* but a new opening of consciousness.

The final thematic picture of *To the Lighthouse* would have an even greater austerity were it not for the new consciousness introduced (though passed over) in the brief middle section. While the impersonal interval links the two major sections of the novel and justifies the acceptance of Mr. Ramsay's truth, the emotional content is at odds with the idea. As she was writing "Time Passes," Woolf found with astonishment that she was writing with great ease and joy. On April 30, 1926, she says:

> I cannot make it out—here is the most difficult abstract piece of writing—I have to give an empty house, no people's characters, the passage of time, all eyeless and featureless with nothing to cling to; well, I rush at it, and at once scatter out two pages. Is it nonsense, is it brilliance? Why am I so flown with words and apparently free to do exactly what I like?[8]

"Time Passes," though it should show the falling away of human meaning in organic death and decay, and the coming of chaos, is an experience of liberation and joy into which a note of common human suffering intrudes as parenthetically as does someone's arrival by train. It ought to be important that "[Mr. Ramsay stumbling along a passage stretched his arms out one dark morning, but, Mrs. Ramsay having died rather suddenly the night before, he stretched his arms out. They remained empty.]"

However, only the abstract mind tells us that this is tragic, and that the inconsequence of the event in time is a use of tragic irony. The ebullient style tells us something quite different. With Mrs. Ramsay dead, all nature flourishes, and for the first time animal life is free. The stylistic animism, in which the wind and its random airs enter the house like an entire zoo loosed, points up the restraint that has been exercised in "The Window" and will be used again in extreme form in "The Lighthouse." Fertility, sensuality, curiosity, amorality attend the process by which the house is undone by wind, wet, rats, and swallows. The senses being freed in this natural invasion, the visual and auditory richness of this passage is unlike any description elsewhere in the novel. Further, the elements against which the Ramsays have defended themselves, the ones Virginia Woolf has identified with fear or threat, are now without terror: the wind, the dark.

> . . . Only gigantic chaos streaked with lightning could have been heard tumbling and tossing, as the winds and waves disported themselves like the amorphous bulks of leviathans whose brows are pierced by no light of reason, and mounted one on top of another, and lunged and plunged in the darkness or the daylight . . . in brute confusion and wanton lust aimlessly by itself. (Pp. 208-209)

Such passages reveal most clearly the identification of sexuality with the wind and the dark, and suggest that a cosmic orgy is needed after a tyranny of reason.

Without the visionary eye, which is too firmly mated to pure intelligence, sound and silence can be heard as an intermittent music offering another meaning in art, not abstract like Lily Briscoe's painting but in its original sensuous integrity:

> And now as if the cleaning and the scrubbing and the scything and the mowing had drowned it there rose that half-heard melody, that intermittent music which the ear half catches but lets fall; a bark, a bleat; irregular, intermittent, yet somehow related; the hum of an insect, the tremor of cut grass, dissevered yet somehow belonging; the jar of a dor beetle, the squeak of a wheel, loud, low, but mysteriously related; which the ear strains to bring together and is always on the verge of harmonising. . . . (P. 218)

But "Time Passes" is not characterless, and the possibility of a harmonizing ear is present in a female figure which presides over he disintegration and restoration of the house. Mrs. McNab, the cleaning woman, is similar to the mythic old woman, the street singer, in *Mrs. Dalloway,* and in strong opposition to Mrs. Ramsay.

How long, she asked, creaking and groaning on her knees under the bed, dusting the boards, how long shall it endure? but hobbled to her feet again, pulled herself up, and again with her sidelong leer which slipped and turned aside even from her own face, and her own sorrows, stood and gaped in the glass, aimlessly smiling, and began again the old amble and hobble. . . . (P. 203)

Without beauty or dignity, she endures and sings an old music hall song. But in her is the human light and a vast adaptation to the world of mutability. At last she is the force determining that the cycle shall return, after death and disintegration, to rebirth:

But there was a force working; something not highly conscious; something that leered, something that lurched; something not inspired to go about its work with dignified ritual or solemn chanting. (P. 215)

This female figure over which neither the bourgeois moral tradition nor the great Western intellectual tradition has empire, is a major guiding figure for the progress to *Orlando, The Waves,* and *Between the Acts.*

chapter 4

Orlando

Although *Orlando* was written in 1927 and 1928, between *To the Lighthouse* and *The Waves*, and *Flush* was written in 1932, between *The Waves* and *The Years*, these pseudo-biographies fill similar functions in the rhythm of Virginia Woolf's work, placing previous novels in a new perspective and establishing a working distance. *Orlando* sets aside *To the Lighthouse* and prepares for both *The Waves* and *The Years*.

As Virginia Woolf states in her *Diary*, the completion of *To the Lighthouse* left her desiring "to kick up my heels and be off,"[1] and in part the ensuing frivolity is a result of the freeing of personal memory. "I used to think of him [her father] and mother daily," she writes on November 28, 1928, "but writing the *Lighthouse* laid them in my mind." Thereafter a great rush of ideas, situations, and characters came to her. The ideas sketched between September 30, 1926, and June 30, 1927, contain germs of *A Room of One's Own, The Waves, The Years,* and *Between the Acts* as well as of *Orlando;* but all these ideas are departures from the idea of truth triumphant in *To the Lighthouse,* and also rejections of the style and the social propriety implicit in it. Freedom from high seriousness is the first psychological movement towards the definition of *Orlando;* wildness informs the entirety of the new conception, and is to be found in the action of the omniscient narrator as well as in the action of the protagonist.

After the euphoria of writing *Orlando* and the anxiety about its reception after publication, Woolf's final estimate before going on to something new was that "*Orlando* taught me how to write a direct sentence; taught me continuity and narrative and how to keep the realities at bay. . . . I never got down to my depths. . . ."[2] However, this is a very modest self-judgment, and in fact *Orlando* has depths unlike those of preceding novels, as well as extraordinary scope.

On a first reading, *Orlando* seems to be precisely what Woolf intended in October of 1927, a book satiric in spirit, wild in structure, and fluid in style. The satiric spirit, though it boldly attacks only a few elements in man and society, pervades the entire fantasy if one considers style and structure as implicit satire on pedantry and the traditional ordering of history. In a work which takes us from the reign of Elizabeth through the reign of Edward, we find royal processions, bills of Parliament, wars, trade treaties, and strikes are notably absent, and political history is known largely by the amorous inclinations of the reigning monarch. The smell of the streets of London, the quality of light from the sky, the clothing worn by Orlando and Nick Greene, the use the great house of Knole is put to, the mating habits of young men and women, tell us the truth of history. In short, English history is given to us in terms of the quality of life enjoyed by the people rather than in the sensational events which provide dates to remember.

All the forms of pedantry are mocked—biography, literary criticism, history of ideas, ethics, theology—with the same end in view. A house, a mind, an oak tree are the enduring signs of the progress of a civilization, and if one reads the mind as one reads the rings of a tree, he can define the relationship of the past to the present and of the individual to his milieu. Every satiric and comic development leads to a very serious center; and yet the surface of plot, style, and character is one of brilliant and light-hearted raillery.

In mockery of the convention of the omniscient narrator, Woolf defines herself as a character—and perhaps the central character—of the novel. The narrator is in part sedulous and earnest biographer, in part moral and literary parodist; she is also arch and flighty female, and roué. But consistently she has the light, irreverent freedom (even when Orlando is earnest) of the moths which (in contrast to the ant and grasshopper) "breathe in our ears such wild nonsense as one hears from telegraph wires in snow storms; tee hee, haw haw. Laughter, Laughter! the moths say." The narrator has no commitment to the past, no need to uphold any institution, and so the distance is an ideal distance devoid of fear or rancor. As Virginia Woolf indicates in *A Room of One's Own,* that dispassionate position is rare in novelists who are women. The stance is maintained not by emotional distancing but by the eradication of anything resembling conventional morality. She is, on a very elegant level, a picaresque narrator. Though this is one of the major styles of Virginia Woolf's unpublished diaries, its wicked potential has not been exploited in fiction before *Orlando.* Here it proves capable of functioning in harmony with a symbolic structure.

In spite of the laughter and the wildness, an extremely complex web of commentary on the relations of men and women to the world and to one another is constructed in *Orlando.* For the sake of clarity, I have separated the various strands and used the vocabulary of medieval biblical exegesis in describing them. On the most obvious level, the level of history and allegorical plot, the history of England is defined by action of two sexes in one house, and (using conventional sexual distinctions) the nation advances from its condition of adolescent male to one of mature female and ends (in

1927) as androgyne. The Elizabethan is bold, ribald, reckless, hot as a sparrow, physically active; as a Jacobean he becomes disillusioned, morose, introspective. As a Cavalier in his twenties he has dash and manners, is adept at amours, restless, a dilettante. That decadent moment of history ends in conflagration or civil war, and Orlando becomes woman. The adventuring of manhood gives way to the civility, delicacy, and shrewdness of a womanish eighteenth century, where decorum rules in the lady's salon and license prevails in the back streets. In the nineteenth century the dark age descends, and life is mufflled in sentiment, smut, and timidity; it is a period of lachrymose fecundity in the green world, in families, and in art.

Corresponding to the changes in man, the condition of his house reveals history. In the Elizabethan age, it is a dwelling and a town, roughly furnished, largely bare, and allowing space for a barbaric severed head as a boy's plaything. In the succeeding period, with the bold venturing spirit checked, the house becomes a showpiece, causing a great waste of resources for its elegant furnishings and hectic entertainments. In the nineteenth century, it becomes a dark prison with the view to the outer world blocked by creeping ivy, and the bare bones of the structure muffled by pictures, wallpaper, tablecloths, chair coverings, and rugs. At last, in the twentieth century, the house has become a museum; with the chairs of past grandeur secluded behind velvet ropes, it is to be valued for the life it has contained, not for the life still to be lived in it.

English history as revealed by the plot here sketched, and English society as exemplified in the house, have been a process of the segregation of forms, paralleled by the segregation of the sexes, until in the nineteenth century the forms of nature and civilization have become tyrannically exclusive. Whereas in the sixteenth century Orlando moves freely from the oak tree to the house and within it to the attic containing acts of imagination beyond the house and the oak tree, in the course of centuries the categories of thought have become so fixed that easy and natural movement becomes virtually impossible in the nineteenth century. The twentieth century must take a new departure, one more complex and difficult than the spontaneity of Orlando's Renaissance.

Seen tropologically, the evolution just discussed provides a lesson concerning the conduct of men and women. The change of sex which occurs at the time of the Restoration, when Orlando is thirty, is the key to an understanding of civilization. Being male is most satisfactory before the turn of the seventeenth century, or in adolescence. Being male is increasingly disillusioning as falsity of sex roles brings failure of love, artificiality of literary modes ends in ridicule, and emptiness of the forms of public office leads to futility. Crisis by fire and a return to tents in the desert mark the point of revolutionary destruction and learning again from an alien earth. Significantly, Orlando's induction into womanhood is in a world without history, permanence of place, literary tradition, or social amenities; it is a world in which roles are elemental, and Orlando as woman milks goats, makes baskets, bakes bread, and is in danger if she thinks. She therefore returns to the world she knew as a boy, and finds means of accommodating her complex and altered nature to it. Yet society becomes increasingly unsatisfactory to her as a woman, just as it had failed her as a man, until the end of the Victorian age finds her immobilized in voluminous skirts and misty sentiments, to be rescued only by the magic circle of a wedding ring. Society has become so hostile to authentic individual life that a new mutation must occur for the restoration of life. The necessity for the ring (treated most satirically at first) shatters the unity and sufficiency of her being, but makes possible a new integration. She enters into a new relation with her house, her England, and her art; all these new relationships depend on her mating with a new man, for union of man and woman figures forth the entire mystery of relationships with the world.

Here we are necessarily brought to the symbolic or anagogic level. Beyond social or historical determinism or biological determinism, the human being is a creative consciousness. At this level Woolf uses a complex but coherent
structure of imagery and symbol to make a configuration of
reality. Protected by the avowed intention of satire and the
ambivalence of the comic mode, and freed from the temporal
and logical necessities of realism, Virginia Woolf is here
able to state and resolve the fundamental intellectual and
emotional problems informing the first period of her work.
These problems which have come to definition as they
emerged in the images of *The Voyage Out* and subsequent
novels arrive at a more theoretical and self-conscious ordering in *Orlando*.

If one returns to the range of problems outlined in chapter 1 as threatening or dangerous, one finds that they recur
in *Orlando*, together with their familiar definitions in imagery,
but that Woolf has for the moment found strategies "to keep
the realities at bay." The threats of society, the alien earth,
and chaos, are disarmed. The mastering of society and the
accommodation of alien nature are, it is true, achieved largely
by the magic that fantasy allows, but there is a solid underlying structure of thought.

Orlando at the beginning of the novel is a creature in total
harmony with his world. The house is his without question
or self-consciousness, and he moves in its freely, even though
he hides some of his life from its inmates. His place in
society is unquestioned, and he receives gratification from
above and below. More important because more basic, nature
is not alien to Orlando in any of its manifestations. In a
passage which will be echoed at the conclusion of the novel,
Orlando goes to the oak tree:

> He sighed profoundly, and flung himself—there was a passion
> in his movements which deserves the word—on the earth at the
> foot of the oak tree. He loved, beneath all this summer transiency,
> to feel the earth's spine beneath him; for such he took the hard

root of the oak tree to be; or, for image followed image, it was the back of a great horse that he was riding; or the deck of a tumbling ship—it was anything indeed, so long as it was hard, for he felt the need of something which he could attach his floating heart to . . . gradually the flutter in and about him stilled itself; the little leaves hung, the deer stopped; the pale summer clouds stayed; his limbs grew heavy on the ground; and he lay so still that by degrees the deer stepped nearer and the rooks wheeled round him and the swallows dipped and circled and the dragon-flies shot past, as if all the fertility and amorous activity of a summer's evening were woven web-like about his body.[3]

Elements which have elsewhere been found opposed are here parts of an entire organism. Creatures of air and creatures of earth meet at the tree which makes the organism whole, as the spine makes brain and viscera parts of the same structure. Further, man is part of the cosmic structure, not an alien mind in it; he is linked to the animal world, the green world, and the life of the upper air. Horse and tumbling ship, introduced as emblems of the sexual drive in *The Voyage Out* and *Jacob's Room,* do not cause fear or disrupt the harmony, and at the end of the cited paragraph the amorous quality of the harmony is made explicit. Order in amorous abundance and variety is the new design.

The symbolism here introduced, supporting that design, is systematically developed in *Orlando.* Since symbolism in the novel is not restricted by any realistic necessity, the symbolic structure is essentially one of the imagination; it is as significant and dramatic as the plot. For this reason, *Orlando* is the most revealing work for a close consideration of Woolf's symbolism. The dramatic conflict and resolution are concentrated in three pairs of opposites: *house/tree, ice/fire,* and *light/dark,* with a secondary emphasis on *horse/bird* and a brief but unequivocal definition of the nearly mystic symbol of the *fish.*

Though one might argue that *house* is virtually compulsory, given the plot and the aristocratic protagonist, still the oak tree is not a necessity; and these two symbols play against one another. *House,* in two fairly traditional senses, is society and the mind; *tree,* again traditionally, is nature and sensibility (sensibility defined as the response of the total organism). As we have seen in *Mrs. Dalloway* chancily and *To the Lighthouse* radically and deliberately, harmony of being demands both house and tree. Whereas Mrs. Ramsay was limited to a house and was related to the tree by vision and imagination only, Orlando identifies his being with the root and feels it in his body as a spine. The contrast with *Mrs. Dalloway* is even more marked, for that consciousness exists largely in air, and even the identification with trees is with branches in air. The instability of Septimus Warren Smith is defined when he thinks, "Leaves were alive; trees were alive. And the leaves being connected by millions of fibres with his own body, there on the seat, fanned it up and down." *Orlando* marks the point of the rooting of the imagination in nature. The fundamental security of Orlando is in adherence to the order of nature; and, to make the symbol inescapably obvious, Orlando carries his/her poem "The Oak Tree" at heart through all vicissitudes, sexual, social, and temporal. In the evolution of these symbols *house* and *tree,* the house becomes oppressive, the tree never. At last the great house must fall into memory and the person must go out into nature. At the oak tree again in the end, "Flinging herself on the ground, she felt the bones of the tree running out like ribs from a spine this way and that beneath her. She liked to think that she was riding the back of the world." This is the Tree of Life at the source, firm in earth, hard and secure, the skeleton on which all the clothing of society and the imagination may hang momentarily and then be put aside.

As a result, the aspects of nature that terrify Rachel in *The Voyage Out* and also the ones from which Clarissa recoils in *Mrs. Dalloway* can be understood and placed in perspective. The bare earth, seen without amenities of cities and gardens, is awesome and splendid but not wholly alien. The fierce and elemental human life belonging to such a landscape is finally known and, though ultimately transcended, admired. To the very end, the primitive Gypsy remains as a strong fiber of Orlando's being. Beneath the oak tree at night, Orlando remembers the blaze of noon on a baked hillside in Turkey, and the warning of the Gypsy not to think much of great houses with four hundred bedrooms. The doubleness of all things announces itself in the need to be reconciled to the bare earth, but not to be satisfied. The hills of Turkey represent a hard reality, something as radical as the roots of the oak tree but without the surrounding plenitude. With the stark hills, Woolf associates the blocking of full human development, for they are compared to "a sheep's skeleton; to a gigantic skull picked white by a thousand vultures." Bones, the fetishes of little boys like Jacob and James of *To the Lighthouse,* are related to the abstract mind; even as a boy Orlando chooses a less skeletal memento mori as a plaything, for he jousts with a shrunken head.

Another motif of death from nature is the Great Frost. The ice age, the frigid world which threatens to still life in *Jacob's Room* and *To the Lighthouse,* is a place of carnival in *Orlando,* and the blaze of life is merely intensified by the Great Frost. Amorous Orlando is incandescent, "like a million-candled Christmas tree" skating over a river of ice. Later, as a woman, Orlando continues to possess such power, "for all about the looking-glass were snowy lawns, and she was like a fire, a burning bush. . . ." Although snow and ice show nature at its most inhospitable for the animal man, a vital society in all its splendor builds pavilions even upon the ice. However, the context of references to ice and snow here and elsewhere indicates that they are also a psychological condition, and one not adequately described by "frigidity." The human cold is essentially the cold of Mr. Ramsay, and it is the denial of life by abstract mind. The moral equation is given in *Orlando* in the allegorical figures of Purity, Chastity, and Modesty, which are defined by snow, ice, and sterility; life can thrive if the ice is outside on river and lawn, but not when sensibility is checked by the tryrannical mind. Triumph over this essential

cold is by the flame unequivocally affirmed in *Orlando* as
natural desire:

. . . The secrets of all hearts are hidden so that we are lured on
for ever to suspect something, perhaps, that does not exist; still
through our cigarette smoke, we see blaze up and salute the
splendid fulfilment of natural desires for a hat, for a boat, for
a rat in a ditch; as once one saw blazing . . . a fire in a field
against minarets near Constantinople. (P. 264)

Natural desire, and the flame in which it is manifest, ranges
far beyond the domain of sexual desire in the usual sense of the
word, and the apparent inconsequence of the objects cited
(hat, boat, rat) conceals the sketching of impulses to intellectual, physical, and sensual freedom. But all flames have
their origin in the primordial energy of the body, striving for
expression in eroticism, physical beauty, art, and religious
feeling. For Woolf as novelist, this affirmation is a crucial one,
for the purely esthetic and spiritual expressions of vital energy
in *Mrs. Dalloway* and *To the Lighthouse* have been tenuous,
like rootless blossoms. Woolf's recognition of the problem has
been signaled by Lily Briscoe's fear of the erotic flame because it threatens the beauty of the house. History is allowed
to teach in *Orlando* that the flame must burn if the house is
to escape being a damp mausoleum. Resolution is offered in
a cryptic and paradoxical image, related to the match-in-a-
crocus of Mrs. Dalloway, of fire burning upon the ice. Incongruous in nature, these symbols represent difficult accommo-
dations of the imagination. In *Orlando* there is a greater fire
because the sexual element in all desires has been affirmed.

Related to the symbol of fire, but more specific in their
references to the vitality of the body, are the animal images
so abundant in *Orlando*. Animal life, virtually exiled from the
Ramsay house, enters Orlando's house freely (Orlando has
always a pack of elkhounds and spaniels at her heels) and
roam the gardens. The horse, formerly a somewhat frighten-
ing symbol of the inner dynamo and physical freedom, is still
associated with the male, but transfers its power in the twen-

tieth century to a mechanical substitute which the feminine Orlando has at her command, the motorcar. All the animals have correspondences in human sensibility, and all are free and joyous, with one exception. The Archduchess Harriet, who pursues Orlando so hotly, is identified with a vulture, allegorically defined as Lust, and the doubleness of animal life is fully stated:

> For Love, to which we may now return, has two faces. . . . Yet, so strictly are they joined together that you cannot separate them. In this case, Orlando's love began her flight towards him with her white face turned, and her smooth and lovely body out-wards. Nearer and nearer she came wafting before her airs of pure delight. All of a sudden (at the sight of the Archduchess presumably) she wheeled about, turned the other way round; showed herself black, hairy, brutish; and it was Lust the vulture, not Love, the Bird of Paradise, that flopped foully and disgust-ingly upon his shoulders. (P. 108)

If this seems to be a recapitulation of attitudes in previous works, the recoiling from sex as something unclean and disgusting, we must remember that Orlando is now in Puritan England; we must also take into account the satiric style and the subsequent humorous acceptance of Harriet/Harry on the periphery of Orlando's world. Still, the evident sensual revulsion remains, a comic echo of the repugnance Clarissa Dalloway felt for Miss Kilman. In both cases the recoil is partly esthetic, partly moral. It would seem that Lust is distinguished from Desire not merely in being appetite divorced from affection but also in despoiling another, or taking by force, and Woolf consistently repudiates power when it signifies power over another. When love finally comes, in chapter 5, it is not precisely the Bird of Paradise, but it drops its feathers seductively rather than seizing its prey. Predatory nature has no place in the nature worship of *Orlando*.

The threat of chaos, as it is present in loosed forces of nature beyond man's mastery and also in uncontrolled or discordant passions within himself, loses its force when mind owes allegiance to nature rather than to society. The chaos of

the Great Flood in chapter 1, which can be tropologically
explained in terms of Orlando's ignorance of (female) nature,
has its answer in the tumultuous union of Orlando and Shelmerdine at the end of chapter 5. Light and dark, thunder and
lightning, a clamor of bells, slamming of doors, growling of
organ, rain falling, horse bounding, hawks circling "till they
crashed and fell in a shower of fragments to the ground"—
all the tumult and all the contraries are contained in being,
and are the elements of ecstasy rather than terror.

If symbols of house and tree, ice and fire, are related as
the outer and inner ordering of man's perception of his own
doubleness, which may be somewhat grossly stated as the
conflict between the need for society and the need for self-
sufficiency, the final pair of major symbols is more subtle. The
pattern of light and dark takes us to an analysis of the
creative mind which would not have been possible in the
Elizabethan age, or indeed in the Victorian age, and thus
makes itself fully understood only in the twentieth century.

The ambiguous treatment of the dark, terror of it but also
temptation by it, characteristic of the preceding novels, may
be epitomized by the mysterious moment near the end of
Mrs. Dalloway when Clarissa, having learned of the suicide
of Septimus Warren Smith, looks across the way and sees an
old woman climb the stairs and put out the light. Clarissa
feels serene pleasure, and the pleasure seems to be related to
her affirmation of Septimus's act—the putting out of life—
and the incident suggests an abiding death wish in Clarissa.
However, in the development of imagery in *To the Lighthouse*
Woolf has begun to recognize the dark not as a death, literally or in terms of mind, but as another kind of consciousness.
Orlando clarifies the meaning of this darkness, alters the proportions of the world of light, and reassesses the faculty of
vision so central to *Mrs. Dalloway* and *To the Lighthouse*.

Though the Elizabethan chapter takes place largely at sunset, no emphasis is placed on the movement from daylight
to dark; symbolic dark is not an issue until late in the second

chapter, when Fame, like social identity, "curbs the heart" and obscurity offers freedom. "Over the obscure man is poured the merciful suffusion of darkness" provides an echo of the "profusion of darkness" liberating the Ramsay house in "Time Passes." In another turn of the symbol, dark is a restorative memory and a hallucination on the stark hillside in Turkey, when the image of the green land of home comes to Orlando in a shadow. Neither of these passages is given theoretical expansion by Woolf, but an extended incident in the eighteenth century explains both. In an encounter between Orlando and the witty Mr. Pope, Woolf begins satirically:

A man who can destroy illusions is both beast and flood. Illusions are to the soul what atmosphere is to the earth. Roll up that tender air and the plant dies, the colour fades. The earth we walk on is a parched cinder. It is marl we tread and fiery cobbles scorch our feet. By the truth we are undone. Life is a dream. 'Tis waking that kills us. He who robs us of our dreams robs us of our life—(and so on for six pages if you will, but the style is tedious and may well be dropped). (Pp. 184-185)

Driving home with Pope, Orlando's attitudes shift as the coach passes from lamppost to darkness and to lamppost again; but the conclusion is more sardonic than satiric:

The light blazed in her eyes, and she saw, besides some degraded creatures of her own sex, two wretched pigmies on a stark desert land. Both were naked, solitary, and defenceless. The one was powerless to help the other. . . . Looking Mr. Pope full in the face, "It is equally vain", she thought, "for you to think you can protect me, or for me to think I can worship you. The light of truth beats upon us without shadow, and the light of truth is damnably unbecoming to us both." (P. 187)

Truth here defined is Mr. Ramsay's truth, which categorizes emotion and the senses as a world of illusion and rests with deadly security on the facts of man's infirmity, his mortality, and his finiteness. From this truth, irrefutable on its own ground but frail on any other, Orlando must depart to the night life of Drury Lane and the conversation of light women, as Woolf left *To the Lighthouse* behind for the fantasy of *Orlando*. The problem now is not one of accepting the dark but of understanding and justifying doing so. The theoretical analysis occupies much of the final chapter of *Orlando*.

The relentless light of Pope's wit, a hillside in Turkey, and the eye of the present moment represent a partial truth which becomes a falsity if taken for truth whole. The bare hills of Turkey may say to Orlando, "We perish, each alone," but simultaneously in a remembered England an oak tree of the world joins man, bird, leaf, and sky. The eye of the present observes life with shattering distinctness, sees things in clinical isolation:

Here the shadows of the plants were miraculously distinct. She noticed the separate grains of earth in the flower beds as if she had a microscope stuck to her eye. She saw the intricacy of the twigs of every tree. Each blade of grass was distinct and the markings of veins and petals. (P. 288)

The salvation, the form-giving shadow, comes from something Proust might call involuntary memory, or from the unconscious, "at the back of the brain (which is the part farthest from sight)". Vision is distinguished from sight by its dependence on something beyond the stimuli of the present moment; it demands the dark. Woolf's speculation begins in psychology and moves into esthetic theory, or theory of creativity:

She now looked down into this pool or sea in which everything is reflected—and, indeed, some say that all our most violent passions, and art and religion, are the reflections which we see in the dark hollow at the back of the head when the visible world is obscured for the time. (P. 290)

As a theory of art, it is contrary to that of Lily Briscoe, who "saw the colour burning on a framework of steel; the light of a butterflys wing lying upon the arches of a cathedral." Art in *To the Lighthouse* has its chiaroscuro ("A mother and child might be reduced to a shadow without irreverence. A light here required a shadow there"), but the interplay is on the level of abstraction and it is dominated by light. Briscoe art is the development of the sensibility of Rachel in *The Voyage Out;* beauty, fragility, and transience are in the light, and its opposite is not only the dark but also inert permanence. But in *Orlando* the entire symbolic structure has been reversed. Light is not here identified with color, nor is it the force imposing creative order. Rather, it presents the data for form, the separate grains of earth, the buttons on Stubbs's gaiters; but its information is inert and begins to have life only with the coming of the shadow. Just before the passages quoted, the daylight of the present is metaphorically offered as the domain of ice: Orlando's body "quivered and tingled as if suddenly stood naked in a hard frost."

The threat of the present is that visual daylight (related to fact and reason) denies affective meaning (in the fluidity of shadow). In the repudiation of chaos, which contains mystery as well as unreason, sight is sterile; the observing eye has no connection with the vital forces, cosmic or emotional:

Braced and strung up by the present moment she was also strangely afraid, as if whenever the gulf of time gaped and let a second through some unknown danger might come with it. The tension was too relentless and too rigorous to be endured long without discomfort. (Pp. 288-289)

An analysis of the sense of alienation or disconnection, in consciousness, and the mystery of integration, occupies the final chapter of *Orlando*. It is related to the historical lines of the novel by the fact that these lines are the external design of consciousness; and the study of history has led the narrator to see the future—for civilization as well as for the individual consciousness—in terms of revolutionary change. Thus, the new social consciousness runs the risk of disconnection from the mind or culture of the past, just as the exclusively present moment of Orlando's mind is in danger of closing out the body's memory of the past. Pursuing the parallel a little further, one finds a salvaging of the mind of the past in literature rather than in fact, like the recovery of individual affective memory by nonvisual senses. The time sense, and with it affective memory, is linked to the kinetic and auditory experience of life, in which there is a danger of chaos. But the risk must be accepted.

With the shadowing of the purely visual and intellectual sense of the present, Orlando can find radical identity and the novel can conclude on a passage which recovers the sense of duration. There can be no question, then, that the visual art forms celebrated at the end of *To the Lighthouse* are placed in a new perspective. One of the new dimensions of Woolf's art is emphasized by Orlando's return to the oak tree and to the physical sense of harmony. On a more mythic level, the night and the dark pool of the mind reveal their meaning in an ecstatic anticipation of the beloved, the traumatic moment conveyed by kinetic and auditory impressions: "The wind roared in her ears," and "Her pearls burnt like a phosphorescent flare."

Even allowing for the element of romantic parody, the return of Marmaduke Bonthrop Shelmerdine is the affirmation of the male principle contrary to the one which has dominated Woolf's novels. He belongs rather to the night world of the interval in *To the Lighthouse:* "They would see then night flowing down in purple; his head crowned; his sceptre jewelled; and how in his eyes a child might look."

None of the personages in the novel is a character, and none could exist outside the world of fantasy, but Shelmerdine, even more than Sasha, is an animate symbol. He is for the woman Orlando what Urania is for Milton, the muse of transcendental union, the fertilizing principle in the congress of the individual and the universe. Katherine in *Night and Day* sought such a transcendent union, but dimly and warily, and Woolf made the desire known in cryptic figures; in *Jacob's Room, Mrs. Dalloway,* and *To the Lighthouse,* the desire was displaced and sublimated; in *Orlando* it can find bold and extravagant expression because the vehicle is fantasy. For the male figure sought is not only mythic man as mate nor even symbiosis of the *other.* Shelmerdine comes to Orlando twice (three times, with the birth of the son), each time associated with an ecstatic moment in nature; and when this occurs, the style of narration loses its satiric distance to become religious in tone and mythic in its emblems.

At the end of the nineteenth century, when Orlando is on the verge of despair because she is unmarried, she wanders into the park and under the guidance of falling feathers comes to a mysterious pool which is compared to the lake into which the magic sword of Arthur was cast. There she finds "strange ecstasy" and declares herself as nature's bride, come to gather the feathers of wild birds. She lies upon the wet moor; at length she hears "deep within, some hammer on an anvil, or was it a heart beating? . . . the anvil, or the heart in the middle of the earth. . . ." Again this is the experience of unity which deflects intellectual doubt, for the body supine on the earth has the authority of its sensations. Yet the quality of this passage is radically different from those describing Orlando's harmony with the earth at the oak tree. In imagery anticipating the sea in *The Waves* (the beating of the anvil, the hooves of horses), Orlando feels the presence of a force beyond the solid earth.

Whereas Orlando, even as a boy, is associated with earth, Shelmerdine is associated with bird and sea. He is a sea captain from the opposite pole of the world (and here the symbolism is cheerful burlesque, as is the description of the life of male heroism "which is to voyage round Cape Horn in the teeth of a gale"), and his union with Orlando is the union of contraries in which neither is fettered. He is also associated with "the steel-blue gleam of rooks' wings, the hoarse laughter of their caws, the snake-like twisting descent of their feathers in a silver pool." The principle of wildness is in the birds he represents, the rook and the wild goose, but the true symbolic bird of *Orlando* is the kingfisher, which is natural desire and creative power, the child born of Orlando and Shelmerdine. Shelmerdine gone, Orlando sits beneath an oak at Kew "waiting for the kingfisher, which, it is said, was

seen once to cross in the evening from bank to bank." The
coming of the kingfisher is not the coming of Shelmerdine but
a new birth, in which both the eye and the body are instinct
with life.

> . . . We are not going, this time, visiting the blind land. Blue,
> like a match struck right in the ball of the innermost eye, he flys
> [sic], burns, bursts the seal of sleep; the kingfisher; so that now
> floods back refluent like a tide, the red, thick stream of life
> again. . . . (P. 265)

Images of completion taking us back to *Night and Day* and
to *Mrs. Dalloway* (the globe, the fecund fluid) are joined to
images of creative artistic power, and both are found in a
dynamic rather than a static condition. For the first time,
fertility of the imagination is inescapably linked to the biological life; the freeing of the mind occurs with the beginning
of the menses, here given symbolically as the birth of a
child. The rhythms of the inner tide of women now inform
the literary style.[4]

The brilliance and boldness of the kingfisher are certainly
significant, but so also is the name, the right name for the
creative imagination of a writer for whom the fish is virtually
a mystic symbol. In *A Writer's Diary* Woolf has noted on
September 30, 1926, after *To the Lighthouse,* a comment on
her anxiety about the reception of her novels.

> I wished to add some remarks to this, on the mystical side of
> this solicitude; how it is not oneself but something in the universe
> that one's left with. It is this that is frightening and exciting in
> the midst of my profound gloom, depression, boredom, whatever
> it is. One sees a fin passing far out. What image can I reach to
> convey what I mean?[5]

One could not ask for a more explicit statement of the nature
of the truth Woolf seeks in the various forms—the nets—of
her novels. But parts of this diary entry found in the unpublished diaries (omitted from Leonard Woolf's selection)
indicate that the sea is that of solitary being, unconscious
life being linked to the universal force. In the final chapter of
Orlando, we learn that "fish . . . who have lived in green

caves, solitary for years to hear them speak, never, never say, and so perhaps know what life is." One of the more obscure lines of *Orlando* is in fact the suggested inadequacy of verbal art to capture a truth which is silent, spontaneous, and elusive.

"Haunted! ever since I was a child. There flies the wild goose. It flies past the window out to sea. . . . I've seen it, here—there—there—England, Persia, Italy. Always it flies fast out to sea and always I fling after it words like nets . . . which shrivel as I've seen nets shrivel drawn on deck with only sea-weed in them; and sometimes there's an inch of silver—six words—in the bottom of the net. But never the great fish who lives in the coral groves." (Pp. 281-282)

The final chapter of *Orlando*, which Virginia Woolf suspected of violating the unity of the fantasy, is a new mode in style, imagery, point of view, and conception. In terms of its argument, on every level but that of history, it is not a breaking of unity so much as a new departure, for in the present age the sharp distinctions between subject and object, or physiology and metaphysics, disappear, and a new mind emerges.

Orlando is optimistic in its analysis of history, finding the present time a new birth for society; the past is lightly sifted for its true wealth, the dross is left behind, and men and women can make new social structures which do not pervert or suffocate life. What is to be salvaged from the past may be recognized in *Orlando* by the lapses in the satiric mode: the experience of love in nature in chapter 1, and the poet who is beyond his society, Shakespeare; contemplation and Sir Thomas Browne in chapter 2; libertinism in the eighteenth century; worship of nature in the nineteenth centry. The danger of fragmentation and triviality in the present age (conveyed in the confusion of details flashing past Orlando's eye as she motors through London) is to be averted by the individual's radical attachment to natural life and by the discovery of truer relationships than in the past.

Yet the evolution of civilization and the individual toward greater complexity and freedom (the plot structure of *Or-*

lando) satisfies neither Orlando nor Virginia Woolf, and declaration of the covert and symbolic quest is made by the style of the final chapter, in which satire is abandoned, and with it the comic distance of earlier chapters. The narrator is now truly omniscient, and the blank intervals and mysterious sleep of former times are filled with new consciousness and an analysis of it. The ecstatic mode which begins to break through shows much more than "natural desire." Woolf at the end of *Orlando* is frankly moving towards exploration of the religious unknown in life, and preparing for *The Waves.*

chapter 5

The Waves

When Virginia Woolf noted, after the completion of *Orlando,* that she would like never to write a novel again,[1] she was chafing primarily against plot—the orderly sequence of chronological time and the consequent lapses of meaning—and its exclusion of the depth she was seeking. Even before she began *Orlando*, Woolf was looking toward an action outside of time, in which sequential event would be abandoned as well as character. Orlando, in spite of flourishing through centuries, comes in the final chapter to the compression of history into the few minutes needed to stride through a house. Yet it would seem that the continued struggle against conventional forms, or ways of seeing, is now rather different from that begun in *Jacob's Room*; the halo of light can still surround a man in a railway carriage if the storyteller Bernard is traveling in the carriage, but the experience of being now to be captured is that which is antecedent to the shaping eye of the observer. When Woolf notes that her new book is to be "an abstract mystical eyeless book—a playpoem,"[2] however, she seems to be suggesting another step as well: the escape from the tyranny of sight with which we order our own beings, also sequentially, in space. In *The Waves* Woolf seeks a form and a style to convey vision in the symbolic or anagogic sense rather than the literal sense.

147

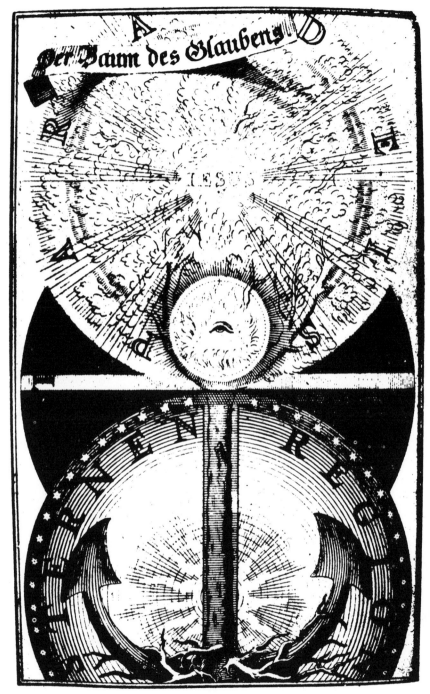

Figure 1

The word "mystical" occurs frequently in her diary entries, and on November 23, 1926, she sketches her first theme for *The Waves*:

Yet I am now and then haunted by some semi-mystic very profound life of a woman, which shall all be told on one occasion; and time shall be utterly obliterated; future shall somehow blossom out of the past. One incident—say the fall of a flower—might contain it. My theory being that the actual event practically does not exist—nor time either.[3]

An entry on September 10, 1928, shows the beginning of the struggle to define an idea that was essentially inarticulate.

Often down here I have entered into a sanctuary; a nunnery; had a religious retreat; of great agony once; and always some terror; so afraid one is of loneliness; of seeing to the bottom of the vessel. That is one of the experiences I have had here in some Augusts; and got then to a consciousness of what I call "reality": a thing I see before me: something abstract; but residing in the downs or sky; beside which nothing matters; in which I shall rest and continue to exist. Reality I call it. And I fancy sometimes this is the most necessary thing to me: that which I seek. But who knows—once one takes a pen and writes? How difficult not to go making "reality" this and that, whereas it is one thing.[4]

The contemplative and the mystic notes have been struck in every novel but have been overborne by other notes; the most obvious example perhaps is *Night and Day,* in which Katherine's dilemma and her double perception of being are presumably resolved by the expediencies of a Jane Austen world. The novel is unsatisfactory because marriage does not seem to answer Katherine's question:

Why, she reflected, should there be this perpetual disparity between the thought and the action, between the life of solitude and the life of society, this astonishing precipice on one side of which the soul was active and in broad daylight, on the other side of which it was contemplative and dark as night?[5]

In order for the contemplative side to emerge more fully than is possible in an intermittent pattern of mystical symbols, the human being has to be removed from the novel of society, in which he is a character, and followed into his essential solitude. Moreover, the style that Virginia Woolf had mastered was a style of the active soul and, though highly individual, linked to a tradition in that it imitated the example of novelists of the past in constructing a written language on the basis of spoken cadences. In *A Room of One's Own* Woolf suggests that women novelists must find their own cadences from speech; but she discovers in writing *The Waves* that speech is no longer the source of style. The reality sought is not only unspoken—outside the range of social realism—but also largely unconscious—thus outside the range of stream-of-consciousness novel. The difficulty of such an exploration of reality within any known literary form caused Woolf to re-structure and revise her work to the very end. In the final, intricate structuring, Virginia Woolf was able to include the dichotomy of *Night and Day* within a mythic unity. The con-taining frame (not to be found until two years after the initial idea) depends on a state of tension between an absolute and mystical perception of reality on the one hand and a multitudinous flux of realities on the other, resolved in an abstract symbolic structure.

There is in fact a double mystery to be explored: first, the source of individual souls, involving multiple realities and a flux in time, and second, the relation of individual souls to the single cosmic reality. Both mysteries are suggested in the opening pages of the novel, in which the primary perceptions of the six children rapidly prefigure all their later visions and responses. As has been noted by Robert Collins,[6] the key to soul-making is given in the first episode, as Bernard responds to the bath: "Water pours down the runnel of my spine. Bright arrows of sensation shoot on either side. I am covered with warm flesh." In old age Bernard is to speculate on this formation of identify by sensation: "But we were all different. The wax—the virginal wax that coats the spine melted in different patches for each of us." So each child perceives the great circle of unity differently: Bernard as a loop of light, Neville as a globe, Susan as a curled caterpillar, Rhoda as a bowl of mackerel, Jinny as bubbles in a saucepan. All except Louis respond with delight to sound, light, and color, yet each has only a single intense perception. The only relationships known are those of metaphor, and each child is in a closed circuit of object (like) subject. The *world* as a configuration is more unreal than the basin in which Rhoda rocks her petal ships. A world grows from the accretion of sensation in memory. "The back of my hand burns," said Jinny, "but the palm is clammy and damp with dew." A little later causality and space begin to appear: "I burn, I shiver," said Jinny, "out of this sun, into this shadow."

However, the first episode reveals the origin of being in sensation as something to be accepted less easily. In another metaphor of the soul, several times suggested, the soul is like the soft snail on which sensations tap like the beaks of birds; if the beak strikes before the shell is firm, the soul is presumably injured. To the solitary world, the microcosm of the body, come sensations arising not from the presence of objects in an external world but from the willed act of another. The scullery maid "scrapes the fish-scales with a jagged knife"; a bird pecks a worm and leaves it to fester. Louis, imagining himself as a hidden tree, is kissed by Jinny and feels the kiss as a blow shattering his safety. The motif, its first childish manifestation appearing harmless perhaps to an adult, is picked up again and again in subsequent episodes: "An axe has split a tree to the core," or "The hatchet must fall on the block; the oak must be cleft to the center."

The deadly seriousness of these blows is known even in the first episode, for Neville has felt a blow from which he will suffer all his life.

He was found with his throat cut. The apple-tree leaves became fixed in the sky; the moon glared; I was unable to lift my foot up the stair. . . . I shall call this stricture, this rigidity, 'death among the apple trees' for ever. There were the floating, pale-grey clouds; and the immitigable tree; the implacable tree with its greaved silver bark. The ripple of my life was unavailing. I was unable to pass by. (P. 17)[7]

The formative events are the arrest of sensation and understanding by the presence of another as obstacle, terrible
because uncontrollable. For Neville the hideous image of
death by the apple trees; for Louis the kiss; for Susan the
rejection of her love; for Bernard the sight of a garden which
denies his existence. With Rhoda alone the arrest is not the
result of the act of another person; and the significance of
Rhoda's destiny lies outside the range of sensation.

As the children depart from the garden of childhood with
their defensive hardness beginning to form, they recognize
complex external structures into which they must fit. They
do so; they make appropriate masks against which the blows
of the other—now less overt—strike harmlessly. One must
"interpose something hard between myself and the stare of
housemaids." There is then a change in the literary style
recovering the inarticulate life; fewer and fewer of the immediate and intense sensations of life come through the pro-
tective screen of the forming ego, but the ones that do filter
in are those that support the original vivid sensations of
being. Because the shell is not only a fortification but also
a prison, a keen longing arises not to be defended but to
find a way of making contact and, in so doing, to find identity
beyond the limits of the body. The terror and the pain of
being—the fall of the axe, the man with his throat cut
beneath the apple tree—evolve inevitably from the ecstasy
and the beauty of the life of sensation, which is the life of
relationship. As there is one character who tries to escape
totally from the ecstasy and terror of the world of sensation,
so there is one who casts herself into it without fear or
hesitation. This is Jinny, who in spite of her vitality tends to
be passed over because of the overmastering symbolic structure and its metaphysical implications. However, Jinny,
touched by the mystery of life in the unmoved mover of the
first episode—the leaves moving in the garden without cause
—questions the mysterious rhythm of the world in her own

body: "What moves my heart?" Her response is to be the mover—"I" as vitality—and send the rhythm outward again. In Jinny, Virginia Woolf has explored the limits of eroticism and has shown its harmony with the cosmic mystery.

To the extent that *The Waves* can be said to have a plot, the rise and fall of narrative and dramatic interest follows the moments in which six people focus their desires upon another, Percival, and have intimations of completion. Only at these moments is there interaction among the six; only then does the isolation of existence permit communication. For these times the presence of others is not a threat and a sundering, but an opening of awareness. "I do not believe in separation. We are not single," says Bernard, but his act of union is to weave a web of words, "a wandering thread, lightly joining one thing to another." He needs the stimulus of other people to weave his web but avoids the intensity of contact.

In the fourth episode, however, as the friends unite in the leave-taking of Percival (which is also a Last Supper, for Percival goes to his death), the dimensions of being expand, even to the fourth dimension, and the six friends feel themselvse existing in time and space. The full meaning of this episode emerges only when it is examined in the light of the abstract, mystical pattern; but in terms of the first pattern, of sensation and psyche, it is clear that Percival is the desirable body of the world, and that he calls up each essential existence and enables it to communicate with the others. The six are able to say "we" instead of "I," not because they remember the same childhood, or see the same things in the present, but because they return to their most authentic condition, the spontaneous and elemental life exterior to ego, in which other people were forces and sensations. The communication is of course nonverbal; yet such a moment breaches the limits of physical existence and enables one character to share the awareness of another. The pattern of symbol and image reveals the process whereby the initial

image of being is modified by a relationship. In the following passage, in which each of the six states his truth, the
process has already begun with Rhoda and Louis.

"Now let us issue from the darkness of solitude," said Louis.

"Now let us say, brutally and directly, what is in our minds,"
said Neville. "Our isolation, our preparation, is over. The furtive
days of secrecy and hiding, the revelations on staircases, moments of terror and ecstasy."

"Old Mrs. Constable lifted her sponge and warmth poured over
us," said Bernard. "We became clothed in this changing, this
feeling garment of flesh."

"The boot-boy made love to the scullery-maid in the kitchen
garden," said Susan, "among the blown-out washing."

"The breath of the wind was like a tiger panting," said Rhoda.

"The man lay livid with his throat cut in the gutter," said
Neville. "And going upstairs I could not raise my foot against the
immitigable apple tree with its silver leaves held stiff."

"The leaf danced in the hedge without anyone to blow it," said
Jinny.

"In the sun-baked corner," said Louis, "the petals swam on
depths of green."

"At Elvedon the gardeners swept and swept with their great
brooms, and the woman sat at a table writing," said Bernard.
(Pp. 88-89)

Paradoxically, Percival, of whom they make an ikon of
contemplative love, is desired by them in order to make
articulate the secret life of terror and ecstasy. He is not a
composite of their knowledge of life, but of their ideal forms
denying the reality of life. "We have come together . . . to
make one thing, not enduring—for what endures?—but seen
by many eyes simultaneously." He is thus a flower, and a
"globe whose walls are made of Percival, of youth and beauty,
and something so deep sunk within us that we shall perhaps
never make this moment out of one man again." Though
Percival is described as monolithic and godlike, this fullness
and intensification does not occur because he is a god, for
Woolf shows him to be imperfect. ("Yet I could not live with
him and suffer his stupidity. He will coarsen and snore.")
Rather, he is an external image in the atmosphere of light,
giving the reverse of the dark and private knowledge of each

and yet satisfying the need which all their masks have been laboriously constructed to satisfy. When Percival enters the restaurant for the reunion, Neville says: "The reign of chaos is over. He has imposed order."

In *The Waves* Virginia Woolf has at last confronted the threat of chaos directly and in its full power. The word itself recurs with the ominous force of the great beast stamping on the shore, and the life of each person, except that of Rhoda, has been organized as a conquest of chaos. For Louis chaos shows itself as the flux, disorder, and despair of survival in shoddy coffee houses and attic rooms; his efforts to master it have taken the forms of a mythic identification with history, commercial power ("I roll the dark before me, spreading commerce where there was chaos") and of the effort to "make a steel ring of clear poetry, that shall connect the gulls and the women with bad teeth." For Neville nature is chaos, opposed by the ecstasy or trance of sacrifice. Confronted with the terror of the dead man under the apple tree, he has identified truth with the knife which cut the man's throat. The knife, blade, or rapier is his symbol, and it establishes ascendancy over chaos by the power of destruction. As he sees Fenwick in the garden with raised mallet, his response is religious: "Then suddenly descended upon me the obscure, the mystic, sense of adoration, of completeness that triumphed over chaos." For both Louis and Neville, man is in a state of siege and must impose his own form. History, myth, the cult of love, worldly power, and art are the strategies of conquest. Bernard shares this attitude intermittently: "We too, as we put on our hats and push open the door, stride not into chaos, but into a world that our own force can subjugate and make part of the illumined and everlasting road."

Whereas the men at maturity have created bulwarks against the forces of chaos, Susan and Jinny have established limited strategies of exposure to them. Indeed, none of the girls has an abstract conception called "chaos." But Susan, perceiving as a child a drama of sexual wildness acted out by the servants, gives us images of chaos as experience rather than as a concept:

He was blind as a bull, and she swooned in anguish. . . . Now though they pass plates of bread and butter and cups of milk at tea-time I see a crack in the earth and hot steam hisses up; and the urn roars as Ernest roared, and I am blown out hard like the pyjamas, even while my teeth meet in the soft bread. . . . I am not afraid of heat, nor of the frozen winter. (P. 18)

Jinny, a child, perceives a leaf moving for no reason, and the entire mystery of death strikes her. Both encompass the unknown, Susan with a "fell" acceptance, Jinny by casting the fiery light of her own power over the world physically. Rhoda has no defense against chaos; on the contrary, in *The Waves* she is the constant presence of chaos.

Let me pull myself out of these waters. But they heap themselves on me; they sweep me between their great shoulders; I am turned; I am tumbled; I am stretched, among these long lights, these long waves, these endless paths, with people pursuing, pursuing. (P. 20)

The strategies of protection and containment of the others are to be read against the destiny of the defenseless Rhoda, who lives out all their intimations of chaos and is Bernard's opposite. Though the summation of all terrors is the terror of chaos, it includes not only the overwhelming of human forms by wild forces in the cosmos and in the body but also the distintegration of human meaning, emotional or intellectual. The waves which sweep Rhoda away are fundamentally the same waves that Jinny feels slapping against her ribs and drumming in her forehead; love ends as surely when Jinny feels indifference after the moment of ecstasy as when Percival falls from his horse and is killed; and the death of the universe is as complete when Bernard loses the thread of his story as when the sun goes into eclipse.

But the moment of union with Percival is the moment of illusion, when it seems that chaos and death are conquered at no expense, and the early intuitions of ruin are transfigured in Bernard's image of the crimson carnation which is the transcendence of egoism. For Neville, Percival is an object of adoration because he embodies the vision of sacrifice at the apple tree, transfigured in a splendid barbaric rite of eroticism. Yet contained in the moment of unity is the fore-warning of disintegration, and part of the ecstasy is the result of the secret knowledge that the image of youth and beauty leaves out much of reality. As Neville indicates, affirmations of identity are "crazy platforms" on the "roaring waters" of chaos. Before the episode ends, and before Perci-val's death, the magic circle has been broken by elements which do not fit into the perfect design but confirm Louis's first intuition of life: "The great brute on the beach stamps." Egoism returns, and at this point it is seen as an imperious and predatory egoism; the moment of perfection has depended on something akin to contemplation, and alien to instinctive savagery: "Their eyes burn like the eyes of animals brush-ing through leaves on the scent of the prey. The circle is destroyed."

The interlude following the moment of union confirms Louis's premonition, for it ends with the sound of the waves "like the thud of a great beast stamping." After the death of illusion, life becomes increasingly an act of will in solitude, facing the knowledge of death. For a time the sensual en-chantments of the life of the body seem to offer sufficient meaning, as in the sixth episode, in which the creatures of fire and earth content themselves in a present function or a tran-sitory delight. Neville says: "Time passes, yes. And we grow old. But to sit with you, alone with you . . . in the firelit room . . . is all." Susan, bound to her sleeping child, is som-nolent in yielding to the cycles. Jinny throws herself into the flux, confident that she can seize her body's satisfaction:

Now I hear crash and rending of boughs and the crack of antlers as if the beasts of the forest were all hunting, all rearing high and plunging down among the thorns. One has pierced me. . . . And velvet flowers and leaves whose coolness has been stood in water wash me round. . . .

Louis, feeling the weight of the world on his shoulders, experiences the keenest joy in mastering a world felt to be alien. But from this episode, in which the depths are not to be sounded, Bernard and Rhoda are absent; they return only in the seventh episode, in which the fullness of possibility for each of the characters reveals itself. Greatest depth and dignity come to Jinny, Louis, and Neville in the fading light of failure, disillusion, decay, and death, and this final expression of the forms of their inner lives belies the later summation by Bernard. Of Louis, for example, Bernard will say:

He fascinated me with his sordid imagination. His heroes wore bowler-hats and talked about selling pianos for tenners. Through his landscape the tram squealed; the factory poured its acrid fumes. He haunted mean streets and towns where women lay drunk, naked, on . . . Christmas day. (P. 179)

The inadequacy of such a caricature is shown by all the soliloquies of Louis, but in particular the last ones:

My destiny has been that I remember and must . . . plait into one cable the many threads, the thin, the thick, the broken, the enduring of our long history, of our tumultuous and varied day. There is always more to be understood; a discord to be listened for; a falsity to be reprimanded. (P. 144)

At this stage the forms of life are fixed; indeed, from the moment of the first perceptions of the children there has been a degree of tragic inevitability in the choices. For Susan, Jinny, and Neville the irreversible decay of their forms—the downward journey of time-bound man in his decaying flesh—leads them to a silent end. Bernard and Rhoda, however, leave the old forms behind. Bernard yields the past to its ruin and looks for what may appear by chance, the "fin in a waste of waters," and Rhoda journeys into the totally unknown.

The incompleteness of each life in isolation has been apparent from the third episode (perhaps from the beginning), as has been Bernard's function as observing eye and interpreter seeing things on the periphery of life unseen by the others, glimpsing inarticulate motives and relationships. Less obviously, his shaping of reality, like theirs, has been limited. Although the ease and fluency of his mind and his dexterity in outwitting the forces of chaos have provided comfort to the reader, one is not left with the final comfort of believing that, through Bernard, he has come to the truth. As much as can be done in a condition of mortality, moving through a world of gardens and cities in a pattern of childhood, youth, mating, and aging, is done by Bernard with the gift of story-telling, which places him in touch with solid reality but free of a fixed position in it, like the spider's web floating between earth and sky, or the bubble blown between water and air, or the smoke ring blown between fire and air. These are his symbols. Insubstantial they may be, but Bernard, ever-changing, creates a new form when a bubble bursts or a drop falls. The story he has been preparing for, all his life (and finally renounces) is the story of the ninth and final episode. As he has foreseen in youth, a final summation will be made, as by Louis the accountant, and "our total will be known; but it will not be enough."

In a dramatic monologue, he reveals himself and the form of his life to an unknown listener who cannot see the form or hear the story. Bernard himself no longer believes in stories, especially not the one he is to tell; it is in fact a fairy tale, elemental, yet safe for children. He recounts the childhood scene and the process of formation of sensibility and identity as a response to arrows of sensation. He composes stories about his friends, partial truths—"a convenience, a lie"— placing them beside a willow tree which is a symbol of per-manence. Intermittently new strains are heard—an "almost wordless, almost senseless song"—but Bernard persists in the story of common life, the life of Monday and Tuesday, of domestication, until the death of Percival. At this point the tenor of his narrative changes, for he leaves the surface. He becomes philosophic, not on the basis of his responses re-

corded in the fifth episode but on the basis of the response of
Rhoda. Something, it seems, was suppressed in the fifth episode. We recognize suddenly that Bernard, as he moved
lightly over the surface of things, excluded the violence of
passion, fear, hate, desire, present in all the others; and that
he begins cautiously in his final solitude to encompass their
sensations. As he continues to tell stories, he moves deeper
into the reality of the others and into a philosophic acceptance of the limitations of each life—each being "committed
to a statement"—moving towards extinction. "Fight!" has
been Bernard's response at the end of the sad reunion of the
eighth episode, where there is no gathering together in the
pronoun "we." At length, in middle age Bernard undergoes
symbolic death in the eclipse of the sun, and can no longer
create an *I*. Now, with the loss of self he begins to merge
with the others, but the creative force rises to a new threat,
another death, and this the final one.

The final paragraph of *The Waves* is in a mood of exaltation, a frankly heroic rhetoric of defiance to the inevitable
defeat; but the last few pages of Bernard's monologue, beginning with the earth's revival after the eclipse, insist upon a
double reading, for the mystical line emerges. Bernard can
do no more than herald it, but the cryptic conclusion *"The
waves broke on the shore"* is not fully comprehensible without the symbolic pattern.

The bare outlines of the abstract structure are contained in
one of the earliest sketches, made when the book was still to
be called *The Moths*. Abstract lines, vertical and horizontal,
are made by a flower and the flight of the moths, the total
meaning contained in the consciousness of a solitary being,
a woman. Thus is derived the abstract figure

which is the
basic structure of the final version, in which the presiding
female figure, though present, has become a gigantic mythic

shape on the horizon of the interludes, and the horizontal and vertical lines are represented in character, natural imagery, and geometric figures. Although in the process of vision and revision Woolf altered her attitude to the design, complicating it and placing emphasis on unanticipated aspects, the basic tension remains. It is partially dependent on the nature imagery already familiar from the preceding novels, but Virginia Woolf has here attempted an abstract art for the conveying of the mystical theme.

Before the new book became articulate as an idea, it had an "angular shape" in her mind; she anticipated that it would be "sharply cornered,"[8] and in the finished work we find geometric figures with a traditionally religious or occult significance counterposed to images of nature:

Although the abstract patterns could presumably have been found without intellectual precedent, if one takes seriously the idea of a collective unconscious, it is certain that Woolf would have found precedent for geometric and numerical symbolism in the work of three thinkers with whom she was familiar: Sir Thomas Browne (who is Orlando's guide in the second stage of his life), Carl Jung, and W. B. Yeats. It is immediately evident that the figure first sketched (p. 160) is one of the designs found by Jung to be symbols of "self-collection";[9] it also resembles the one which is the basic figure of the esoteric system of W. B. Yeats;[10] and it is one of the cabalistic symbols used by the Rosicrucians, in fact one of the emblems of the Rosy Cross.[11] (See fig. 2.) In its natural as opposed to its divine unity, it contains the four elements—fire, air, earth, and water—with which the characters of *The Waves* are identified.

Figure 2

However, the true evidence of the occult symbolic structure is to be found in the completed work *The Waves,* and the reader is awakened to the nature of the structure by the first of the omniscient interludes as well as by the first episode. In a densely metaphoric introduction, Woolf presents the world of nature as it is emerging from chaos, just at the entrance of light, and before the familiar objects of our world have received their names and become distinct from one another. Sky is described as liquid, like the sea, but of a different color; air is felt as fibrous, like a plant; and the sky is woollen, like a blanket. The waves of the sea are scarcely defined, but are submerged movements of dark bars. When the lamp of the sun is raised, the world begins to be a world.

The introduction of *The Waves* sketches a cosmogony. In the beginning is chaos as a reservoir of the elements of form. In the beginning of the universe of *The Waves* (as both macrocosm and microcosm), chaos is not a condition of strife, or warring of elements, but of unconscious, unknown rhythm, and of quiescence. The creative force is light, a lamp in the hand of the mythic woman at the source of creation. In the mythic figure of which the world is made, Woolf presents the horizontal and vertical lines for the first time, and indicates a correspondence between the horizontal body of the woman and the bars of the waves, and between her raised arm and the bars of color spread across the sky. The arc of the sun is the emerging globe which serves as a major motif in the episodes; it is emphasized by the first responses of Bernard and Neville, "I see a ring," and "I see a globe." Words of circularity appear on every page of the first half of *The Waves.* Ring, loop, ball, bubble, wheel, balloon, circle, drop, and globe are signs of the awareness of the six characters of a master design, a completeness that is spontaneously and intuitively known at the dawn of being, before identity has separated the parts from the whole. Separate, they will seek the knowledge again in all the bodies

of the world. It would seem that the elemental forces are in
the circle, as in the cabalistic diagram, and the
thoughtless child is reminded of the great circle by the little
circle of his blood: intuition of the macrocosm then comes
through knowledge of the microcosm. When the circle is not
present to the senses in the external world (as it is in a ring,
a wheel, or a bowl), the mind constructs steel rings of poetry,
or blows bubbles of language, or dances a sphere. The characters whose physical relationship with the world is halted
early, Neville, Susan, and Rhoda, think least in images of
circularity; and the culmination of the movement toward a
physical and sensual recovery of the circle is in the presence
of Percival, who is the epitome of spontaneous life, having
no need of thought or language. But, as Rhoda suggests at
the end of the fourth episode, neither Percival nor any other
person can be the true and transcendent whole. For the most
part, Bernard, Louis, and Jinny—in whose minds circular
images play—are aware of a need for a ring of life in the
world of action, but Rhoda states the larger desire, and the
mystical significance of the circle, at the time of the second
reunion:

Yet there are moments when the walls of the mind grow thin;
when nothing is unabsorbed, and I could fancy that we might
blow so vast a bubble that the sun might set and rise in it and we
might take the blue of midday and the black of midnight and be
cast off and escape from here and now. (P. 159)

The failure, and the enclosure of each of the six in his
own partial life, can be understood by a design of verbal
abstraction. In the preceding circle with its four elements,
Susan is the element of earth; Rhoda, water; Bernard, air;
Jinny, fire. Neville is outside of nature; having no relation
with women, he must construct his elements by artifice. Louis
is from the beginning an integrator, for he identifies himself
with the tree joining earth and air. The true circle, and its

alchemical permanence, depend on the harmonious mixture of the elements. In *The Waves,* it would involve the self-definition of each character in terms of the powers of the others rather than in defense against the others. Bernard, Jinny, Susan, Rhoda, Louis, and Neville meet in various combinations, usually the least fertile ones in terms of a finite world. For example, the earliest known encounter of Louis with another is in the amorous attack by Jinny in the first episode; but for Louis, experiencing himself as a tree, the attack by the element of fire can only be destructive. Bernard seeks to console earthy Susan, to whom he can give no real comfort. Symbolism of the elements is to some extent related to the Grail symbolism suggested by the central use of Percival, although the relationship is not entirely clear (as the Grail symbols themselves are ambiguous) nor is it simple. Cup, Lance, Sword, Dish, and Stone, though the talismans of the Grail quest, have a less arbitrary place in the symbolism of *The Waves,* with the exception of the Stone, with which Percival is identified. Percival as questing hero and restorer of the land offers a salvation which proves to be illusory. His myth would have to be considered a failed quest, for he does not succeed in "freeing the waters," the result Jessie Weston finds to be the radically restorative act.[12] But fire and air are the dominant elements of the episodes, the meaning of water being left to the interludes and the isolated Rhoda. Thus the Quest hero, exploring the esoteric meaning, is Rhoda.

Louis and Rhoda provide a guide through the mystical structure of *The Waves,* with Rhoda establishing the geometric figures of it. The basic text for elucidation of an abstract structure is the first soliloquy of Rhoda:

Now the terror is beginning. Now taking her lump of chalk she [Miss Hudson] draws figures, six, seven, eight, and then a cross and then a line on the blackboard. What is the answer? The others look; they look with understanding. . . . I see only figures. The others are handing in their answers. . . . But I have no answer. The others are allowed to go. . . . I am left alone to find

an answer. The figures mean nothing now. Meaning has gone.
The clock ticks. The two hands are convoys marching through a
desert. The black bars on the clock face are green oases. The
long hand has marched ahead to find water. The other, painfully
stumbles among hot stones in the desert. It will die in the desert.
The kitchen door slams. Wild dogs bark far away. Look, the loop
of the figure is beginning to fill with time; it holds the world in it.
I begin to draw a figure and the world is looped in it, and I myself am outside the loop; which I now join—so—and seal up, and
make entire. The world is entire, and I am outside of it, crying,
'Oh save me, from being blown for ever outside the loop of time!'
(P. 15)

Doing sums is the business of life: adding up, making
connections, understanding the symbol + as a sign, a direction to do something. The clock also presides over the world
of action, keeping us informed about the cosmic facts we
must consider: time and space, the movements of the sun.
Five of the children who begin *The Waves* learn these les-
sons; they learn to establish sequences and to recognize themselves as creatures of time. For Rhoda + is a cross, the clock
is a desert promising death, and the numbers of her lesson in

$$\begin{aligned}6\\7\\+8\\\hline\end{aligned}$$

arithmetic become occult symbols.   for Rhoda does not

signify 21 but ∞. It is probable that the figure Rhoda finally
draws is the figure 6.[13] Six, the number of characters in *The
Waves,* is considered by Philo to be the perfect number.[14]
Paradoxically, Rhoda is a part of that number, but the part
destined to be forever outside the circle of the world and
time. Her position is illustrated by an engraving from Robert
Fludd's *Apologia*[15] in which the circles of the microcosm and
the macrocosm wind off, like a 6, to infinity or the unknown.
(See fig. 3.)

Over the basic cosmic circle, however, other abstract figures are superimposed. The + in Rhoda's soliloquy, defined
by her as a cross, has Christian connotations which are rein-

Figure 3

forced by Neville's image of death beneath the apple tree, and by the ostentatious presence of the crucifix in the third episode, in which it is a symbol of traditional authority and historical continuity. Even for Louis, however, that meaning is transitory, an externally presented definition of a condition known much more existentially. The horizontal line is the line of time, the condition of flux; the vertical line is the condition of permanence. Louis desires the vertical; he is the tree whose roots reach to the hard center of the earth and whose leaves move, vulnerable, in the air; his tree is also a world tree, reaching from the mysterious desert on the Nile to twentieth-century London, with Australia an accident on the under side of the world. Only painfully can he accept the line of flux:

> I oppose to what is passing this ramrod of beaten steel. I will not submit to this aimless passing of billycock hats and Homburg hats and all the plumed and variegated head-dresses of women. . . .
> . . . .
> I see the gleaming tea-urn; the glass cases full of pale-yellow sandwiches . . . and also behind them, eternity. (Pp. 68-69)

Bernard on the other hand lives on the horizontal line. He resists any permanence (becoming engaged is to him like walking "bang into a pillar box"), and he is described again and again in terms of a wandering thread, a dangling wire, or the flight of a bee moving irreverently through chapel and out of the window.

For Susan, Jinny, and Rhoda, the pattern is more complex. Susan has no abstract figures but blindly adheres to farm life, which is both flux and permanence; Jinny's characteristic pattern (the dance) is a spiral, which is a simultaneous horizonal and vertical movement; and Rhoda's patterns are beyond the reach of the senses, or body, of common life. Earth is not Rhoda's element; she is, as Bernard sees, a nymph of the fountain. Her first story about the world is about a basin of water in which petal-ships float, and in which the lighthouse is a blossom. All the story elements and symbols of *The Waves* are here, including the stone (Percival) which makes "bubbles

rise from the depths of the sea," and including also the survival of a solitary ship, Rhoda's own. She is, as Woolf thus
indicates from the beginning, a manifestation of the mythic
figure of the interludes, and though out of her element in the
finite world of action, a reminder of transcendence. The images
she presents cannot be understood in bodily terms or in
familiar rational relationships, as can the symbols of the
others. One who tries to relate her images to the perceptual
world and the exigencies of men in Homburg hats is likely to
say that Rhoda is slightly mad. However, in the Western
tradition the distinction between madness and mysticism has
not often been clear; Woolf apparently accepts such an
ambiguity in *The Waves,* and offers two readings of Rhoda,
corresponding to the two readings of the novel in the contexts
of time and of eternity.

For Rhoda the vertical symbol of permanence is known only
in a dream-landscape: a mysterious column. The horizontal
line of time is not precisely a line, but a succession of attacks
by sensation: "The tiger leaps. Tongues with their whips are
upon me. Mobile, incessant, they flicker over me." When
through a knowledge of eroticism she succeeds in understanding the tiger and brings the two lines into conjunction, she
offers a key image for the entire work.

Before we describe Rhoda's pillar, however, the significance
of the square, a more mundane symbol, should perhaps be
considered. Even though explicit statements about the square
occur only in the second half of the novel, the opening section
introduces the square in the incident that is repeated again and
again in Bernard's memory; it is Elveden, the "ringed wood
with a wall round it," which Bernard sees as hostile country.
The square is also, to Rhoda, the world of "hard contacts and
collisions" from which she would escape; the square of a room
is for Neville the private being protected from nature and
society. Susan gives the square a humanistic meaning:

But I have seen life in blocks, substantial, huge; its battlements
and towers, factories and gasometers; a dwelling-place made from

time immemorial after an hereditary pattern. These things remain
square, prominent, undissolved in my mind. I am not sinuous. . . .
(Pp. 152-153)

However, the abstract significance at its most intense satura-
tion is given by Rhoda, who upon hearing of the death of
Percival goes to a concert and there attempts to define reality:

'Like' and 'like' and 'like'—but what is the thing that lies beneath the semblance of the thing? . . . There is a square; there is
an oblong. The players take the square and place it upon the
oblong. They place it very accurately; they make a perfect dwelling-place. Very little is left outside. The structure is now visible;
what is inchoate is here stated; we are not so various or so mean;
we have made oblongs and stood them upon squares. (P. 116)

The juxtaposition of the square and the oblong is a sign of
disorientation and disharmony, in either position. Rhoda's own
vision has been temporarily lost, to be replaced by a figure
which demonstrates esthetically a moral disproportion. The
oblong is both inelegant and inert through lack of a dynamic
harmony, like the hall and the crowd within which the
musicians attempt to compose the square of a musical quartet.
In this sharply cornered design, religious or cosmic harmony is

unknown. The true figure would be 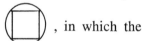 , in which the

human act is contained within a larger, harmonious whole,
touching upon the whole at all vital points. The acceptance of
the square/oblong superimposition is an acceptance of alienation and, especially for Rhoda, betrayal of the self. Later,
remembering, Rhoda is to see that the art form of the music
is as much an oblong as is a palace by Wren; neither provides
a place for the square of the ideal dwelling place, and Rhoda
ultimately must leave them, seeking the pillar of her vision.

In the central episode, the valedictory dinner with its acts of
self-definition and confession, Jinny has confessed: "My body
goes before me, like a lantern down a dark lane, bringing one
thing after another out of darkness into a ring of light. I dazzle
you; I make you believe that this is all." Yet it is not all, and

Rhoda sees, as Neville knows, "far away over our heads, beyond India." Rhoda offers a truly occult vision:

> . . . A hollow where the many-backed steep hills come down like birds' wings folded. There, on the short, firm turf, are bushes, dark leaved, and against their darkness I see a shape, white, but not of stone, moving, perhaps alive. But it is not you, it is not you, it is not you; not Percival, Susan, Jinny, Neville or Louis. When the white arm rests upon the knee it is a triangle; now it is upright— a column; now a fountain, falling. It makes no sign, it does not beckon, it does not see us. Behind it roars the sea. It is beyond our reach. Yet there I venture. (P. 99)

Against this background the rites of adoration of Percival take place. Rhoda sees the farewell dinner and the worship of Percival as a splendid and savage ritual of love:

> "The flames of the festival rise high," said Rhoda. "The great procession passes, flinging green boughs and flowering branches. . . . They deck the beloved with garlands and with laurel leaves, there on the ring of turf where the steep-backed hills come down. The procession passes. And while it passes, Louis, we are aware of downfalling, we forebode decay. (Pp. 100-101)

Rhoda's vision, a mythic rather than a naturalistic landscape, has a druidic cast which is, I think, echoed in Bernard's awakening to fatality in the ninth episode "as if one had woken in Stonehenge surrounded by a circle of great stones, these enemies, these presences." The occult ring of Rhoda seems to be Delphic and to contain the omphalos. The triangle associated with this mystery is unlike the other geometric figures in *The Waves,* not only because of the rarity of its appearance but because of its separation from nature and the world of action, like Mrs. Ramsay's "wedge of darkness." Thus, while the circle and the square exist on both the exoteric and esoteric levels, the triangle appears solely on the esoteric. The only approximations to it in the world of the senses are in partial perceptions such as that of Louis, seeing the shadow of a tree like a bent elbow, and that of Bernard, glimpsing a fin in the sea. To speculate about trinitarian religious significance seems irrelevant in terms of the larger structures of *The Waves;* and indeed all speculation seems both futile and contrary to

Woolf's intention, for the triangle, and the white form which Rhoda sees, seem clearly to be signs of the unknown, having power because they are beyond knowledge.

The ritual of the sacrificed god is the horizontal line moving against the background of the mysterious column and the sea; it belongs to the world of mutability; with its ready analogies in the world of action and its more or less efficacious offer of sustenance to the living, it is a passing pageant. The food of life offered is a tragic knowledge which enables each of the six to go to his end with the vision of dimensions beyond the circle of his body. Rhoda's sacrifice too, like her vision, is only partly efficacious. Her act is that of "freeing the waters," but it is an act that must be carried to completion by Bernard, in the knowledge communicated in the ninth episode. In her last soliloquy, in the seventh episode, Rhoda defines her life as "the white spaces that lie between hour and hour." She is the intuition of the timeless and of the sea behind the mysterious forms; her silence is to the verbal forms of speaking and writing what the white spaces of the page are to the printed word: the necessary condition of existence. The mythic "freeing of the waters" in *The Waves* is in part the acceptance of the terrifying life "in the white spaces" beyond the reach of language; it is also acceptance of chaos.

Language is the net with which Neville fishes the waters of life: "And so (while they talk) let down one's net deeper and deeper and gently draw in and bring to the surface what he said and she said and make poetry." Bernard even more consistently seizes life with words: "I netted them under with a sudden phrase. I retrieved them from formlessness with words." In another metaphor he compares the world to a cauldron from which he has drawn a sentence of six little fish. In neither case does the mind subject itself to the element; it seizes the fruit of the sea while remaining safely on the dry land of forms. In contrast the white spaces and the roaring waters known to Rhoda are the formless, inarticulate, dangerous places of the macrocosm and microcosm. Rhoda's terror of her being is evident from the beginning; one refrain of her soliloquies is the crying out against waves which overwhelm her, yet simultaneously she desires to drift on the waters. In the end she consents to know her element, not only as a dream-lake or a story-sea whose motions she can control but also as the turbulent unknown. Her journey to a Spanish inn[16] at the end of the seventh episode is her consent to experience the chaos against which the other five defend themselves with hard forms:

We launch out now over the precipice. . . . The cliffs vanish. Rippling small, rippling grey, innumerable waves spread beneath us. I touch nothing. I see nothing. We may sink and settle on the waves. The sea will drum in my ears. . . . Rolling me over the waves will shoulder me under. Everything falls in a tremendous shower, dissolving me. (P. 147)

One function of the interludes is to remove Rhoda's dilemma, and her resolution of it, from the level on which it could be read as simply psychotic, and to emphasize the cosmic pattern to which she is intimately related.

The interludes in their totality may be read as terrestrial history: emergence from chaos, proliferation of life, intense individuation, exhaustion, breakdown of the forms of life, and return to chaos. They may also be read as the natural cycles of day and night, organic mortality, or the seasons. In all these readings, they offer multiple meanings for the human creature, who is snail and bird, wave and leaf, moon and sun, circle and square: in short, Woolf offers an intricate web of correspondences between the macrocosm and the microcosm. Since these correspondences have an ancient history in literature and art, they are readily understood and offer little difficulty except in the richness and compression of the literary form Woolf has created. However, the unusual aspect, and one that may seem nihilistic, is the correspondence established between the formless, dimensionless forces of external nature and man, and the affirmation of it.

If we return to the second interlude, we see that there is a growing fever of life as the world emerges from chaos. As forms become more and more sharply defined under the intensifying rays of the sun, they also become more and more separate as the earth loses its wetness. While the day is young, the slime of chaos persists, now seen by daylight as repugnant:

> *Down there among the roots where the flowers decayed, gusts of dead smells were wafted; drops formed on the bloated sides of swollen things. The skin of rotten fruit broke, and matter oozed too thick to run. Yellow excretions were exuded by slugs. . . . The gold-eyed birds darting in between the leaves observed that purulence, that wetness, quizzically.* (P. 54)

Yet this is the reservoir as well as the graveyard of forms—and the source of sustenance for birds. Under the impact of fire in air, the fertile ooze disappears, until at last, at sunset, the world has become a desert:

> *The hard stone of the day was cracked and light poured through its splinters . . . the waves, as they neared the shore, were robbed of light, and fell in one long concussion, like a wall falling, a wall of grey stone. . . .* (P. 147)

In external nature, as in human nature, the evolution towards perfection of form becomes a movement towards the death of form. Fiercely vital individuation may be at the zenith, yet its greatest beauty is in the moment before disintegration begins, when the forms of nature have become fixed, like ikons: *"A deep varnish was laid like a lacquer over the fields. . . . If a cow moved a leg it stirred ripples of red gold, and its horns seemed lined with light."* At this moment of blazing but metallic color, the design wavers under a swift shadow of dissolution. This is the moment of nature corresponding to the moment in human life (in the seventh episode) in which Neville, Jinny, and Louis recognize the forms of their individual lives and accept them in the knowledge of death; for Bernard and Rhoda it is the moment of departure from known forms.

Intermittently, in both episodes and interludes, Woolf has placed peculiar emphasis on shadows, as in the third interlude:

"The real flower on the windowsill was attended by a phantom flower. Yet the phantom was part of the flower, for when a bud broke free the paler flower in the glass opened a bud too." The early references, for the most part, occur in a realistic optical world in which the tangible flower is the real flower and the shadow is the illusion of a flower. However, in the eighth episode Rhoda sees that "Every tree is big with a shadow that is not the shadow of the tree behind it," and she sees her friends, in symbolic shadow, emerging from the night mythic in their proportions: ". . . As they pass that tree, they regain their natural size. They are only men, only women. Wonder and awe change as they put off the draperies of the flowing tide." For Rhoda, with her thirst for the infinite, the shadow is the reality, as in a poem of Yeats, "Who can distinguish darkness from the soul?" The moth, as opposed to the bird of the ego, is a delicate movement of the soul, and its light shadow is a presage of the greater darkness. In the fourth episode, for example, as the friends gather around Percival, they "become nocturnal, rapt. Their eyes are like moth's wings moving so quickly that they do not seem to move at all." So the moth of the seventh episode casts in doubt the daylight world which "bent in uncertainty and ambiguity, as if a great moth sailing through the room had shadowed the immense solidity of chairs and tables with floating wings."

Darkness, silence, impulse are the qualities of the unconscious mind as well as of the soul, but in *The Waves* the greater design—larger than persons, forces of nature, or social structures—must be considered a religious or mythic one, partly because the point of view of the omniscient narrator of the interludes is transcendent, seeing, in the eighth episode, "The land . . . so distant that no shining roof or glittering window could be any longer seen." Still, the mythic unknown is reflected in nature. Darkness is to air as water is to land, a solvent of forms; in the cosmic dark, the objects of day disintegrate like images under water. At the end of the ninth interlude, the world is flooded with darkness explicitly compared to waves of the sea: "Darkness rolled its waves along grassy rides and over the wrinkled skin of the turf. . . ." The total dark at the end of this interlude is the return to chaos; the waves no longer break upon the shore because there is no longer any shore.

Rhoda, as indicated, is the continued presence in daylight of the intuition of night, the sea, silence, and chaos; her death occurs in the interlude just discussed. In the ninth episode, Bernard, who has been the element of air and has moved lightly on the horizontal line, touching land intermittently and toying with fire, finds himself alone, earth having drowned in the dark. The final disappearance of form is the end of sound, in particular the sound of human speech and the structures it makes.

From the beginning Bernard has been the speaker who served to tell time: to establish an experienced duration for the absolute experience of the others. Since the fourth episode, he has also been a commentator rather than a recorder, and has defined himself: "When I cannot see words curling like rings of smoke round me I am in darkness—I am nothing." By the seventh episode, he has acquired the flexible and varied rhetoric of a raconteur and is truly the speaker, not only the dominant thematic voice establishing the intellectual form of *The Waves* but also the one who has captured identity by speech. His style encompasses the dimensions of the body, the rhythm of movement, the dallying of perception, and duration; at the same time, he defines a listener and a situation containing duration beyond his own.

In the end, then, this most intimate voice is played against the severity of the omniscient narrator's voice, and the final monologue, while it tells stories of the seven persons, tells the human story omitted from the interludes, drawing the human analogy for the flourishing and desiccation of nature. Bernard has seen an eclipse of the sun, and has felt his vitality cease—analogous experiences—and the parallel to the world of the interludes just before darkness is apparent. The miraculous return of life after the eclipse gives an outline of the cyclic pattern and of the relations between forces in the microcosm as well as the macrocosm:

It is a hoop to be fractured by a tiny jar. There is a spark there. . . . Then a vapour as if earth were breathing in and out, once, twice, for the first time. Then under the dullness someone walks with a green light. Then off twists a white wraith. The woods throb blue and green, and gradually the fields drink in red, gold, brown. Suddenly a river snatches a blue light. The earth absorbs colour like a sponge slowly drinking water. It puts on weight; rounds itself; hangs pendent; settles and swings beneath our feet. (P. 203)

The initial perceptions of Bernard, Susan, Jinny, Louis, and Rhoda are echoed in this description of the insubstantial earth become substantial, reinforcing the abstract pattern of meaning for the novel. However, the passage also suggests another reversal of traditional relationships of the elements. Light here is not a power of air but of water, and Bernard's last adventure will be in leaving the element in which he has been a wandering thread in order to recognize the element which he has avoided. Intimations of the meaning of water have come to Bernard largely when "the drop that has formed on the roof of the soul" falls. He has defined the drop as time and as silence: both, for him, intimations of mortality. He has also had, as in the fourth episode, a passing fancy "to go under; to visit the profound depths; once in a while to exercise my prerogative not always to act, but to explore; to hear vague, ancestral sounds. . . ." In the ninth episode, he explores the depths. When he has gone under, that is, has lost his self, he sees at last the true "nymph of the fountains" of the interludes, the girl with "watery fire-hearted jewels," perhaps the Aphrodite at the source of the Grail quest.[17] His final monologue acquires its freedom and authority from Bernard's having moved beyond his stories, his poses, bubbles, and conviviality; through disillusion, solitude, and silence; to the reverent recognition of the harmony of the elements and the greater circle beyond chaos that miraculously remakes order. Both the breaking of forms and the recommencement of forms are suggested by the final line, no longer an interlude, *"The waves broke on the shore."*

Figure 4

chapter 6

Flush and *The Years*

No work of Virginia Woolf was completed with as little joy as *Flush,* if *A Writer's Diary* indicates the writer's mood; no work was undertaken with more excitement than *The Years.* However, both became burdens and left Woolf unsatisfied. She judged *The Years* a failure even after Leonard Woolf had praised it and after it had become a best seller in the United States. Some serious critics have tended to agree. A. D. Moody for example finds *The Years* unsatisfactory because of its "indictment of an historical order, based, quite incongruously, upon fragmentary and trivial details, upon a disobligingly undeveloped awareness of social realities,"[1] and David Daiches sees no formal necessity in it, considering that it might well have stopped at 1917 rather than 1937.[2] Some criticism indeed seems to have begun from inappropriate assumptions, for example the assumption that Woolf needed a lighter and more conventional mode after the high pressure of *The Waves.*

Different as *Flush* and *The Years* are in form and style, they have in common an impulse to encompass the element of social protest touched upon and put aside in *Night and Day.* In a sense *Flush* was a preparation for the more ambitious work, for the subject offered her a biographical-whimsical disguise for a plot which is essentially a parable or allegory, and the major literary problems with which she struggled in writing *The Years* did not arise. The physical similarity between Elizabeth Barrett and her spaniel, pointed up at the beginning and end of *Flush,* was present in Woolf's sources, and the extension of that similarity to include a commentary on the invalidism of society was not a difficult step. Flush's subjection, after a clean and free infancy in nature, following the smells that called to the hunt and sex, to the stifling atmosphere of an invalid's bedroom which is a scented prison, and to the leash-laws of London parks, and to the perverse, putrid, and mechanical smells of London streets has obvious parallels in the breaking of Elizabeth Barrett's spirit, which made her a recluse and led her to disguise her prison as an exotic nest. The means of subjection, by implication, are similar; and here Woolf touches a criticism of society so deep and primitive that it is almost inaccessible to remedy. Quite possibly for this reason, Woolf became restive before the end and felt drawn away by the new idea, *The Pargiters.*

Yet in *Flush* she undertook a problem which had been omitted from the psychological structuring of *The Waves* and was also to be omitted from *The Years,* though tacitly present in both: the psychic and emotional life which does not develop freely in the privacy of the soul but is limited by and subjected to the life of another. More directly than in any work which is entirely fictional, Woolf explores the inarticulate and vulnerable center of life from which the sensuous organization springs, and which is the source of love. Love is a tool of tyranny:

He could not help dancing round the room on a windy autumn day when the partridges must be scattering over the stubble. . . . He could not help running to the door with his hackles raised when a dog barked outside. And yet when Miss Barrett called him back, when she laid her hand on his collar, he could not deny that another feeling, urgent, contradictory, disagreeable—he did not know what to call it or why he obeyed it—restrained him. He lay still at her feet. To resign, to control, to suppress the most violent instincts of his nature—that was the prime lesson of the bedroom school. . . . (P. 35)[3]

At an extremely elemental level, the animal is torn by powerful feelings, some of them calling to the free play of his body and senses but one of them, love, making him respond to the desires of his mistress rather than to his own desires. He must lie still. So Elizabeth Barrett also has been taught to lie still.

This is the dilemma that cannot be resolved by social argument, and perhaps not even by social change, for it is the basic problem posed by love. Any society of two contains the danger of such subjugation. Woolf uses this slight work to expose the problem, but since Flush is merely a dog, the full implications of the human dilemma are not developed. The line of social criticism moves to the level of institutionalized subjection, which is more external and therefore more available to rational argumentation, leaving the problem of love to be disposed of partly by our automatic distinctions between animal and human. In the hierarchy of being, we accept the sacrifice of the dog to mankind, while we do not usually accept the sacrifice of one human being to another. On a more philosophic level, relevant to the organization of the psyche, the problem of love is resolved by sublimation. The primitive animal instincts and powers are sacrificed to a higher spiritual power: to Elizabeth Barrett Browning or the imagination. If one reads *Flush* as an allegory of the relation between libido and ego, in Freudian terms, he may find a creative potentiality in the animal dilemma. Elizabeth Barrett Browning's justification, if not Virginia Woolf's, is placed at the end:

> . . . I knew Flush, and rose above
> Surprise and sadness—thanking the true Pan,
> Who, by low creatures, leads to heights of love.

However, Woolf's primary interest is clearly in the revelation of the evil of English society, and the center of the novel is the fourth chapter, "Whitechapel," in which Flush is seized for ransom by an underworld society of the slums. Here the commentary moves beyond the tyrannies of love and family life to establish analogies in the society as a whole, in which the existence of Wimpole Street requires the existence of the Rookery of St. Giles, just as the authoritarian power of Mr. Barrett requires the quiescence of Elizabeth. The invalidism of half of respectable society, touching in the case of Elizabeth, becomes loathsome in the disease (whether cholera or vice) in the disreputable back streets. In the Whitechapel incident, the indictment extends to the high-minded intelligentsia (including Robert Browning) whose virtues grow inhumane out of the corrupt soil of the system. In majestic posturing, father, brother, and lover would defy the dogstealers and blackmailers in the name of Right; they would make a stand against evil and tyranny. They would rest virtuously in the abstract principle, even when the dog's bloody head was brought to the door; and the true evils would not have been attacked. Elizabeth Barrett's reply is clearly congenial to Virginia Woolf: "Have I a right to sacrifice *him* in his innocence, for the sake of any Mr. Taylor's guilt in the world?"

The intricate net of corruption which extends from the wielding of familial power to the upholding of an aristocracy of blood or money continues to reveal its strands as the Brownings and Flush escape to Italy, where freedom intensifies the awareness of previous bondage:

Where was "must" now? Where were chains now? Where were park-keepers and truncheons? Gone, with the dog-stealers and Kennel Clubs and Spaniel Clubs of a corrupt aristocracy! . . . He ran, he raced; his coat flashed; his eyes blazed. He was the friend of all the world now. (P. 110)

A glancing connection to the human counterpart is made a few lines further on: "Fear was unknown in Florence; there were no dog-stealers here and, she may have sighed, there were no fathers."

The urbanity and charm of the style, the whimsicality of the idea of a dog's biography, the sentimental history of Elizabeth Barrett and Robert Browning, and the sentimental

distance of the past tend to conceal the relevance of the criticism, which does not restrict itself safely to nineteenth-century
London slums. The abuse and perversion of natural life, the
sacrifice of some creatures for others, the spurious use of
rational intelligence to avoid real human issues, were as easily
found in 1932 as in 1847, but only by those ready to look.
Flush offers the suggestion without insisting, and for Virginia
Woolf the major commentary remains to be made.

If in the course of years and novels Virginia Woolf managed
to master her fear of certain violent emotions, at the time of
writing *The Years* she had not come to terms with anger, nor
found a form for it.[4] During the writing of the second version,
the *Diary* notes the dilemma:

> Let me make a note that it would be much wiser not to attempt
> to sketch a draft of *On Being Despised,* or whatever it is to be
> called, until *The Ps.* is done with. I was vagrant this morning and
> made a rash attempt, with the interesting discovery that one can't
> propagate at the same time as write fiction. And as this fiction is
> dangerously near propaganda, I must keep my hands clear.[5]

As a result, apparently, the original conception sketched on
November 2, 1932, which was to have been an "Essay-Novel"
taking in "everything, sex, education, life etc,"[6] was modified
in such a way that the original central speaker Elvira could no
longer say, "It is an utterly corrupt society . . . and I will take
nothing that it can give me."[7] The searing rage that Woolf
shows now and then fleetingly in her diaries had to be tem-
pered into genial satire, whimsy, or eccentricity: the initial
rebel, Delia, can only say "O my God!" and spend most of the
novel in exile on the isle of rebels, Ireland, and the rejecter of
corrupt society becomes the queer creature Sara, who is
allowed merely to twitch the fringes of respectable society, or
"thorny Rose," the laughable reincarnation of Pargiter of
Pargiter's Horse.

A heat of social intention and active revolt against the ills of
society seemed to Woolf to be propaganda,[8] to be left to *Three
Guineas,* and it was thus imperative to return to a realistic

mode—or what Woolf calls "representational"[9]—in order to avoid the danger of writing from within the world of someone like Doris Kilman. Even so, she felt that realism was intractable material for art: "And conversation: argument. How to do that will be one of the problems. I mean intellectual argument in the form of art: I mean how give ordinary waking Arnold Bennett life the form of art?"[10]

The various strategies of art in containing her argument may be indicated by the sequence of titles: *The Pargiters, Here and Now, Music, Dawn, Daughters and Sons, The Pargiters, Ordinary People, The Caravan, The Pargiters, The Years,* the final one chosen on September 5, 1935. These titles suggest three or four disparate kinds of structure of plot and theme, and also perhaps different conceptions of the relations of persons to time. The title of *The Years* and the final structuring indicate a return to the four dimensions and an intention to see human identity in terms of historical time, in which selves are as mutable as manners and subject to a larger, abstract organism. Woolf's comments in her early diaries on existence within the artifice of time called a "year" indicate that she saw its possibilities as a fictional form; as with a novel, she could attempt to give the year a meaningful design. In *The Years,* however, the year invites us to recognize it not as an artifice but as an organism; the writer has found rather than constructed its design. Each year has a body, a soul, and a spirit, known by the condition of nature (the season, the weather), the feelings manifested by people, and the patterns of public behavior. The rainy spring of 1880 is a reminder of Woolf's definition of the nineteenth century in *Orlando;* so the year is oppressive with a wet fecundity and piety. The year 1913, a midwinter year, is the empty shell of a life as the old dwelling is abandoned to a fall of snow, and no vital human force remains in the master/servant relationship.

With four exceptions—1891, 1910, 1914, and 1918—the years are not moments of history which have an obvious and recognized identity; even in those years, the definition Virginia

Woolf has found would not be a historian's definition, particularly not for the year 1914. The choice of certain years may be arbitrary, or may mark epochs in a very personal history of Woolf's mind, but as they follow upon one another, in spite of the completeness and finality of each year, they show the stages of evolution of a species, including the atrophy of certain parts, death of certain branches, hybridization, and mutation.

The nineteenth century of the species is long in dying. *The Years* begins with its death, for the Victorian family passes with Rose Pargiter in 1880. Although the family is dead, the convolutions of spirit associated with it persist; in 1891 the double morality associated with the tragic fall of Charles Stewart Parnell continues in Colonel Abel Pargiter, who wistfully courts his slightly scarlet sister-in-law, simultaneously censuring her in the name of family propriety. The century continues to die; the death of King Edward in 1910 marks the end of a moment of intense frustration bordering on despair as the old adaptation persists, impeding the birth of the new. In 1914 the old order ends in ironic glory (although Martin sees only "the nineteenth century going to bed") with a visit to St. Paul's, the sounding of the bells of London, the burgeoning spring, a pompous dinner party, and Kitty's long exodus from London to the land itself. Spring, the traditional season of death and resurrection, occurs three times in *The Years:* in 1880, 1908, and 1914.

This structuring is not obvious on a first reading, partly because the first chapter establishes expectations of a comfortable pursuit of family history, and partly because the techniques of realism have been subtly altered by the addition of techniques from music. The relationship of the Pargiters to the larger organism of Society 1880 or Society 1914 is dual, even though the full import of its duality is not obvious until "The Present Day." On the one hand, they are creatures of the year in a complex of determined and determining roles; they are subjected to the forces of nature and society but are also

energies of soul and spirit animating those dominating forces
or struggling against them. In these terms, each year disposes
of them with finality, and there is no return to the life of a
previous year. Kitty can never return to the sudden love of
1880 for Jo Robson hammering the chicken coop; at the
same time, that love has subtly altered the spirit of all the
years to come. Some people follow a course laid out in deter-
ministic finality by the time, the place, their status and sex:
Crosby, the servant, could easily be placed in a nineteenth-
century naturalistic novel of France; she is kin to the heroine
of Flaubert's "A Simple Heart." For others the line of destiny
is not a straight, clear prospect. The unchosen, unconscious
pattern taken by the movement of time is illustrated by the
destiny of Edward: no one in 1880, certainly not Edward,
would have guessed that the flower of the family was to wither
into a dried academic beauty in the course of years.

The structure just discussed might be described as a poetry
of naturalism; it presents the major social argument of the
novel largely in objective terms. The juxtaposition of scenes
involving Edward and Kitty in 1880, for example, dramatically
reveals a contrast between society's preparation of the young
man and of the young woman, and its accommodation of the
desires of the man while it thwarts the desires of the woman—
virtually the same injustice that Woolf explicitly exposed in
the England of 1928 in *A Room of One's Own*. The vested
interests of landlordism involved in the fall of Parnell are
suggested in Eleanor's discomfort in 1891 in playing the roles
of the moneyed Establishment, landlords, and judges, and her
hasty departure in the true direction of social reality, looking
for Parnell's disciple Delia in the squalid byways of the slums.
Raw anger is generally absent because the intense identification with persons in their moments of passion is avoided.
Direct statement is unnecessary because the evidence has been
selected to speak.

The exceptions are the scenes involving Sara and Rose
(1907, 1908, and 1910). Some of the ferocity behind the

pervasive genteel frustration of both men and women is conveyed by Sara's unladylike comments, like a sudden dissonance
shattering all civility: "But the Jew's in my bath, I said—the
Jew . . . the Jew. . . ." Similarly, the brick-throwing of Rose
and her memories in 1908 of childhood violence have added
intensity because of a hiatus in causation. In both women
there is clearly a core of rage which is partly unknown and
cannot find direct outlet. One cannot say that Rose attacks the
system because she was exiled from the schoolroom to the
nursery in childhood, nor that Sara sniggers at society because
she was dropped as a baby. Nor can the growing alienation in
the women of *The Years* he ascribed merely to a reaction
against the narrow range of roles offered to them, the con-
stricting walls of their houses, or the opulence of displays of
masculine privilege: the men, who have the universities, the
lawcourts, the empire, the City, show even greater malaise.

Problems which arise entirely from sexual roles are not
primary but secondary. In order to expose the larger problem,
Woolf offers two scenes more sharply defined and explicit than
most, scenes of 1907 and 1910 which avoid the usual sexual
tension felt when both sexes are present. The first of these
scenes is Sara's midsummer. The hot, exciting night and
society's salute to it in the mating dance make a sensual background for Sara's state of withdrawal as she lies in bed reading
philosophy and *Antigone*. The unrest of Sara is in part the
result of the thwarting of the sexual élan involved in respectable encounters between men and women. That aspect is
largely left to the suggestions of the dramatic scenes; Maggie's
bored return from a dinner party where she sat beside a man in
gold lace who did not say "O my broken heart," and the young
couple whose conversation in the moonlit garden is limited to
"Going to the match tomorrow?" But Sara's alienation has
passed the stage of erotic deception; it is more philosophic and
more general, for she already knows that the impulse of love
meets a blank wall in the outer world. As she hears the music
of the dance outside, she reads philosophy and she reads

Antigone. The little brown book which offers to explain away
the chasm between her room and the outer world, as she
translates it, could be the work of any number of philosophers
from Berkeley to Bradley.

> "And he says," she murmured, "the world is nothing but..."
> She paused. What did he say? Nothing but thought, was it? . . .
> Well, since it was impossible to read and impossible to sleep, she
> would let herself *be* thought. . . . Legs, body, hands, the whole of
> her must be laid out passively to take part in this universal
> process of thinking which the man said was the world living.
> (P. 142)[11]

As Sara attempts to prove the dependence of the world on
her will, she merely proves to herself that the abstract intelligence and the will belonging to her can only induce a
momentary hallucination, an illusion that the outer world
reflects the desires of the inner world. Though Sara begins
with the microcosm which includes mind and body, the extension of the body is limited to a few feet of bed in a closed
room, and the mind which attempts to impose itself outside of
those limits is impotent. The tree in the dark garden does not
become dappled with sunlight because she wills it.

The inadequacy of such concepts, and perhaps of the entire
orthodox idealist tradition, is reinforced by Maggie, who asks
first a standard academic question, "Would there be trees if
we didn't see them?" and then the fruitful question, "What's
'I'?" Though the answer is not explicitly to begin until 1917,
the tendency of resolution is presented dramatically when
Eugénie enters her daughter's room. Throughout the scene
there have been bursts of dance music; Sara's meditations and
her wandering dream of valleys of the moon with nightingales
calling and answering have been picked up by the rhythms of
the waltz, which coarsen them, just as they render her reading
of the martyrdom of Antigone trivial. Moreover, the music
testifies to the existence of an outer world which is not merely
inert in the face of her will but contains other wills, other
ideas, which act upon her own. The lines of argument and
meditation here meet in the suggestion that the error under-

lying all the specific falsities as well as the tyrannies of social intercourse is perhaps the idea of making a world by extending the shape of one's own mind over it, like the nets of *To the Lighthouse* and *The Waves.* With these expectations the meeting of two people on any terms but those of conquest becomes virtually impossible.[12] The dilemma is not to be resolved by philosophic discourse but by relaxing the concentration of mind in action. Eugénie, attending to the outer music, uses it to dance her youth, and during this union of inner and outer—which is not that of the imposition of will—Sara's walls of isolation for a moment disappear.

This kind of music, inconsequential, even nonsensical, is one of the motifs of *The Years,* present throughout in Sara's antic snatches of song, in the music of the organ grinder, dance music, and most decisively in the song of the children at the end of the novel. At this point we must recognize that the historical structure of the novel has a counter-structure which provides further distancing from realism. Woolf's comment on Chekhov, a writer whom she revered, is particularly illuminating for the method of *The Years:*

... We need a very daring and alert sense of literature to make us hear the tune, and in particular those last notes which complete the harmony. . . .

We have to cast about in order to discover where the emphasis in these strange stories rightly comes. . . . Tchekov, too, is aware of the evils and injustices of the social state; the condition of the peasants appals him, but the reformer's zeal is not his—that is not the signal for us to stop. The mind interests him enormously. . . . But again, no; the end is not there. Is it that he is primarily interested not in the soul's relation with other souls, but with the soul's relation to health—with the soul's relation to goodness?[13]

Like Chekhov, Virginia Woolf intends to go beyond social reform, and she uses musical motifs and musical structuring to take her argument beyond the known society. Vulgar music composes one of the lines of the musical structure of *The Years,* but in both melody and rhythm it moves against serious

music, the large sound of Wagner, for example, or the highly
refined, abstract form of the quartet used symbolically in
The Waves. Street music is a repudiation of the austere transcendence of such music, which the earlier sketch "The String
Quartet" has shown to be antithetical to life:

> But this city to which we travel has neither stone nor marble;
> hangs enduring; stands unshakable; nor does a face, nor does a
> flag greet or welcome. Leave then to perish your hope; droop in
> the desert my joy; naked advance. Bare are the pillars; auspicious
> to none; casting no shade; resplendent; severe. Back then I fall,
> eager no more, desiring only to go, find the street, mark the
> buildings, greet the applewoman. . . .[14]

Both the music of the string quartet and that of the organ
grinder oppose experienced duration to conceptual time, but
the vulgar music subverts abstraction and fixed forms just as
the waltz of 1907 shattered the continuity of Sara's adherence
to a philosophic argument. It succeeds in doing so because it
is not itself a fixed art form, complete, final, and reverend; it
does not demand that the body be stretched out in silence and
passive acceptance but that the body catch its rhythm and use
it. By its nature it is completed only in a physical experience,
and has meaning in a place and a relationship of people—in
short, in an affective whole. As in *Mrs. Dalloway,* it is fecund,
rousing the irrational joy of the body, a radical vitality below
the threshold of the esthetic sense. Yet it is the link, like Mrs.
McNab in *To the Lighthouse,* between the mindless inhuman
energy of the natural world and the intelligence, rather than
the intellectuality, of a civilization.

The musical intelligence, which is essentially nonverbal,
functions perhaps most constantly for *The Years* by rhythm,
in which syncopation and silence are even more meaningful
than tempo. These are also the techniques that leave readers
haunted by a sense of something missing, an incompleteness
of form, or a lack of social awareness, for the syncopation
consistently occurs at a moment of obvious significance, when
the expected stress is displaced or the passionate development
is left in silence. For example, in 1908 the passionate recall

of childhood by Martin and Rose is punctuated by the sound of shattering glass, but the promise of depths, "What awful lives children live," dwindles with a non sequitur which invites an end to the kind of communion which depends upon sharing dreadful memories of the past.

"Miss Pym's conservatory?" said Martin. . . .
"Miss Pym?" said Eleanor. "She's been dead these twenty years!"
(P. 171)

The entire complex defining the year 1914 is off beat, since it is a year of lonely people obsessively feeding pigeons in the shadow of St. Paul's or talking to themselves in the park, giving and attending stiff formal parties, attending religious services that have lost their meaning ("The father incomprehensible; the son incomprehensible," Sara reads from her prayer book). Only by implication do we read that this is a world falling into a great conflagration, like the dead leaves Sara and Maggie once cast ecstatically into the flames. The pattern of syncopation is used for individual lives as well, for the 1910 scene between Sara and Maggie, conveying the desolation and squalor of their poverty, replaces the scene which presumably, for Maggie, should have been one of the great scenes of her life; but Rennie's courtship is alluded to in passing, almost as one of Sara's fantasies:

But she did not see the notes, she saw a garden; flowers; and her sister; and a young man with a big nose who stooped to pick a flower that was gleaming in the dark. And he held the flower out in his hand in the moonlight. . . . (P. 201)

Such displacements of the usual accents of plot, though they require the collaboration of a knowing reader, speak quite clearly. These rhythms with their new accents and their silences enable Woolf to be faithful to "things in themselves" while escaping the net of realism; they silently indicate that traditional values do not apply and that a new pattern is emerging. The new pattern is basically a new family, a new conception of relatedness, to replace the blood-family of the Pargiters and the nineteenth century, to replace the old rhythms of society which emphasize the possessiveness of tribal relationships and the rituals of tribal continuity. For this reason, I think, the new father is Nicholas Brown, a homosexual, and the new mother is Eleanor Pargiter, a spinster; and the literary motif is drawn from the epic poet of transcendent love, Dante. Without quite understanding, Eleanor reads, at the time when her father's death has freed her,

> For by so many more there are who say 'ours'
> So much the more of good doth each possess. (P. 228)

The new seed is planted by Nicholas during the raid in 1917: "It is only a question...of learning. The soul...." However, his arguments as arguments are feeble, and the speeches he would make are never heard. The convincing argument is the history of the Pargiters and Eleanor's role in it.

Eleanor appears at first to belong to the naturalist organism of the year; her role in 1880 seems to be a finished one, and one of little importance: the young woman destined to be a spinster, to serve as substitute mother for the younger children, to keep the household accounts, act as sister of mercy, and provide an audience for the exploits of the more dynamic members of the family. In 1880 there is little indication that Eleanor is more than this or that she suffers discontent. The note of criticism of her world, in the beginning, is not personal but sympathetic, for her good works have taken her beyond the safety and comfort of her house; she has seen beauty and dignity in the poor, she has seen the cloistered boredom of her sisters, and she has concluded that "the poor enjoy themselves more than we do." As she continues to play her part as kindly spinster whose intellectual powers are slight, she discovers more of the tedium and falsity of her class, as landlords, as lawyers, as reformers, as families, until she is freed from her auxiliary roles in 1911 (now a woman of 53) to begin life.

Among the generations at Wittering in 1911, Eleanor is no longer placed in time but has begun to move into space—in this novel, departure from England and its fringes of empire— and the opening of worlds is towards the east rather than the west. She has gone to Spain and will go to India and the Far East. Spain is the precipice of Europe, looking out to Africa and the Orient;[15] when she returns to an England which is apparently unchanged though on the precipice of war, she returns as a detached observer, one who looks back not only on the vanities and fidelities of her youth but also on the pageant of her society, in affection and goodbye. When she appears again, during the raid, she begins to assume a religious distance—as Maggie says, she looks like an abbess in a dressing gown which hides her garb as middle class Englishwoman.

Here Nicholas Brown appears, the dark man about whom Eleanor notes, "There was something queer about him . . . medical, priestly?" Nicholas' queerness is not homosexuality, for he is never presented as homosexual, but the priestly quality, the absence of acquisitive or egotistical drives. His message, which Eleanor embodies, is given with extreme brevity:

> "The soul—the whole being," he explained. He hollowed his hands as if to enclose a circle. "It wishes to expand; to adventure; to form—new combinations?
>
> "Whereas now,"—he drew himself together; put his feet together; he looked like an old lady who is afraid of mice—"this is how we live, screwed up into one hard little, tight little—knot?" (P. 319)

At the moment of survival on the brink of extinction, they have found the bare realities: the natural family, which is that of Maggie and Rennie, has none of the power-organizations or civilities of the old family, but in it there is a place for true conviviality as well as eroticism ("That is the man," Eleanor thinks, "that I should like to have married"); the spiritual family, which Nicholas defines and Eleanor lives, includes but transcends the natural family, and includes but transcends a particular civilization. Its vigor derives from its affirmation of an expanding life.

The new world, and the promise of freedom, are clearly bound to a prior destruction, both in the plot structure of *The*

Years and in the motif of fire. At the moment when the possibility of freedom becomes a desire in Eleanor, Maggie strikes
the fire with a poker, sending sparks up the chimney. Sara,
roused from a doze, claims to have heard what they said:
"The soul flying upwards like sparks up the chimney." The
symbolic act of striking the fire has occurred several times
before and has consistently been an act which broke the
rigidity of a moment of life; in a less domesticated form, the
dangerous flare of autumn leaves in 1891 conveyed the necessity for destroying the dead residue of the past even with some
risk and wildness.

These elements are carried into "The Present Day," the
most intricate of the episodes because it contains the past as
well as the present and the presentiment of a future. In the
present Eleanor and Nicholas continue to have presiding roles
and to offer a coherent meaning for the time, even though
they are in danger during most of the action of the party of
being engulfed or overwhelmed by the confusion of desires
around them. The postwar world has lost the social formalities
of former times; Delia's party is deliberately disorganized,
inelegant, "democratic," and Dionysian. The present day has
been conquered by the pace of machines rather than that of
men, as North discovers when he meditates in London traffic.
The present views the past with derision; the old members of
the Pargiter family, seen as objects down the ruthless perspective of years, have lost their humanity. North defines the lives
of his aunt Milly and Hugh Gibbs:

> That was what it came to—thirty years of being husband and
> wife—tut-tut-tut—and chew-chew-chew. It sounded like the half-
> inarticulate munchings of animals in a stall. Tut-tut-tut, and chew-
> chew-chew—as they trod out the soft steamy straw in the stable;
> as they wallowed in the primeval swamp, prolific, profuse, half-
> conscious. . . . (P. 404)

The past is revalued, including the presentation of hitherto
tacit knowledge, and is judged from the point of view of
rational egotism. With the younger generation, however, the

skepticism and scorn of judgment do not derive from self-congratulation. Peggy in particular is gnawed by the sense of having been deceived into buying a false freedom. The arguments of protest and anger which have been left unspoken in previous years become articulate as the point of view of narration becomes increasingly introspective, and North and Peggy rage inwardly against their elders and the world that is their heritage.

The contemplative and sensuous life—for Peggy, the owl flying at dusk through the garden—has been replaced by the anatomizing mind, and on that basis Peggy has purchased freedom—the power to follow a profession, to be considered brilliant, to have money, and to belong to no family. The price of freedom has been harmony of being. Though she can observe and analyze with a well-trained clinical eye, she cannot sympathize, not even with herself. She knows her state of mind by physical symptoms—a thrill down the thigh signifies bitterness—but in the dynamo of the party her unconscious sense of humiliation and resentment come to the surface in an attack on her brother North, who is after all her own kind by spirit as well as blood:

> "Here you all are—talking about North—" He looked up at her in surprise. It was not what she had meant to say. . . .
>
> "What's the use?" she said, facing him. "You'll marry. You'll have children. What'll you do then? Make money. Write little books to make money. . . .
>
> "You'll write one little book, and then another little book," she said viciously, "instead of living . . . living differently, differently." (P. 421)

The unspoken motive behind Peggy's outburst is obviously like the motive in former times of Rose's rage against Martin, for the boy in the family assumed dominant status and privilege, but it is also an appeal. Peggy has not broken a revolutionary trail as Rose has, but has tailored herself to the tradition of her father. Nevertheless, behind her hostility and spite is the cry of protest, to which North responds. Both have the guilty knowledge that their lives and thought are in the wrong.

Herein perhaps lies the weakness of the novel; in "The Present Day" a distinction can be made between form and content, the two demands diverging, and each having great affective power for Virginia Woolf. It is questionable that a containing form has been prepared for the energy of anger in Peggy. Avenues of action available to Rose are no longer open to Peggy (in 1935), for Rose belonged to an era of romantic political unrest largely defined by the Irish struggle, a motif present in Delia's devotion to the Irish cause and to Parnell, but also in the suggested association of Rose with the rose poems of W. B. Yeats's period of mystical nationalism:

> I, too, await
> The hour of thy great wind of love and hate.
> When shall the stars be blown about the sky,
> Like the sparks blown out of a smithy, and die?
> Surely thine hour has come, thy great wind blows,
> Far-off, most secret, and inviolate Rose?[16]

The toasts to Rose Pargiter at the end of *The Years* are salutes to the fighting heart; but the innocence of her combative spirit is not possible in "The Present Day." After the war the entire configuration of attitudes and methods of social protest is revealed as futile and destructive—destructive even to those who protest—and Peggy's anger is unresolved, or resolved only by its containment in the world of Eleanor. In terms of "the soul's relation to health," the broad acceptance of Eleanor is undoubtedly best, but the example of her life in all the years from 1880 to the present offers no means of getting beyond Peggy's position except by the abdication of will and desire. The full force of this truth strikes perhaps too suddenly and too harshly in "The Present Day," after the basically comic containment of previous years. Considered in the abstract, Eleanor's stance, at least from 1880 to 1917, might seem to support a Schopenhauerian pessimism, with its sense that the world of desire, especially physical desire, is evil.

Although the alternative disposition of desire, associated with oriental philosophy and the progression of Dante's *Divine Comedy,* is left on an allusive level, it is Eleanor's wisdom to find in old age a desire which is purely sensuous and imaginative and has no hint of conquest, defense, or avarice. It is, in short, a desire of the spirit and not of the will. At this final moment of the novel, she is placed at a mythic distance and approaches the condition of complete and spontaneous ease discussed in chapters 1 and 4, of the fish in water; she is without fear.

The freedom of such a condition serves society as well as personal happiness. At the end of *The Years,* at the dawn of a new day, a totally alien element is introduced when the children of Delia's caretaker are brought in to eat cake[17] and to sing in gratitude. Their Cockney song disconcerts their audience:

> Etho passo tanno hai,
> Fai donk to tu do,
> Mai to, kai to, lai to see
> Toh dom to tuh do— (P. 463)

Social realism has moved towards surrealism. The lower classes, which were servants or not very interesting oddities to the Pargiters of 1880, subsequently became reminders of social guilt for Eleanor, but also for Sara a reminder of her own relationship to animal squalor. At Hyams Place Sara and Maggie lived surrounded by the filth, drunkenness, and quarrelsomeness of the slums:

> "In time to come," she said . . . "people, looking into this room—this cave, this little antre, scooped out of mud and dung, will hold their fingers to their noses . . . and say, 'Pah! They stink!" (P. 203)

The lower classes, especially those in great poverty, are reminders of everything the middle class repudiates. The history of the Pargiters has shown the scope and the achievement of English civilization of the past, a middle class civilization. Its values, viewed positively, have been duty (extending from the family to the class system, upwards and downwards), piety, reason, propriety, control, and, at the patrician end of the spectrum, a massive morality of art, representational art, and elegance of manners. Members of the family who lacked the virtues of duty or decorum, either socially or intellectually, almost dropped out of the society (for example, Delia and Sara).

But at the party, which Delia intends as a repudiation of the society of her youth, the middle class culture is obviously a relic, like the don Edward and the country squire Hugh; in the new society, the hitherto despised elements will assume significant functions. Only those Pargiters who have not become fossilized in an old adaptation can move into the new day, or indeed see that the new day is not merely a repetition of the days already known. The song of the children establishes the point of recognition. To most of the tired ·guests, the sound is hideous, and it signifies the discordance of the class to which the children belong, the inadequacies of modern education, the end of elegance of manners, and a gulf of incomprehension between two worlds.

To Eleanor it signifies the advent of a new sensibility and new social possibilities, moving towards the "new combinations" which Nicholas has promised in 1917. What they will be is unknown. As Peggy says, "The younger generation don't mean to speak." In their wordless dignity and hideousness they are beyond Eleanor's vocabulary as well; she is uncertain of the word she tries, "beautiful?" However, the children and their song are related to the simple singers of Virginia Woolf's previous novels, and to the restoration of the fertility of life by seeking human meaning at its nonintellectual and amoral roots.

Formal farewell to the old family of the Pargiters occurs at the end of *The Years*:

> The group in the window, the men in their black-and-white evening dress, the women in their crimsons, golds and silvers, wore a statuesque air for a moment, as if they were carved in stone. Their dresses fell in stiff sculptured folds. (P. 467)

The past is not rejected but left behind as a completed and inert art; in the new day Eleanor as the guiding consciousness will look beyond the family, as she does at the end, for she lives in an expanding universe: the cosmic expansion or dispersion of modern physical theory, seen repeated in human life, does not imply loss.

Perhaps *The Years* is a failure in terms of Virginia Woolf's original desire to speak out strongly in relation to the world which is not art; in the esthetic discipline of desire in the course of tortured rewritings of the novel, the affective power of fact, the social anger, has largely been lost. Yet the exiled force of anger had to find expression before Woolf could be content; the completion of *Three Guineas,* though it was to make her feel something of a pariah, left her in a state of "immense relief and peace,"[18] and reconciled her to *The Years*: "Anyhow, that's the end of six years floundering, striving, much agony, some ecstasy: lumping the *Years* and *Three Guineas* together as one book—as indeed they are."[19] However, *The Years* is more than an argument or a pamphlet. Although Woolf may have failed in her first intent, the novel became greater than the intent; in a more spacious context it succeeds as an objectified vision of history as a meaningful process.

chapter 7

Between the Acts

Between the Acts fulfills a tacit promise of *The Waves* and *The Years,* for the great circle of being intermittently glimpsed in *The Waves* has been given its definitive form in *Between the Acts,* and equilibrium of inner and outer forces desired for *The Years* has been achieved. In significant ways, however, it is a departure from the previous works. Its central theme does not grow from *The Years* as *The Waves* and *The Years* grew from *Orlando;* its ancestor is perhaps *Mrs. Dalloway,* yet in character, symbolism, and emotional aura it belongs to a different world. The two novels invite comparison for several reasons: both are contained in a day, both attempt to define personal existence by intangible links in communal life, both focus upon a ritual which draws together the various meaningful elements of a civilization. But whereas *Mrs. Dalloway* moves from morning to morning, triumphantly controlling death, darkness, and madness, *Between the Acts* proceeds from nightfall to nightfall, serenely opening towards darkness and violence. Woolf's last novel is without the tension of fear in Clarissa Dalloway, which intensified the gallantry of her action and the keenness of her pleasure but cast doubt on the safety of her civilization.

Three Guineas liberated Virginia Woolf from fear. In a diary entry of April 26, 1938, she writes: "But now I feel entirely free. Why? Have committed myself, am afraid of nothing . . . enfranchised till death, and quit of all humbug. . . ."[1] When she had accepted herself as an outsider, and perhaps even more when war came, she lost all inclination to remain silent about inconvenient truths or to defend an old order which was increasingly irrevelant. She no longer felt obliged to keep a shrine in imagination for the world of Leslie Stephen (the man who said "never again" to having ladies on the board of the London Library)[2] or to remain in the context of "Bloomsbury" thinkers G. E. Moore or Roger Fry. Free of the old pieties and resentments, Woolf could move into another conceptual world with extraordinary elegance and ease.

The departure from previous forms is indicated physically as well as psychologically. *Between the Acts* is set outside the context of the automated flux of London, in a rural scene which shows the relationship of the house to the land at an elemental rather than a political or economic level. The presence of nature is constantly felt, as in *To the Lighthouse,* rather than intermittently received almost as a vision, as in *Mrs. Dalloway,* or known by a conscious effort of departure, as in *The Years.* As a consequence, human movements include the green world at almost every moment. The characters who wander through Pointz Hall—itself a dwelling attached to Roman antiquity and the primitive native past—and the terraces and lawns are oddly assorted. Although the four people of the Hall are related by blood or marriage, in their true consciousness of life they are as disparate as the neighbors who drive in for the pageant. Isabella Oliver's mind establishes connections with Rupert Haines and William Dodge, men she does not "know," as significantly as with her husband Giles Oliver; and Giles finds in Mrs. Manresa a contact with life that is largely unexpressed in the continuity of his ordinary domestic life. The people who attend the pageant make connections with others and with their own being, in that brief time and that place, which are as significant as the routine of their lives which goes on from year to year. The free and shifting relatedness is in part caused by the random mobility of people who have nothing to do (in the sense of a purposeful action); largely, however, it is not a matter causality, but of Woolf's altered conception of character, which permits the simultaneous experience of two or more states of being without a wrench of transition from inner to outer. The narrative gives the impression of a single unbroken consciousness because the separateness of human individuality has been radically modified. The problem of the self and the disparition of the ego have been the subject of much critical analysis based to a large extent upon Woolf's theoretical wrestling with the problem in *Mrs. Dalloway* and in the mind of Bernard in *The Waves*. However, in *Orlando* and *The Years* the problem has been resolved with the liberation of the concept of self from external social definition; in *Between the Acts* the problem no longer exists.

The writing of *Between the Acts* was a pleasure, not a duty or an economic necessity, from the beginning, and at the end Woolf, with the scarce butter of the war years fresh in mind, called it "a richer pat" with "more milk skimmed off." It seemed to her to be a new method, more quintessential than anything that preceded it.[3] The method to some degree derives from *The Years,* at least from the lesson learned in 1907, for the structure involves a constant bombardment of the willed forms of each life by the music from outside, the unforeseen and transitory movements of external life. Each life is like the tree, at the end of the pageant:

> Then suddenly the starlings attacked the tree behind which she had hidden. In one flock they pelted it like so many winged stones. The whole tree hummed with the whizz they made, as if each bird plucked a wire. A whizz, a buzz rose from the bird-buzzing, bird-vibrant, bird-blackened tree. The tree became a rhapsody, a quivering cacophony, a whizz and vibrant rapture, branches, leaves, birds syllabling discordantly life, life, life, without measure, without stop devouring the tree. (Pp. 244-245)[4]

In contrast to the symbolic trees of *Orlando* and *The Waves,* the tree here is not merely a fixed upright, slowly and silently moving through its green changes, offering to the human mind an image of permanence, standing firm against the flights of fancy, passion, or egoism. The tree may remain a solid and rooted form (and Miss La Trobe, like Orlando, seeks refuge behind it), but it can also become at a given moment a gigantic birdsong; its branches and leaves are ravished from the green world, taken into the animate world and the airy world of sound. Overwhelmed and devoured, the tree returns a moment later to the quietude of its essential form. The stable form is no more real, however, than the dynamic form it had with starlings. This is the basic duality of the world in *Between the Acts,* a doubleness shared by natural objects, dwellings, historical facts, and persons.

Traditional distinctions between "subjective" and "objective," of questionable value for understanding Virginia Woolf's work since *Jacob's Room,* have now lost all point for the underlying perception of reality (although they may still apply, for example, in understanding Isa or George) in which things in themselves demonstrably have both qualities. The distinction is very clear if we compare a significant image from *The Voyage Out*—that of the patch of light moving over the inert objects of a room[5]—to the living tree of *Between the Acts.* In Woolf's first novel, the conception of mind and of art shared the insubstantiality of a fleck of sunlight, which reveals an object but is extraneous to it; subjectivity in the early work had similar elements of fragility and fancy. Lily Briscoe in *To the Lighthouse* retains much of this attitude, even though her subjectivity has become much more abstract and sophisticated, when she defines her art metaphorically as "the light of a butterfly's wing lying upon the arches of a cathedral."[6] In Woolf's last novel, the stark contrast between mind and object has disappeared, perhaps because the object has lost its sanctity—that is, the external world is not a prior *given,* with the irrevocable meaning suggested by Lily's choice of *cathedral* as image of reality. The "things in themselves" that Woolf sees are no longer simple, and certainly not static: Piccadilly was once a rhododendron forest; the scullery of Pointz Hall was once a chapel; the brightly festooned hall for tea was once a barn. The land itself, the "view,' changes' from hour to hour. These changes are not fancies of a perceiver, but facts. Moreover, the last two historically complex images do not require an action of disengaged mind in memory. This undebatable argument by evidence stands behind the show of flux in human identity and human relatedness.

In the brief introductory episode, the night before the pageant, the action opens with a social encounter between Isa and Bart and Mr. and Mrs. Rupert Haines, people who mean little to one another outside of the accident of communal relationship, and they talk about a community problem, the cesspool. While the action and the characters of the novel remain undefined at the end of this brief introductory scene, important motifs are declared. The unity of life, in spite of the apparent incongruities of social roles, high-flown dreams, and brute facts, is suggested by the placing of this scene in history and in nature in such a way that the ludicrous cesspool is no more incongruous than the description of Bart as "Mr. Oliver, of the Indian Civil Service, retired." The glamour of a summer night may seem to be more in harmony with Bart's recollection of Byron's line, "She walks in beauty like the night," but in fact nature is present in its less dignified forms, for the awkward conversation about cesspools is punctuated by the cough of a cow and the chuckle of a bird. In Isa most obviously, the divergent elements of life coexist: massive, even bovine, she shatters propriety when she enters dressed in a faded dressing gown, her hair in pigtails; and she drifts into a dream which is at odds with her appearance, turning the line of Byron into two perfect rings in which she and Rupert Haines drift as swans.

The composition of reality is not that of human beings

formed by a time and place, but of the interplay of forces which we agree to call mind and nature, self and other, present and past, for the sake of convenience. That such distinctions are fictions Woolf shows throughout the novel, but most emphatically in the one scene of childhood, when little George grubs for a flower:

> The flower blazed between the angles of the roots. Membrane after membrane was torn. It blazed a soft yellow, a lambent light under a film of velvet; it filled the caverns behind the eyes with light. All that inner darkness became a hall, leaf smelling, earth smelling of yellow light. (P. 16)

Although George tears the flower from its rooted place to put it in another design, beginning the process of "one-making" which may be an exclusively human occupation, the role of the flower is not truly passive; its verbs are active. The object of nature with its energy of color invades the darkness of mind before mind begins to make designs. So later cows, dog, cat, birds, fish and butterflies are described in terms of a powerful and intentional identity, suggesting that the directive energy we call mind does not make man's solitude. The Afghan hound for example who "never admitted the ties of domesticity" shows the power of the unknown animal intelligence which is a significant presence in *Between the Acts.* "Now his wild yellow eyes gazed at her, gazed at him. He could outstare them both." The world is alive with intelligent energy over which the human mind presides precariously. As in "Time Passes" in *To the Lighthouse,* man the caretaker has only to absent himself awhile for the other forces to make themselves known. While *To The Lighthouse* still shows man in fear of the rest of nature, bent on subduing it, the fear is absent from *Between the Acts,* because mankind knows itself as animal; even the ethereal Lucy Swithin recognizes her relation to the prehistoric "elephant-bodied, seal-necked, heaving, surging" ancestor. While the relationship between mankind and the rest of nature is interpreted by the audience of the pageant in terms of the pathetic fallacy, with the rain falling in tears, the relationship prevailing in the novel is not sentimental. The intuitive sense of connections in nature and between people, open to the charge of fantasy or sentimentality in *Mrs. Dalloway,* now finds corroboration in scientific thought, for the link between man and the cosmos can be understood without metaphysical assumptions. Virginia Woolf's reading in modern science was probably not extensive, but she had certainly read Charles Darwin and Sir James Jeans, whose books have a place in the library of Pointz Hall, and both Darwin and Jeans contribute significantly to Lucy Swithin's "one-making": the theory of evolution connects her to the organic sources, and Jeans (with Sir Thomas Eddington, associated with the theory of the expanding universe) takes her into interstellar space. Jeans provides an image for Lucy's transcendental meditation as she gazes into clouds and sky:

Beyond that was blue, pure blue, black blue; blue that had never filtered down; that had escaped registration. It never fell as sun, shadow, or rain upon the world, but disregarded the little coloured ball of earth entirely. (P. 30)

The "real" world is a world of appearances which, by the habit of perception, we may separate into solid, liquid, and ethereal, as we tend to think the sky a blue dome even when science has taught us that all these perceptions are illusions. Lucy Swithin, the most erudite as well as the most religious consciousness of *Between the Acts,* has moved beyond such illusory perceptions to the recognition of a reality millions of light-years away. Isa may interpret Lucy's contemplation as a foolish mysticism, but it represents the joining of scientific thought about the nature of the cosmos and religious thought about a transcendent reality. The connection is explicitly made later by an anonymous voice in the dispersing audience saying that science "is making things (so to speak) more spiritual." Sir James Jeans also clearly corroborates Virginia Woolf's intuition of intangible relationships; in *The*

Universe Around Us Jeans illustrates cosmic interdependence by a domestic event which is echoed in *Between the Acts:* "Each time the child throws its toy out of its baby-carriage, it disturbs the motion of every star in the universe."[7]

But in *Between the Acts* the major theoretical conception joining the scientific, religious, esthetic, and practical modes of thought is the conception of matter as energy. The pulse of energy is everywhere, even in the silence of the vacant dining room: "The room was a shell, singing of what was before time was; a vase stood in the heart of the house, alabaster, smooth, cold, holding the still, distilled essence of emptiness, silence." It is present in the tension of the silent party on the terrace after lunch as people feel one another's presence: "We aren't free, each one of them felt separately to feel or think separately, nor yet to fall asleep. We're too close; but not close enough." The "one-making," the principle of coherence drawing together all of the forces at Pointz Hall, is the power of magnetism working in diverse ways. On a minor level, it reveals itself in the action of the butterflies which hover amorously over the brightly colored dresses of the players, for attraction goes beyond the need of survival or the utility of flowers. The energy of color attracts. Again, near the end the esthetic and religious power of music is related to the force of properties in chemistry and physics: "Like quicksilver sliding, filings magnetized, the distracted united."

Pronouncing upon the pageant, the clergyman Mr. Streatfield offers a simple and homely lesson, "Each is part of the whole," but it is clear that the "whole" of *Between the Acts* is not that contained in the doctrines of his church. Furthermore, *Between the Acts* as a different anatomy of love discovers principles at variance with Christian charity. Supported on all sides by the amorous energy of light and matter, and the drama of mating in English history, the six central human characters are drawn into a play of attraction and dispersion, or as Isa defines the forces, love and hate.

The greater energy bringing all together to a place, a time, and an action, is the creative energy of Miss La Trobe, which little George prefigures in the beginning as he tears the flower from the earth and places it in a new whole, against the tree; in her creation violence is done to the pre-existing order, yet the act is intensely amorous; the pageant is a gesture of love passing between La Trobe and the audience.

Isa, who introduces the love-dream at the beginning of the novel, continues to trace the changing lineaments of love and to show its dynamism, for she blazes like George's flower with the creative energy we call sex. Every detail of her body, her dress, and her desire reveals the inadequacy of conventional descriptions of sexuality; for the ordinary attributes of female attraction, voluptuousness, sensuality, receptiveness, and the beguilements of dress, one must look to Mrs. Manresa; but Mrs. Manresa's energy is without erotic enchantment. With Isa also the usual confinement of love to husband, child, and ideal lover is shown to be not only inadequate to this energy, but also in part hostile to it. The true power of erotic magnetism is known not in coupling or in charity but in the intangible drawing together of two separate bodies, which has occurred for Isa at the moment that she began to love Giles; the moment was of such intensity that its force persists in Isa's memory like a radioactive atom:

> They had met first in Scotland, fishing—she from one rock, he from another. Her line had got tangled; she had given over, and had watched him with the stream rushing between his legs, casting, casting—until, like a thick ingot of silver bent in the middle, the salmon had leapt, had been caught, and she had loved him. (P. 60)

A part of the energy of that moment, which may legitimately be called a moment of ecstasy, still attaches her to Giles. But the magnificently handsome young man who returns to Pointz Hall from business in the City—the father of her children, as Isa constantly reminds herself—is alien to the lambent image of love, which contains both more and less than mating and procreation. The inextricable mesh of love and hate in which Isa feels herself caught is the result of a simultaneous rather than sequential action of the energies of attraction and dispersion. She is powerfully drawn to Giles in her fierce animal nature, which unlike Lucy she will not acknowledge in the daylight world; at the same time, her romantic mind is repelled and offended by him. Isa's torment is the plight of those still caught in the old dichotomy of subjective/objective or mind/matter. It is also, from the point of view of realism, the prevalent attitude of woman in a society dominated by nineteenth-century double morality. Yet the intensity of frustration and revulsion is equal in Giles, for whom these complicated pressures exist in egotistical terms, as he thinks his self, his ego, violated by going to the City for business rather than staying in the country to farm, and as he thinks his identity and his love outraged by Isa's idle maunderings. The sheer force of the sexual energy linking them constitutes also a great force of dispersion. Whereas dispersion may be a condition of lapsing into separateness, with Isa and Giles it is manifest as hate. The connection between eroticism and violence is made in both these characters, when Giles squashes the snake and toad and when Isa plays with the knife, the lethal intent only thinly veiled with bad poetry. However, the inadequacy of "one other" as a focus of all the energies of being is resolved in the main by less destructive action.

Hence the mythic-erotic venturing force in Isa is a wandering beam. She is seeking, as William Dodge recognizes, "hidden faces." Her inclinations towards others indicate what love is, beyond the potency of Giles; since the fish is more than an erotic symbol, Isa must look for the rest of the meaning, for the whole. In part her attitude is humorously treated, as she longs for "the ravaged, the silent, the romantic gentleman farmer," yet the schoolgirl state of being in love with a man who is in no way connected to the objects and actions of her life releases feeling intangibly in an energy which can

"lie between them like a wire, tingling, tangling, vibrating."
To demand of Isa that all her energy be magnetized by Giles
is to assume that human emotion is an anomaly in a world
of seven-dimensional potentiality. Isa's extemporaneous rhyming is a comment upon the falsely static human world implied
by marriage and other regulated human relations: "flying
mounting through the air . . . there to lose what binds us
here."

Although Isa's state is the most obvious, and the electri-
city in Isa and Giles is readily comprehensible because it
touches the most common experience, the same principle is
manifest in the relationship of Lucy Swithin and William
Dodge, and William Dodge and Giles Oliver. The force of
attraction between Isa and Giles, and Mrs. Manresa and
Giles, is a complex response which we tend to simplify by
calling it sex, but when Lucy Swithin takes William Dodge
for a tour of the Hall, William has an experience comparable to Isa's response on seeing Giles catch a salmon;
since we cannot comfortably relegate his experience to
eroticism, we are led further away from stereotyped definitions of the relations between men and women, and shown
a paradigm of love in such a state of compression that the
episode needs to be cited entire, like poetry.

Lucy Swithin, "Old Flimsy," as the servants call her, is
an old and flighty woman, by no means a figure of maternal
warmth. When she murmurs, "Come and I'll show you the
house," she addresses no one and apparently means nothing
in particular; yet William Dodge knows that he has been
chosen, and he follows, docile but reserved, through a conventional tour upstairs. He is, like Isa, attending, and ready
to be caught. Suddenly it occurs:

Old and frail she had climbed the stairs. She had spoken her
thoughts, ignoring, not caring if he thought her, as he had, in-
consequent, sentimental, foolish. She had lent him a hand to help
him up a steep place. She had guessed his trouble. Sitting on the
bed he heard her sing, swinging her little legs, "Come and see my
sea weeds, come and see my sea shells, come and see my dicky

bird hop upon its perch"—an old child's nursery rhyme to help a child. Standing by the cupboard in the corner he saw her reflected in the glass. Cut off from their bodies, their eyes smiled, their bodiless eyes, at their eyes in the glass. (P. 87)

In a few minutes, going from the bedroom in which Lucy was born to the nursery of her brother's grandchildren, William Dodge has gone through all the changes of relations of sympathy to girls and has broken through the veil of dirty water of his childhood:

But her eyes in their caves of bone were still lambent. . . . And he wished to kneel before her, to kiss her hand, and to say: "At school they held me under a bucket of dirty water, Mrs. Swithin; when I looked up, the world was dirty, Mrs. Swithin; . . . I'm a half-man, Mrs. Swithin; a flickering, mind-divided little snake in the grass, Mrs. Swithin; as Giles saw; but you've healed me. ... (P. 90)

All residue of rational causality in understanding human motivation has now disappeared; and Woolf has completed the development begun in *Jacob's Room* and *Mrs. Dalloway*, having found a conceptual structure to defend her against the charge of sentimentality which distracted her in the middle period of her work.

The entire incident reveals the energy of the psyche as an authentic power transcending the physical potentiality of the body. Such a conception of soul is not new, nor is the residence of the soul's power in the eye Woolf's invention, for the love poetry of the troubadours, with its occult religious significance, reflects such a pattern;[8] Donne, one of the four poets named at Pointz Hall, continues the tradition in "The Ecstasy," in which the lovers' contact is solely by "eye-beames twisted." The new element not to be found in the quasi-mystical literary tradition but supported by modern scientific theory, is the literalness with which the power of psyche is understood.[9] It is no longer indulged as fancy, or as an imaginative power functioning only in art, but found to be as real as a physical act. William Dodge does not respond to Lucy Swithin as he does because of the projection of his desire, for he knows nothing about Mrs. Swithin and is not emotionally alert to her. Instead he receives a totally unlooked-for communication from her affective mind (an inadequate term, but more accurate than any of the usual terms, such as "subconscious") which includes the entire configuration of her perceptions and feelings, but more specifically the memory of what she has been in all the years before she became a frail old woman. In her memory there are highly charged atoms, similar to the ones we have noted in George and Isa, which are activated by the bedroom and the nursery and carry their radiance to William by the lambent eye. The entire process is signaled by the only comment Lucy makes which is not suitably conventional: "But we have other lives, I think, I hope. . . . We live in things."

The illuminating moment is not central to Mrs. Swithin's world; her moments of intensity have already occurred. By the time William Dodge comes to say goodbye, she has forgotten him. For William, however, there will be a continuing lambency. He will continue to be aroused by men like Giles, with a desire that is partly esthetic, partly a yearning for his own completion; but Lucy Swithin as gentle child, "ravishing girl," and frail old lady, has touched his imaginative powers in their state of innocence, and he has experienced love. In recognition of it, he seeks everywhere for the old woman in order to thank her for doing she knows not what. These intermittencies of love, union and dispersion, are the design of *Between the Acts*, dance figures encompassing an ever-expanding number of atoms and complexities of movement. On the simplest level, perhaps, is the action between George and the flower; then between Mrs. Manresa and Giles, Mrs. Manresa and Bart, Isa and Giles, and Isa and William; then Mrs. Swithin and the cosmos, Miss La Trobe and the audience, and Virginia Woolf and her audience; and finally the universal mind and its thought.

Within the framework of the novel, the major action of unity is that of the pageant composed and produced by the odd woman Miss La Trobe. The dramatic form that Virginia Woolf began to desire in 1927 is in itself a unifying medium and one which needs the support of irrational and wordless forces, as well as that of other people. While the existence of a novel depends on audience, the audience is singular and may be remote in time; the play demands a communal response and one that is immediate. No sophistication is necessary to recognize the obvious collaboration between the author and the audience; hence, the art form of Miss La Trobe, in contrast to Isa's silent lyricism, unites rather than separates people. Moreover, Woolf, in contrast to D. H. Lawrence, succeeded in devising a form which is perfectly articulate as a form but allows space for the entrance of what is unwilled and unpromised. Miss La Trobe's composition, as written, contains the metamorphoses of a place, Pointz Hall, and of the various classes in a local community (with the lower classes performing for the upper class), both easily connected to a spectacle which draws upon English history and literature. The unexpected and random forces are written in only in the mirror-play of the present day, with its orts and fragments. As it is performed, additional chance powers have their part: the interplay of the six central characters of *Between the Acts*, the movements of accidental circumambient nature, the vagaries of audience response to nature, and, most subtle, the effect of the largely unseen presence of Miss La Trobe herself.

To call Miss La Trobe's pageant a pageant of English history is to agree to read history in a very special way, even more eccentric than in *The Years,* for the wars and heroes of the past are forgotten (and the omission, for the year 1939, is striking), as are the great moments of English literature. There is no echo of the great Shakespearean tragedies of public life, or of the epic vision of Milton. If Elizabeth I and Spenser have a place at Pointz Hall, it is surely because heroism and nationalism fall back into the stream of myth in these two figures. In Miss La Trobe's pageant, Elizabethan romantic fantasy, Restoration love-games, and undramatic Victorian courting mark the course of history, with interludes of nearly wordless life cycles dominated by the anonymous workers of the earth. Even more remarkable perhaps is the fact that the audience acquiesces almost without a murmur, except at the end. They accept because they do not understand the negative implications, but are amused and touched where they live (i.e., in love-games and games of mutual recognition): thus they are appropriately playing their parts as the anonymous generations of the earth.

In the scenes themselves, Miss La Trobe presents the elaborate artifices by which the reality of love masquerades. None of these masquerades is entirely a thing of the past, for Isa is living evidence of the continuance of Elizabethan romance, as Mrs. Manresa is of Restoration comedy, and a fair share of the audience is of Victorian hypocrisy. So also, England, a child at the beginning of the pageant, is a child at the end. In short, one of the themes of the pageant, relating it to the rest of the novel, is the illusory movement through time, whereby society appears to progress, relationships appear to change, while in the authentic life—as opposed to the false life of event—all is recurrence. What truly was, is. The monsters of Piccadilly persist, as Lucy knows, and the fierce drives of men and women are present under every mask.

As a commentary on love, the pageant is very complex. On the simplest level of plot, it reveals the fatuity of the love-conventions of any time; Miss La Trobe feels that the audience has seen what she meant when someone says, "All that fuss about nothing!" during the Restoration flutter. Yet Miss La Trobe has exposed her play to the elements, staging it on the terrace rather than in the barn, to invite the true expression of love. Here she is in harmony with Mrs. Swithin, who refuses to protect apricots in muslin bags: "They were so beautiful, naked, with one flushed cheek, one green, that

Mrs. Swithin left them naked, and the wasps burrowed holes." In this action love and art meet, for both occur when two forces are in play (as with George and the flower), and not when a form is imposed or an object seized. The central part of *Between the Acts*, containing the pageant, is an analysis of love when the partners are not a boy and a blossom but the components of a sophisticated civilization and a highly evolved consciousness.

In comparison with Miss La Trobe, the other characters of *Between the Acts* are artifices similar to the characters of the scenes of the pageant; it may be said that they are equally her fictions, playing out similar if more complex roles. For Virginia Woolf's novel, however, Miss La Trobe is the dramatic reminder of a different plane of reality, psychologically as well as socially. By every available means Woolf places her outside the society for which she plays. Her name is foreign; her origins are unknown; she looks suspiciously Russian. She smokes and swears and brandishes a whip: she is not quite respectable, not a lady, and is probably lesbian. In the community as in the pageant, she has none of the safety of assigned roles, and because of this exposure she is constantly, rather than intermittently, in a state of amorous and creative tension. She is unlike Isa, who dissipates the intensity of her feelings of love and hate in snatches of rime:

"She spake," Isa murmured. "And from her bosom's snowy antre drew the gleaming blade. 'Plunge blade!' she said. And struck. 'Faithless!' she cried. Knife, too! It broke. So too my heart," she said. (P. 135)

Miss La Trobe has at every moment a lover's terrible awareness of the object of love, and vulnerability to it: "Every cell in her body was absorbent." In the course of the performance she swears, sweats, stumbles over roots, grinds holes in the turf, and dies.

The immediacy and physical grossness of her responses sets her apart from Woolf's other principal characters, both

men and women, but links her to the key minor figures of
Mrs. Dalloway and *To the Lighthouse*, and she bears some
of the thematic force of the disreputable street singers. In
particular, she serves like them to affirm the complicated
artifice of society while at the same time placing it in a
perspective in which there can be no doubt that it is artifice. In relation to the members of the audience, "the most
respected families" in their Rolls, their Bentleys, and their
Hispano-Suizas, she is as ambiguous as her pageant, for
her art is only partly affirmation. Although only one of the
scenes—the Victorian—is frankly satiric, the entire pageant
invites comment by a larger nature than that tamed by
man; and receives it. The wind blows the solemn words
away and disarranges the splendid headdress of the queen.
The swallows, which playfully skim the stage as if doing
their part in the entertainment, are signs of another reality
which masters the scene when the starlings descend upon
the tree in the passage cited earlier; but from the beginning the
narrator emphasizes their untamed beauty, "dancing, like
the Russians, only not to music, but to the unheard rhythm
of their own wild hearts." The bird and the woman are as-
sociationally linked for the reader by the word "Russian,"
and, more pervasively, she is akin to the untamed, uncivil
life of the Afghan hound and the simpleton Albert.

Because of the incalculable dimensions beyond the fourth,
some of which are suggested by the mind of Mrs. Swithin,
the sense of power and glory Miss La Trobe has when her
art is successful must be considered in a larger artistic design, that of Virginia Woolf. Miss La Trobe, with a traditional but largely romantic conception of artistic creation,
blazes with triumph when one of her themes has been
grasped by Mrs. Swithin:

"You've twitched the invisible strings," was what the old lady
meant; and revealed—of all people—Cleopatra! Glory possessed
her. Ah, but she was not merely a twitcher of individual strings;
she was one who seethes wandering bodies and floating voices in

a cauldron, and makes rise up from its amorphous mass a re-created world . . ." (Pp. 179-180)

But an anonymous voice in the dispersing crowd is allowed to question the creator: "He said she meant we all act. Yes, but whose play?" The conception of literary creation of Miss La Trobe is comparable to the earlier conceptions of Virginia Woolf herself, those demonstrated most fully in *Mrs. Dalloway* and *The Waves* (the cauldron symbol also is a salient one in *The Waves* and evokes Grail symbolism); in the latter Woolf has begun almost secretly the departure from that theory to a larger, more metaphysical one.[10] The new theory, present imagistically in the experience of George and of Isa, and in that of William Dodge in greater complexity of feeling, thought, and memory, is most completely formed in the brief revelation of the working of Miss La Trobe's creative mind.

In the beginning, at the moment of conception, even preceding conception, the external objects to be reordered are not inert, nor are they merely "wandering bodies." Before the scene of the new play can form in Miss La Trobe's inner vision, her mind must be invaded by the energies of the external world. In the pub, after the pageant, she drinks:

She took her chair and looked through the smoke at a crude glass painting of a cow in a stable; also at a cock and a hen. She raised her glass to her lips. And drank. And listened. Words of one syllable sank down into the mud. She drowsed; she nodded. The mud became fertile. Words rose above the intolerably laden dumb oxen plodding through the mud. Words without meaning—wonderful words.

. . . .
. . . Smoke obscured the earth-coloured jackets. She no longer saw them, yet they upheld her, sitting arms akimbo with her glass before her. There was the high ground at midnight; there the rock; and two scarcely perceptible figures. Suddenly the tree was pelted with starlings. She set down her glass. She heard the first words. (Pp. 247-248)

It would be difficult to find a passage which would demonstrate more powerfully the distance Virginia Woolf has come from the intellectual formulations of her brothers' Cambridge circle, for "organic form" is alive in a way unprepared for by the theories of G. E. Moore. On the one hand, the mind is a womb which creates a life only when a living sperm enters it; on the other hand, the creation that occurs is a radical reconstituting of the original elements. The given components of Miss La Trobe's mind at this moment are the brute life of the farmyard, the dingy bar, the dull men, the glass of beer, and a visual image for a play which came to her as she looked at the darkening and unpeopled landscape. The words, until now, have not come.

The passage begins, then, with an action of dispersion, in which the components of creation have separated and broken down, leaving the earth and the mind an amorphous mass like the slime and ooze of the early morning interludes of *The Waves*, or like the Darwinian origins of life. The seeds of a new creation are human sounds, simple words spoken by unsophisticated men; and the earth and the mind grow fertile. But the electric shock which mobilizes all the growing energy is an intense action in the world external to the mind: the descent of the starlings. The mind is not fertilized but ravished. Present here and throughout *Between the Acts* is the open space through which the unknown enters. Also implicit is the parallel between life—cosmic life—and art, and a partial parallel between the creator and her work and the transcendent creator and its design. The parallel must be left incomplete because of a final mystery, for Virginia Woolf does not make a final anthropomorphic assumption.[11]

The idea is conveyed also in sky-images which clarify the area of mystery, and in which Miss La Trobe recognizes the transience of her glory: "What had she given? A cloud that melted into the other clouds on the horizon." And in the evening at Pointz Hall, Mrs. Swithin thinks about the play in the same terms: "Still the play hung in the sky of her mind—moving, diminishing, but still there." Shortly thereafter it has dissipated. There is constant allusion, however, to an art form, a meaningful order beyond the limits of the eye's vision, just as there are invisible stars, and clouds belonging to a different order from the ephemeral clouds of the day's forming. All the cloud references echo a note struck in Mrs. Swithin's first revery:

There was a fecklessness, a lack of symmetry and order in the clouds, as they thinned and thickened. Was it their own law, or no law, they obeyed? . . . One, high up, very distant, had hardened to golden alabaster; was made of immortal marble. Beyond that was blue. . . . (P. 30)

Beyond, when the cloud of one creation has passed, there is the mysterious sky. The presence of this larger order is felt throughout *Between the Acts*, so that the author has transcended not only the limitations of Miss La Trobe's creative mind but also of her own finite self. The universal mind is transcendent as well as immanent. To this unknown order, music—not "God Save the King" but Bach, Handel, Beethoven, or Mozart—can correspond more accurately than drama, reflecting as it does the higher mathematics of the cosmos, beyond the impurity of words. Still, it is meaning, to be described as "somebody speaking."

Like quicksilver sliding, filings magnetized, the distracted united. The tune began; the first note meant a second; the second a third. Then down beneath a force was born in opposition; then another. On different levels they diverged. (P. 220)

The entire description, which goes on for a page, conveys in the absoluteness of musical notes the pattern of attraction/ dispersion or love/hate within an order which all recognize and to which they respond with reverence, but one which is unformulated in their lives (as their lives are organized by caste, money, politics, relatedness, or time) and which can not be adequately verbalized. The ambiguous title of Woolf's book, *Between the Acts*, again suggests the transcendent mystery, for in addition to pointing to the flux of life which occurs between the formalized and official actions of existence, it refers to a cosmic interlude between the moment of creation (Darwin) and the moment of extinction (Jeans) of life within the humanistic spectrum, and it affirms a design, or an act, beyond our range.

The moments of recognition of the unity and of its greater design are brief. The action of dispersion is constant, only less obvious than the action of attraction or union because it conforms more readily to the observable action of ordinary life. Every pair coming together must part; every act must end and be dissipated; every vision must be shattered in order for a new act or vision to occur. The larger design of plot, the coming together of diverse people to see a play, emphasizes the essentially creative nature of the pattern; the largest design, that of a cosmic plot, seems beneficent in terms of the creative mind if not in terms of the finite ego. Rhododendron forests disappear, and a city is made; elephantine barking monsters disappear, and man replaces him; English imperialism disappears, and a new society is made. The first law of thermodynamics still applies for the universal mind of *Between the Acts*; the second law of thermodynamics seems not to apply, for the transformation of energy (when it is not cyclic) pursues an upward rather than a downward way. While human life contains the potentiality of all the brutality of past life, and indeed must preserve the power of animal ferocity, it moves unconsciously towards what it must inevitably desire, an approximation to the all-inclusiveness of the universal mind.

chapter 8

Figures of Thought

This study began with an outline of fear which provides the approach to the energy of Virginia Woolf's genius and to the direction her literary venture was to take, for all the anxiety and terror of the young writer derive from an incompatibility between intelligence and knowledge—that is, between the reality of experience and the reality of education. Although the resulting emotional dilemma might be biographically demonstrated, it is by no means so eccentric that reference must be made to facts of Woolf's life; it is perhaps more definitely a result of the historical moment. The imperative to think what is approved and to feel what one is supposed to feel results not in proper thought and feeling but in terror of any sign of the reality to be suppressed and a recognition of the fragility, not the inevitability, of the order of decorum. For the writer Virginia Woolf, a divestiture of education was necessary.

As *The Voyage Out* demonstrates, inherited forms of fiction could serve only to describe the product of the conflict between reality and convention; they could reveal the alienation of the person, but could neither plumb the mysteries of cause nor reveal the truth of effect; nor could they discover a vital replacement. All these acts required new modes of thought: a new syntax, a new vocabulary, and a new structure. Like her French contemporary Paul Valéry, Virginia Woolf distrusted logical abstraction. The finesse of language would serve to convey multiplicity and the flux in time and individuation; beyond the flux and the plenitude of the moment, Woolf was inclined to seek a thoroughgoing abstraction which was nonlinguistic. Verbal images fall into configurations which extend to the meanings of mathematical, geometric, architectural, and musical forms, the basic figures of which are mathematical and geometric. The clear implication of this level of abstraction is that such forms are linked to the perceptual and affective and metaphysical orders much more closely than are the verbal abstractions of philosophy, and are means of breaking down the isolation which has its source in verbal concepts.

In somewhat more than thirty years of writing and thinking, Virginia Woolf discovered the verbal modes which could express thought accessible to no traditional literary or philosophic mode. Furthermore, her unwillingness to remain permanently within any of her own finished literary forms is an indication of the intent not merely to write novels but to discover truth. For her as for Mr. Ramsay, there is an entire alphabet of reality, but she is not halted at Q nor afraid to try for a complete design. Her Z is not an absolute finality (and one would perhaps not dare to entertain the idea of absolute conclusion in any mind), but it completes the revision of an old alphabet.

The vocabulary of Virginia Woolf is one of images; the syntax derives from painterly perceptions; the larger syntax of structure is related quite literally to architecture, depending as it does not merely on the arrangement of masses, but on an arrangement in space. The new syntax, although it began in something that could be called "stream of consciousness" in early sketches such as "The Mark on the Wall," is not adequately described by that term at any period of

Woolf's work. Even in the germinal story "Kew Gardens," the new mode depends on a new consciousness deliberately opened rather than on reportage of automatic associational processes. With reason, Woolf's early techniques have been compared to the methods of impressionistic painting, for both are highly analytic and far from naive. For Virginia Woolf the method involved learning not to see from the point of view of the educated ego; so the vocabulary of her thought, beginning with "Kew Gardens," is the primitive and universal vocabulary of image, and the conceptual world of each work is built of these images, the space in which they are contained, and the rhythm of relationships of color and space. Since these abstract generalizations would require extended illustration to prove, and particularly to prove as a mode of thought distinct from the mode used in making a general statement, a few brief illustrations will have to suffice.

First, the vocabulary of images: the elemental words-of-one-syllable with which Woolf works are "tree," "bird," "dog," "fish," "horse," "wave," "sea," "crocus," "snow," "wind," "cloud," "knife," "house," "window," etc. With rare exceptions, these are data of experience before they are psychological or metaphysical symbols. They become symbols because the passion of existence has been known through them or in their company, not at one moment but in a continuity and in diversity. For this reason, an image does not lend itself to abstract definition outside its context. The function of any given image is not very different from the function of the nouns in the following sentence: "The armless boy stood before the closed door." We may have a generalized concept of *boy* and *door,* but without the qualifications of the context and without the syntactical relationship we do not really know what *boy* means. In Woolf's natural imagery, the tree is one of the most consistent forms, and yet it has a different meaning when viewed by a child from that when seen by an old woman; it changes meaning as seen from inside a house rather than from outside, in the dark rather than in the light, in motion rather than at rest. Likewise, the verbal abstraction *wave* cannot replace the image of the sea's movement, for a wave presents a different image according to factors of context, the season, the time of day, the quality of the atmosphere, the height of the viewer. Presentation of the image establishes the specific quality and the fluidity that the discursive and rational modes miss. Although the discursive mode is used by various characters, it is used by Woolf herself (after the early works) only with comic or ironic intent.

The exception to mutability in images is found in a natural image which has consistently transcendent implications, and one which is not associated with any of the philosophic problems. The fish appears with marked symbolic intent—indicated in part by the fact that it is not a perceptual but a visionary image—in *To the Lighthouse, Orlando, The Waves,* and *Between the Acts,* and is an organic rather than a constructed link between the chaotic order of nature and the nature of the garden. Bernard's refrain in the last part of *The Waves,* summoning a fin in the waste of waters, indicates the power of the life-force in the fish to endure in something comparable to the sun-dried wasteland Rachel saw; in *Between the Acts* the mystery of the fish is contained in a pool in a domestic garden. Further, the design and the action of the fish offered Virginia Woolf a subject for meditation and a symbol of the ideal in art. As early as 1917, in "The Mark on the Wall," Woolf dreamed of a human world as natural as that of the fish, "a world which one could slice with one's thought as a fish slices the water with his fin"; the fish in water is at ease in his element, almost passive in it (lying beneath the waters, looking dreamily up), and effortless. In 1926 in "Genius," the symbol becomes less passive as she comments on Haydon's mind "tossing and tumbling like a vigorous dolphin in the seas of thought." Two years later "The Sun and the Fish" gives the definitive symbolism: "The fish themselves seem to have been shaped deliberately and slipped into the world only to be themselves. They neither work nor weep. In their shape is their reason."

The fish as symbol thus provides a link between the human creative act of making literary forms, the world of nature, and the area of metaphysical mystery. The final, metaphysical dimension is partly within the tradition of Christian religious feeling, as is hinted by the biblical allusion of the quotation above, but by no means entirely so.

The second element, the unit of meaning in the sentence or complete statement, is also removed from dependence on the categories of logic. Whereas the basic literary syntax of description depends on a copula, a linking of two abstractions, as in "The tree is green," Virginia Woolf's syntax is like that of the impressionistic painter who does not see the tree as a silhouette or structure but as a composition of its qualities, as "The tree with fish-shaped leaves is." The virtue of the statement is in the wholeness of the image and in its liberation from quality judgment: "things in themselves" rather than segregation of qualities. One of the most obvious examples of the power of this syntax, and its strangeness, is the opening episode of *The Waves,* but it is found throughout the later works; the concluding chapter of *Orlando* and most of *Between the Acts* could be cited.

Third, architectonics: Virginia Woolf's preoccupation with the relationships of masses becomes obvious in her struggle with the structuring of *Mrs. Dalloway* and her triumphant discovery of a "tunneling"—and opening of space—to connect the masses. Lily Briscoe also speculates on the problem of the relationship of masses in *To the Lighthouse,* but does not solve the problem for Virginia Woolf, for her abstract design depends on a fixed or frozen relationship. The mastery of Woolf's architecture is found in *Between the Acts,* in which every act, every mass is a transient form and is constantly surrounded by space, the latter often indicated by a sound (the cough of the cow outside the house) or movement in air (the flying of birds or clouds), and in which the art form of the play, instead of requiring the artifice of walls to contain it, constructs its own figures upon the empty air.

In the continuing venture of forms disintegrating rational

structures of syntax, character, scene, and plot by means of sound and images, Virginia Woolf progressed through two stages of intellectual negation marked by stylistic innovations, in order to arrive at a truly original philosophic attitude. Although *The Voyage Out* and *Night and Day* were explorations that proved the impossibility of the old forms, a measure of emotional allegiance to them persisted even after *Mrs. Dalloway,* to be dispelled only in the writing of *To the Lighthouse.* One notes at once that, despite the highly original method of *Jacob's Room,* and despite the originality in the treatment of character in the early novels, the men and women are quite ordinary, even conventional, figures, with none of the boldness or eccentricity of Virginia Woolf herself or of her friends. Before *Orlando* Woolf writes of ordinary middle class people finding their way in an England before the wars, and to a degree the novelist herself is trying to find reality in the forms of the same England—not the literary nor even the social forms, but surely the moral forms. Full recognition of the sterility of those forms came with some reluctance, and only after the writer had reached maturity in her person and in her craft. For this reason, perhaps, critics have tended to concentrate heavily on the middle period of Woolf's work, in which the literary innovations are exciting but the attitudes and types of characters are still familiar, and to assume that all the conceptions of later work are to be found there.

Yet the final works, beginning with *Orlando,* prove the bold assertion in "Mr. Bennett and Mrs. Brown" that "in or about December, 1910, human character changed" in a way and to a degree scarcely hinted in *Mrs. Dalloway.* The new conception of character ceases to be exclusively a literary or psychological idea and becomes a social conception, altering the basic roles of society, and a cosmological reality. *The Years* offers a declaration of change, an evidence of the new human nature emerging from the old social order, and much more subtly and more thoroughly *Between the Acts* is the alchemical solution of the entire design, surrounded as it is by the fecundity of chaos, providing the paradox of form-lessness, or the disintegration of form, contained within the hermetic vial of cosmic reality. (See fig. 4 facing p. 179.)

The plenitude of sensation and civilization thus implies a larger design, one beyond the condition of flux or the defini-tion of being by time and role, and the last three novels of Virginia Woolf are three attempted forms of totality, based upon the key geometric-hermetic figure of *The Waves,*

varying in the emphasis on the linear, historical line, on expanding the circumference of the circle, and on intensify-ing the dynamic relation of the invisible circle to that which it contains, until at last division and opposition cease: the structure of the work of art is that of the cosmic design, and the texture of human experience or consciousness is in har-mony with the events of external nature.

Notes

Introduction

1. *A Writer's Diary* (London, 1969), p. 138.

2. An entry of July 11, 1937, in *A Writer's Diary* also suggests this point, but without reference to Leonard Woolf. Thinking of the death of Janet Case, a girlhood mentor, Woolf writes, ". . . How great a visionary part she has played in my life, till the visionary became a part of the fictitious, not of the real life." (p. 285).

3. Some hint of the existentialist approach is found in the work of Jean Guiguet, *Virginia Woolf and Her Works,* trans. Jean Stewart (London, 1965); and Robert G. Collins has done an interesting study of *The Waves* from an existentialist point of view. See his *Virginia Woolf's Black Arrows of Sensation: The Waves* (Ilfracombe, 1962).

4. *A Haunted House* (London, 1962), pp. 44, 46.

5. *Jacob's Room* (London, 1965), p. 34.

6. *A Haunted House,* p. 41.

7. Sir James Jeans, *The Mysterious Universe* (Cambridge, 1930), p. 3.

Chapter 1

1. "Modern Fiction," *The Common Reader* (New York, 1925); the passage appears on p. 155. "Mr. Bennett and Mrs. Brown," first issued separately, is found in *The Captain's Death Bed* (London, 1950).

2. Mitchell A. Leaska, *Virginia Woolf's Lighthouse: a Study in Critical Method* (London, 1970), p. 61.

3. *The Voyage Out* (London, 1965), p. 249.

4. *The Moment* (London, 1964), pp. 19-20.

5. *The Captain's Death Bed*, p. 197.

6. *The Moment*, p. 12.

7. *The Voyage Out*, pp. 321-322.

8. "The Gnostic idea of the dragon or serpent as an evil world-principle identical with the devil, encircling the earth and holding it in his power, may be referred to in the *Hymn of the Pearl*, ascribed to Bardesanes. The pearl is in the sea, hard by the serpent. The sea is the mythic chaotic deep, which, encircling the world, is sometimes compared in Babylonian mythology to a snake—'the river of the snake.'" J. A. MacCulloch, "Serpent-Worship," *Encyclopaedia of Religion and Ethics* (Edinburgh, 1958), vol. XI, p. 408.

9. *The Voyage Out*, p. 86.

10. *Mrs. Dalloway* (London, 1963), pp. 61-62.

11. *Night and Day* (London, 1960), pp. 417-418.

12. *The Moment*, pp. 12-13.

13. *Mrs. Dalloway*, p. 15.

14. *A Haunted House*, p. 41.

15. *The Moment*, p. 171.

16. *Between the Acts* (London, 1965), p. 214.

17. *The Voyage Out*, pp. 180-181.

18. *A Haunted House*, p. 77.

19. *To the Lighthouse* (London, 1963), pp. 158-159.

20. *A Haunted House*, p. 113.

21. Cited by Quentin Bell in *Virginia Woolf: a Biography* (London, 1972), p. 137.

22. Although the psychological problems of creativity are outside the scope of this study, it may be noted that the names of women provide a clue to some of the process; Woolf sought long for the right name for the protagonist of *The Voyage Out*, and the name chosen, *Rachel*, suggests a biblical story which refers us to the *Sara* of *The Years*.

Chapter 2

1. *The Three-fold Nature of Reality in the Novels of Virginia Woolf* (The Hague, 1965), p. 48.
2. Winifred Holtby, *Virginia Woolf* (London, 1932), p. 61.
3. All references to *The Voyage Out* are to the Hogarth Press edition of 1965.
4. Ginguet, p. 204.
5. See p. 47.
6. *Diary,* p. 10.
7. *Diary,* p. 20.
8. *Diary,* p. 24.
9. All references to *Night and Day* are to the Hogarth Press edition of 1960.
10. *Diary,* p. 23.
11. It is a kind of decorum she in fact violates occasionally in *Jacob's Room,* as in ". . . who shall deny that this blankness of mind, when combined with profusion, mother wit, old wives' tales, haphazard ways, moments of astonishing daring, humour, and sentimentality,—who shall deny that in these respects every women is nicer than any man?" (p. 9).
12. "My instinct at once throws up a screen, which condemns them: I think them in every way angular, awkward and self-assertive. But all this is a great mistake. These screens shut me out. Have no screens, for screens are made out of our own integument; and get at the thing itself, which has nothing whatever in common with a screen." (*Diary,* p. 97)
13. All references to *Jacob's Room* are to the Hogarth Press edition of 1965. This quotation is from p. 34.
14. *The Captain's Death Bed,* p. 58.
15. *Roger Fry* (London, 1940), p. 263.
16. *Diary,* pp. 52-53.

Chapter 3

1. On June 23, 1922, Woolf speaks of *Mrs. Dalloway* as if it were nearly finished, and as if the finished product were the first episode of the novel we now have: "*Mrs. Dalloway in Bond Street*" (*Diary,* p. 46). Subsequently she thought of

another chapter, *The Prime Minister;* and in October she saw "a study of the sane and the insane side by side" (*Diary,* p. 52).

2. Guiguet seems to have missed the point somewhat in thinking that Woolf meant that "Clarissa Dalloway was not big enough to bear all the human attributes with which she sought to burden her . . ." (p. 237).

3. All references to *Mrs. Dalloway* are to the Hogarth Press edition of 1963.

4. Virginia Woolf's indignation upon reading Katherine Mansfield's "Bliss" is a reflection of that taboo partly but not wholly defined as the vulgarity of sexuality. See *Diary,* p. 2.

5. *Mrs. Dalloway,* p. 64.

6. All references to *To the Lighthouse* are to the Hogarth Press edition of 1963.

7. *Diary,* p. 80.

8. *Diary,* pp. 88-89.

Chapter 4

1. *Diary,* p. 105.

2. *Diary,* p. 136.

3. All references to *Orlando* are to the Hogarth Press edition of 1928. This passage appears on pp. 20-21.

4. Woolf's explicit recognition of the relationship between menstruation and writing is found in *A Writer's Diary* at the time when she was working on the conclusion of *Orlando,* Feb. 18, 1928 (p. 123).

5. *Diary,* p. 101.

Chapter 5

1. *Diary,* March 18, 1928, p. 124.

2. *Diary,* p. 137.

3. *Diary,* p. 102.

4. *Diary,* p. 132.

5. *Night and Day,* p. 358.

6. Collins, p. 17.

7. Page references to *The Waves* are to the Hogarth Press edition of 1963.

8. *Diary,* p. 142.

9. See Carl Gustav Jung, *Psychology and Religion* (New Haven, 1938):

The image of the circle—regarded as the most perfect form since Plato's *Timaeus,* the prime authority of Hermetic philosophy —was also given to the most perfect substance, to the gold, to the anima mundi or anima media natura, and to the first created light. And because the macrocosm, the Great World, was made by the creator "in forma rotunda et globosa," the smallest part of the whole, the point, also contains this perfect nature. (Pp. 66-67)

A little further on, he cites the Anonymous of the "Rosarium Philosophorum":

Make a round circle of man and woman, extract therefrom a quadrangle and from it a triangle. Make the circle round and thou shalt have the Philosopher's Stone.

Jung indicates a psychological extension, arrived at through dreams:

The application of the comparative method indubitably shows the quaternity as being a more or less direct representation of the God manifested in his creation. We might, therefore, conclude that the symbol, spontaneously produced in the dreams of modern people, means the same thing—*the God within.* (P. 72)

10. During the period of gestation of *The Waves,* Virginia Woolf heard Yeats expounding his theories and was fascinated, as is recorded in the unpublished diaries in the Berg Collection of the New York Public Library.

11. It may be noted in passing that "Rhoda" means rose.

12. Jessie L. Weston, *From Ritual to Romance* (Garden City, N.Y., 1957), chap. 3.

13. According to J. W. Graham, the first draft of *The Waves* specified the number 6. See "Point of View in *The Waves:* Some Services of the Style," *University of Toronto Quarterly,* XXXIX, no. 3 (April, 1970), 199.

14. Christopher Butler, *Number Symbolism* (London, 1970), p. 22.

15. Taken from *A Christian Rosenkreutz Anthology,* ed. Paul M. Allen (Blauvelt, N.Y., 1968), p. 408.

16. As a sketch written in 1923 suggests, Woolf found her journey to Spain an escape from "the hours, the works, the

divisions, rigid and straight, of the old British week," and an entrance into pure experience. As she rode over the Sierra Nevada, she felt the full splendor of departure:

Riders, as night comes on . . . seem to be riding out of life towards some very enticing prospect, while the four legs of their beasts carry on all necessary transactions with the earth. Riders are at rest; on they go, and on and on. And, they muse, what does it all matter; and what harm can come to a good man . . . in life or after death?

"To Spain," in *The Moment,* p. 174.
17. Weston, chap. 4.

Chapter 6

1. A. D. Moody, *Virginia Woolf* (Edinburgh, 1963), p. 73.
2. David Daiches, *Virginia Woolf* (New York, 1942).
3. All references to *Flush* are to the Hogarth Press edition of 1933.
4. Some of the formal changes in the attempt are traced by Charles G. Hoffman in "Virginia Woolf's Manuscript Revisions of *The Years,*" PMLA, 84 no. 1 (1969), 79-89.
5. *Diary,* pp. 244-245.
6. *Diary,* p. 189.
7. *Diary,* p. 195.
8. See the comment on D. H. Lawrence, *Diary,* p. 188: "And why does Aldous say he was an 'artist'? Art is being rid of all preaching: things in themselves. . . ."
   A Writer's Diary indicates that the original conception of *Professions of Women* "about the sexual life of women" continuing *A Room of One's Own* (see *Diary,* p. 166) split, part going to *Three Guineas* and part going to *The Years* (suggested again in the *Diary,* p. 295).
9. *Diary,* p. 225.
10. *Diary,* p. 208.
11. All references to *The Years* are to the Hogarth Press edition of 1965.
12. As has been noted by other critics, the tendency of Virginia Woolf's thought is existentialist; here there is some similarity between the problem Sara finds and the problem of the recognition of the *other* with which Jean-Paul Sartre

deals in *Being and Nothingness*. However, Woolf's resolution of the problem is radically different from that of Sartre.

13. "The Russian Point of View," in *The Common Reader*. pp. 180-181.

14. *A Haunted House*, p. 31.

15. See also Rhoda's last journey in *The Waves*, discussed on p. 173, and note 16 to chap. 5, pp. 232-233.

16. W. B. Yeats, "The Secret Rose," *Collected Poems* (New York, 1950), p. 78. This reference for the triple attributes of Rose seems more convincing to me than the one suggested by Harvena Richter in her book *The Inward Journey* (Princeton, 1970), in which she sees a reference to Crashaw's poems addressed to St. Theresa.

17. This is clearly an ironic allusion to a well-known line from Rousseau's *Confessions:* "At length I recollected the thoughtless saying of a great princess, who, on being informed that the country people had no bread, replied, 'Let them eat cake.' "

18. *Diary*, p. 292.

19. *Diary*, p. 295.

Chapter 7

1. *Diary*, p. 291.

2. *Diary*, p. 243.

3. *Diary*, p. 359.

4. All references to *Between the Acts* are to the Hogarth Press edition of 1965.

5. *The Voyage Out*, p. 358. (See p. 51.)

6. *To the Lighthouse*, p. 78.

7. Jeans, *The Universe Around Us*, 5th ed. (Cambridge, 1953), p. 215.

8. A. J. Denomy, "An Inquiry into the Origins of Courtly Love," *Medieval Studies*, XI (1944), 175-260.

9. Edgar Allan Poe would be the obvious forerunner of Woolf in this line of development, especially in his cosmological poem *Eureka;* but I have no evidence to show that she had read *Eureka*.

10. In the *Diary* Woolf mentions twice an experience of

1933 or 1934 which was a "spiritual conversion." See *Diary,* p. 292.

11. Richter, pp. 137-138, has quoted passages from earlier versions of *Between the Acts* containing explicit references to such parallels, but has not drawn conclusions beyond the stylistic.

INDEX

References to the works of Virginia Woolf

References to authors and persons

236

MAR 1 2 1997
MAR 1 6 200